LEAD THE CLAIM

A NEW STANDARD FOR MODERN ADJUSTERS

NAVIGATING CATASTROPHE, LITIGATION, AND HIGH-PRESSURE CLAIMS

DR. KARISSA THOMAS

Lead the Claim: A New Standard for Modern Adjusters

Navigating Catastrophe, Litigation, and High-Pressure Claims

For bulk orders, training inquiries, or speaking engagements, contact:

https://efficientadjuster.net/

ISBN: 978-1-968277-61-1

Library of Congress Number: 2026909790

Interior Design: Marigold Emal

Published by
Efficient Adjuster Publishing

Printed in the United States of America

DEDICATION

This book is dedicated to the adjusters.

The ones who walk into uncertainty.
The ones who assess damage while others are still processing loss.
The ones who make difficult decisions under pressure, often with limited information and high expectations.

This book is for the adjusters working long days in catastrophe zones.
For those navigating complex claims and rising litigation.
For those balancing empathy with professionalism.
For those leading the claim, even when no one calls them the leader.

Your work matters.
Your decisions matter.
Your leadership matters.

This book is written in recognition of the responsibility you carry and the professionalism you bring to some of the most challenging moments people face.

AUTHOR'S NOTE

Claims work has evolved. Adjusters now operate in environments defined by scale, complexity, and increased scrutiny. Catastrophe events impact entire communities. Litigation risk continues to grow. Claims often involve multiple stakeholders, shifting information, and higher expectations. These conditions demand more than just technical accuracy; they require clarity, consistency, and strong professional leadership from the very beginning of the claim. Modern claims environments require adjusters to operate with structure from the first point of contact.

Modern claims environments leave little room for uncertainty in communication or documentation. Decisions are often made with incomplete information. Timelines shift. Conversations can become emotionally charged. Despite these challenges, adjusters must stay professional, document clearly, and keep the claim moving forward. The margin for error has shrunk, while the responsibility for adjusters has grown. This book is written with that urgency in mind. Clarity and consistency are no longer optional; they are required to maintain professional standards.

This is not a technical estimating manual or a policy interpretation guide. While those skills remain important, they are no longer sufficient on their own. Modern claims require disciplined communication and defensible decisions. Setting expectations early, documenting reasoning clearly, coordinating stakeholders, and maintaining reliability are now essential parts of professional adjusting. These practices stabilize claims and protect both the process and the professionals managing them. This is what transforms technical work into professional claim leadership.

Throughout this book, examples depict catastrophe events, complex losses, and multi-party claims environments. These scenarios demonstrate how quickly claims can evolve and how vital it is for adjusters to provide guidance. Often, the adjuster becomes the primary source of clarity. By guiding communication and maintaining structure, adjusters help steer the claim toward resolution even when conditions remain uncertain. In complex environments, the adjuster's role is to provide direction as conditions continue to develop.

This book aims to help professionals working in challenging claims environments. Whether managing catastrophe responses, complex liability claims, or high-volume workloads, structured leadership practices ensure consistency. Communication, documentation, and disciplined decision-making are now essential skills for effective claim handling. These skills form the foundation of modern professional adjusting.

The purpose of this book is to emphasize leadership in claims. Adjusters shape outcomes through clarity, professionalism, and consistency. When these qualities are present, claims stay organized, communication remains steady, and decisions are more defensible. Modern adjusting requires more than evaluation; it demands leadership under pressure, sound judgment in changing circumstances, and professional discipline from first contact to resolution. The standard you apply to each claim defines the quality of the outcome and the strength of your professional practice.

CONTENTS

PREFACE

Why This Book Exists

Claims work has always required technical skills, sound judgment, and attention to detail. Adjusters assess damage, interpret policy language, document their findings, and help move claims toward resolution. For many years, this process was predictable. Claims were handled one at a time, documentation followed established routines, and timelines were manageable. The adjuster's primary job was to evaluate and report.

But that environment is different now.

Today, claims handling takes place in a world shaped by frequent disasters, more lawsuits, the need to work with many parties, and higher expectations from policyholders and others. Claims are no longer handled in isolation. They develop in complex situations where information changes, timelines shift, and many viewpoints matter. Adjusters now have to balance technical work with communication, managing expectations, and making decisions in a structured way.

This book was written because the adjuster's role has grown. Today's adjuster does more than just document losses. Now, the adjuster leads the claim process. This shift defines the standard required in modern claims environments.

The Shift from Technical Role to Leadership Role

In the past, claims handling focused on technical skills: inspecting damage, reviewing the policy, documenting findings, preparing estimates, and sharing decisions. These steps are still important, but they are not enough by themselves. Today, adjusters often need to work with engineers, lawyers, contractors, and other stakeholders. Information changes over time, and decisions must be made even as situations keep shifting.

Policyholders now start the claims process under more stress. They may be dealing with displacement, money worries, and disruption, which shape what they expect. They look to the adjuster for guidance. The first conversation often sets the tone for the whole claim. Good communication can help keep things calm or, if lacking, make things worse. The adjuster's role is key to keeping things clear.

Technical accuracy remains the foundation, but now leadership shapes how it is shared, recorded, and used. The adjuster's job is to guide the claim, not just process it. Guidance, not just evaluation, is now the defining responsibility of the adjuster.

Complexity Has Become the New Normal

Today's claims environment is complex. Disasters can affect entire communities. Infrastructure failures often involve many parties and shifting responsibilities. Lawsuits happen more often, so documentation and communication are examined more closely. Even routine claims can lead to disputes over scope, value, or coverage.

Adjusters often juggle many demands across several claims at once. Timelines can change because of access issues or contractor schedules. Information comes in stages, and decisions sometimes have to be made before everything is known. These challenges call for discipline, organization, and sound judgment.

In this setting, leadership is part of daily work. Adjusters set expectations early, keep things on track as information changes, and document decisions to keep the claim clear and defensible. Leadership shows through structure, clear communication, and consistency. Complexity is no longer an exception is the operating condition of modern claims handling.

The Human Dimension of Claims Work

Claims work also has a strong human side. Adjusters often talk with people and businesses going through tough times. These conversations can include uncertainty, money worries, and planning for recovery. Adjusters need to show empathy while staying professional.

At the same time, adjusters handle heavy workloads, travel, and make quick decisions. Ongoing pressure can affect how they communicate, focus, and make choices. Staying clear in these situations takes organization, discipline, and resilience.

The human aspect of claims work ensures technical accuracy. Clear communication keeps claims on track. Organized workflows reduce confusion. Consistent documentation maintains smooth progress. Sustainable habits enable adjusters to perform well, even in challenging situations. Professional clarity depends on the ability to manage both the technical and human dimensions of the role.

Why Claim Leadership Matters

You don't need formal authority to show claim leadership. Adjusters work with contractors, engineers, carriers, and policyholders, all of whom shape the outcome. The adjuster's job is to guide this teamwork by offering clarity and keeping things on track.

Leadership in claims is demonstrated through clear communication, well-organized documentation, and setting achievable expectations. When these elements are in place, claims progress smoothly and stay on schedule. Without them, confusion increases, and disputes become more common.

Claim leadership improves both the process and the results. Policyholders know what to expect next. Stakeholders stay on the same page. Decisions are easier to defend. The claim moves forward smoothly. Leadership stabilizes the claim as complexity increases.

How This Book Is Structured

This book shows how the adjuster's role is changing.

Part I looks at how adjusting is changing and how the role is shifting from technical work to claim leadership.

Part II focuses on catastrophe claims and the challenges they pose.

Part III covers litigation risks, documentation, and how to make claims defensible.

Part IV explores leadership in claims, including how to influence without authority and make decisions under pressure.

Part V looks at sustainability, resilience, and the long-term demands of the profession.

Each chapter provides practical guidance for real-world claims situations. The aim is not to replace technical training, but to help you apply it more effectively through disciplined leadership. The design of this book reflects the level of organization and coordination required to manage modern claims successfully.

Who This Book Is For

This book is for adjusters working in today's claims environments, whether you're an independent adjuster, staff adjuster, catastrophe adjuster, or a claims professional handling complex cases. It is also useful for supervisors and claims leaders who support adjusting teams.

Whether you are new to adjusting or experienced in complex claims, the ideas in this book are designed to help you build alignment, reliability, and sound judgment. The goal is not to change your technical methods, but to strengthen how you move claims from start to finish. Every claim depends on professional judgment. Documentation, communication, and decision-making shape the process. Adjusters influence outcomes by establishing clear expectations, maintaining consistency, and applying disciplined leadership.

Leadership begins with the first conversation and continues through resolution. When you stay organized, communicate effectively, and document decisions with care, you stabilize complex situations. These habits lead to defensible decisions, professional communication, and consistent results.

Modern adjusting requires more than evaluation. It demands leadership that brings organization to uncertainty and keeps the process moving forward. The standard you apply from the beginning of the claim defines the outcome.

INTRODUCTION

Leading the Claim in a Changing Industry

The Industry Has Already Changed

The insurance claims industry has already changed. What used to be a structured, process-focused job is now a fast-paced environment marked by more frequent catastrophes, greater legal risks, higher claim amounts, and heightened expectations from policyholders, carriers, and stakeholders. Claims often unfold in urgent situations where information changes quickly, access is limited, and decisions must be made before all the facts are known. Adjusters deal with these changes every day, often without guidance that matches what they actually face.

There are more claims than before. Expectations have increased. Deadlines are shorter. Complexity is now a regular part of the job. The role has grown, and so have the demands. Adjusters are not just managing claims anymore—they are leading them. Modern claims environments require adjusters to provide structure from the outset of a claim.

There is also more scrutiny now. Claim files are reviewed more closely. Documentation is checked in detail. Decisions are judged by changing standards. Lawsuits can happen earlier in the process. Adjusters need to be professional from the very first interaction. There is less room for error, but more responsibility.

These changes have redefined the job. Technical skill remains important, but it is not enough on its own. Today's adjuster needs to provide direction when uncertainty arises, stay consistent under pressure, and guide the claim as it progresses. Clarity and consistency are now required to meet modern standards of claim handling.

Handling the Claim Is No Longer Enough

Traditional claims handling was all about following the process: inspect the loss, review the policy, document what you find, and share the results. That foundation is still important, but today's claims need more. The adjuster's role now starts earlier and lasts longer. The first conversation sets expectations. Early documentation shapes what happens next. Good communication helps reduce uncertainty. Decisions often have to be made even when all the information isn't in yet.

Adjusters now manage the claim from beginning to end. This change is not about having more authority, but about bringing structure. By organizing information, keeping communication clear, and documenting decisions, adjusters shape how the claim moves forward.

This change has reshaped what it means to be an adjuster. The role now includes coordinating, communicating, and exercising sound judgment in dynamic conditions. Adjusters must anticipate questions, set clear expectations, and maintain direction as situations evolve. This is what separates simply reacting to a claim from leading it with purpose. Providing that direction is now the defining responsibility of the modern adjuster.

Complexity Is Now the Baseline

Every day claims are now more complex. The first inspection might only show some of the damage. Experts can add new factors. Coverage rules can change. Different people involved may expect different things. Adjusters have to handle all these moving parts while staying steady.

Catastrophes make this even more challenging. Big losses create many demands at once. Getting access can take time. Resources might be limited. Many people may be involved. Information comes in stages, but decisions still need to be made to keep the claim moving.

Even simple claims can get complicated. People may disagree about the scope, value, or interpretation of the policy. Contractors might give different estimates. Experts may not agree. Policyholders might question decisions. Adjusters need to keep things on track as issues arise.

This takes discipline, good judgment, and clear communication. Adjusters need to explain uncertainty without causing confusion, document decisions as things change, and find the right balance between speed and accuracy. Complexity is no longer occasional—it is the operating condition of the role.

The Policyholder Is Looking for Direction

Every claim involves a policyholder going through a tough time. Their home might be damaged, their business interrupted, or their family displaced. Financial worries often follow. Policyholders rely on the adjuster to explain what will happen next.

Early communication sets the tone for the whole process. Clear explanations help avoid confusion, and realistic timelines help manage expectations. Regular updates prevent problems from getting worse. Professional communication builds trust and keeps the claim moving.

If communication is unstructured, people get frustrated. When expectations are unclear, people seek more opinions. If updates are inconsistent, trust fades. These issues make problems worse and slow down resolution.

Adjusters do not have to promise certainty when it is not possible. Instead, they should be clear about what is known, open about what is still developing, and give direction on what comes next. This helps keep the process steady and shows professionalism. Direction, not certainty, is what stabilizes the claim.

Documentation Has Become Operational Leadership

Documentation is more than just keeping records. It brings structure to the claim. The file explains what was observed, supports decisions, tracks communication, and keeps everyone on the same page. Clear documentation helps avoid confusion and makes the claim easier to defend.

Today, many people review the claim file. Supervisors, experts, attorneys, and other stakeholders depend on documentation to see what happened and why decisions were made. Inconsistent documentation creates uncertainty. Clear records help everyone stay aligned.

Adjusters who use documentation as a leadership tool create files that support accuracy and consistency. They record what they see, explain their reasoning, and note the next steps. This helps with both making decisions and defending them later. Documentation is not just recordkeeping—it is the structure that supports every stage of the claim.

Communication Under Pressure Defines Outcomes

Modern adjusting requires constant communication. Adjusters interact with policyholders, contractors, engineers, attorneys, and internal teams as conditions evolve. Without discipline, communication becomes reactive. A defined approach helps keep the claim steady.

Providing updates, explaining next steps, and maintaining records of conversations improve understanding. Professional communication does not reduce complexity, but it helps manage the situation and prevent issues from escalating.

Pressure influences tone and messaging. Heavy workloads and emotionally charged conversations increase the risk of misunderstanding. Disciplined communication maintains reliability and ensures stakeholders receive accurate information.

Communication is more than exchange; it is a leadership tool. Confusion does not come from complexity; it comes from a lack of direction. Silence creates more work than communication ever will. Disciplined communication turns complexity into manageable progress.

Decisions Must Be Made Before Everything Is Known

Adjusters almost never have all the information. Inspections might not be finished. Reports could still be in progress. Conditions can change. Even so, decisions still need to be made to keep the claim moving.

Adjusters have to balance working quickly with being accurate, write down their reasoning, and review their decisions as new information comes in. Making good decisions in uncertain situations is a key skill for today's adjusters.

Delays create uncertainty. Rushed decisions create variability. A disciplined decision-making approach supports alignment and adaptability. Adjusters assess available information, apply judgment, and communicate next steps. Sound decisions preserve continuity even when conditions are incomplete.

Leading Without Formal Authority Is the Reality

Adjusters often work in teams where authority is shared. Contractors, engineers, attorneys, and policyholders all play a role in the outcome. In this setting, leadership is not about control; it is about establishing alignment. Adjusters move the claim forward by organizing information, aligning communication, and sustaining momentum. This practical leadership keeps the claim progressing even in complex conditions. Leadership is demonstrated through alignment, not control.

Sustainability in a High-Demand Role

Modern adjusting means you have to keep performing well over time. High claim volumes, complex cases, and tough conversations can make it harder to stay clear. Being tired affects how you communicate. Being overloaded affects your decisions.

Having structured workflows, organized documentation, and consistent communication methods helps adjusters maintain their performance. These habits support both doing the job well and maintaining high claim quality. Sustained performance depends on structured and repeatable professional habits.

Professional Responsibility in a Changing Environment

As things get more complex, professional responsibility matters even more. Decisions made under pressure, notes written during busy times, and communication with others may all be reviewed later. The claim file is the record of your professional judgment.

Clear documentation, careful communication, and structured decision-making protect both the claim and the adjuster. These habits build credibility and help you perform well over the long term.

Modern adjusting takes more than just technical skills. It also needs good judgment, clear ethics, and steady leadership, especially under pressure.

This Book Is Written for the Modern Claim Environment

This book is about leadership within the claim process. It covers how to communicate under pressure, use documentation as a leadership tool, make decisions as conditions evolve, and bring alignment to complex situations. It helps you apply your technical skills in real-world environments.

The industry has already changed. Complexity is now the norm. Expectations are higher. Adjusters are being asked to lead. This book is designed to support that role and help you move claims forward with reliability and sound judgment. Professional responsibility is demonstrated through disciplined handling, documentation, and communication.

PRELUDE

The Mosaic Way as the Operating Architecture

This book focuses on practical claim leadership. The chapters that follow are designed to help adjusters bring clarity, structure, and consistency to claims, especially in complex, high-volume environments. The emphasis is on real-world actions, communication, documentation, and workflow leadership throughout the claims process.

Underlying this approach are broader leadership perspectives, the Mosaic Way and the Mosaic Intelligence Method™. Although this book does not formally teach that model, it serves as the operating architecture for the leadership principles presented throughout these chapters. The concepts in this book reflect that approach without requiring adjusters to learn or apply a separate framework.

The Mosaic Way emphasizes leadership in complex, dynamic environments. It focuses on maintaining clarity under pressure, tailoring communication to stakeholders, and guiding outcomes as conditions evolve. These principles align naturally with modern claims adjusting, where adjusters must navigate uncertainty, manage expectations, and maintain direction across multiple conversations.

This perspective is reflected in three leadership capabilities. Emotional Integrity supports calm, professional decision-making in uncertain situations. Cultural Flexibility supports adapting communication for policyholders, contractors, carriers, and technical stakeholders. Identity Agility supports shifting among roles, including evaluator, communicator, coordinator, and claim leader, as conditions evolve.

These capabilities are not presented as a required model in this book. Instead, they serve as the leadership foundation that informs the practical claim guidance that follows. Adjusters do not need to formally apply the Mosaic Intelligence Method™ to benefit from this material. The goal is not to introduce a new system but to strengthen clarity, consistency, and leadership in the claim process.

The chapters that follow focus on practical application. The Mosaic Way remains in the background, guiding the approach and enabling adjusters to apply leadership principles naturally in daily claim management.

This operating architecture supports the consistent application of clarity, communication, and professional leadership throughout the claim process.

PART I

The New Reality of Modern Adjusting

The adjuster's role has evolved from a technical focus on inspection, estimation, and documentation to one that demands leadership, coordination, and professional judgment. Today's claims environments feature higher volumes, greater complexity, and increased expectations from policyholders, carriers, contractors, and other stakeholders. Adjusters are now expected to guide the claim process, maintain structure, and drive claims toward resolution.

This shift has occurred gradually but decisively. Catastrophe events now affect broader areas and generate large volumes of claims simultaneously. Losses often involve multiple stakeholders, changing information, and extended recovery periods. Policyholders seek early clarity, while carriers require organized documentation and consistent decisions. Contractors, engineers, and specialists also contribute to claim development. Internal teams, including supervisors and desk adjusters, require ongoing updates and alignment. The adjuster coordinates these efforts, operating at the intersection of technical assessment, internal coordination, and professional leadership.

Litigation exposure has changed claims handling. Documentation, communication, and decision rationale now face greater scrutiny. Claim files must include observations, structured reasoning, consistent communication, and clear timelines. Adjusters must consider how their documentation and communication affect the entire claim. Tone, timing, and clarity all influence the progression of a claim. This environment demands discipline, consistency, and awareness from the outset.

Policyholders often begin the claims process amid disruption and uncertainty. Homes may be damaged, businesses may be interrupted, and recovery timelines may be unclear. Adjusters are often the first source of structured guidance. Setting expectations, explaining next steps, and communicating calmly help stabilize the claim environment. Clear communication reduces confusion and helps policyholders understand the process. In this context, leadership is defined by clarity, consistency, and professional direction, not authority.

Modern adjusting is defined by leadership amid complexity. Adjusters must manage communication, organize documentation, and maintain continuity as conditions change. They must balance empathy with professionalism, speed with accuracy, and responsiveness with careful evaluation. These responsibilities require discipline, technical precision, and confident claim leadership. Adjusters must guide claims forward while ensuring clarity for all participants.

Modern claims handling requires proactive organization. Tracking inspections, documenting communication, and recording decisions create continuity. Structured documentation keeps claim progression clear, even with multiple participants. Organized files support efficient handling and strengthen defensibility. Consistent workflows reduce confusion and maintain focus throughout the claim lifecycle. These practices help adjusters maintain control in complex environments.

This section examines the shift from traditional claim handling to claim leadership. The following chapters discuss how adjusters set direction early, manage scale during catastrophe events, navigate litigation exposure, and maintain clarity under pressure. These topics reflect the realities of modern claims handling and the adjuster's expanding role.

Modern adjusting requires more than technical evaluation. It demands leadership that guides claims, stabilizes processes, and supports consistent results. Through structured documentation, clear communication, and disciplined handling, adjusters provide direction in complex claims environments. This professional leadership defines the new reality of modern adjusting.

CHAPTER 1

The Adjuster as Claim Leader

Event Spotlight — Maui Wildfires (Hawaii)

Entire communities were destroyed within hours as wind-driven wildfires moved rapidly through Lahaina. Thousands of structures were lost, infrastructure failed, and communication systems collapsed. Policyholders were displaced without access to documents, resources, or a clear path forward, creating immediate uncertainty at the start of the claims process.

Adjusters entered environments where loss extended beyond property damage into stability, identity, and continuity. Homes were gone, records were missing, and expectations were unclear for both policyholders and response teams. Claims often began before any organized process was in place, requiring adjusters to establish direction while information was still developing.

Industry estimates placed insured losses between approximately \$5.5 billion and \$6 billion, making the event one of the costliest wildfire disasters in United States history. This was not simply a claims event—it was a leadership event. Adjusters were required to guide conversations, set expectations, and bring clarity to situations where policyholders had no clear starting point.

CHAPTER FOCUS

Modern adjusters are no longer just documenting losses. They are leading the claim from the first conversation forward. Leadership now begins at first contact, not at resolution.

The Evolution of the Adjuster's Role

The adjuster's role has evolved from a technical position focused on inspection, scope development, and documentation to a leadership function within the claims process. Modern adjusters guide claims from uncertainty to clarity, managing communication, expectations, and direction throughout the claim lifecycle.

Adjusters now operate in an environment defined by higher claim volumes, complex policies, increased litigation, and elevated policyholder expectations. The process is dynamic, requiring adjusters to manage evolving information and multiple conversations simultaneously. Beyond technical evaluation, adjusters must guide discussions, clarify next steps, and maintain direction as claims progress.

Technology continues to reshape claims handling. Artificial intelligence, automated estimating, and digital inspection tools enhance efficiency and organization, but they do not replace the adjuster. Claims still require professional judgment, human interaction, and the ability to provide explanation, reassurance, and direction to policyholders.

As automation expands, the human aspect of adjusting becomes more critical. Adjusters interpret findings, explain decisions, manage expectations, and guide conversations—especially in high-stress situations. While technology processes data, only adjusters can address emotion, resolve misunderstandings, and build trust.

Technical skill remains essential, but it is no longer sufficient. Adjusters must also demonstrate leadership by organizing claims, communicating clearly, and maintaining consistency. They are responsible for guiding claims toward resolution at every stage.

Many adjusters operate across multiple lines of business, including property, liability, and catastrophe response. The core principles of communication, documentation, and structured evaluation apply across these environments.

The modern adjuster is no longer defined by what they document, but by how they guide the claim.

Leadership Within the Claim Process

Leadership in adjusting does not require formal authority. Adjusters rarely control every aspect of a claim, as contractors, engineers, policyholders, carriers, and internal teams all contribute. In this shared environment, adjusters provide structure, maintain clarity, and keep the process moving forward.

Claim leadership starts by reducing uncertainty: identifying completed tasks, explaining what remains, and outlining next steps. Consistent communication ensures stakeholders receive accurate information. Without these elements, confusion and delays increase.

Adjusters create stability by providing clarity. Explaining next steps, decision-making processes, and documenting progress helps align stakeholders. Confirming inspections, communicating review timelines, and scheduling updates all reduce uncertainty and keep claims moving forward.

When adjusters take on this leadership role, claims become more organized, conversations stay focused, expectations are realistic, and the process becomes easier to manage for all parties. Claims do not slow down because of complexity. They slow down because of confusion.

Establishing Direction Early

Initial claim interactions often determine the direction of the process. Policyholders seek early guidance on next steps, timelines, and required information, often while facing disruption or uncertainty. The adjuster's response at this stage sets the claim's direction and establishes trust for future communication.

Establishing direction early does not require all the answers. It involves outlining the process, providing structure, and acknowledging the policyholder's situation. Explaining inspection timing, required documentation, communication methods, and update schedules reduces uncertainty and strengthens engagement.

Early trust brings practical benefits. Clear expectations focus communication, explained timelines make follow-up manageable, and contextual decisions reduce friction. Establishing trust early reduces escalation, supports collaboration, and improves claim efficiency.

Without early direction, claims become reactive. Policyholders request updates without understanding the process, and stakeholders develop conflicting expectations. Adjusters then spend time clarifying issues that could have been addressed from the start. Early leadership improves efficiency and strengthens relationships.

Communication as a Leadership Function

Communication is a key leadership tool for adjusters. Multiple stakeholder conversations shape expectations, clarify decisions, and guide next steps. Early, structured communication keeps claims aligned and reduces disruptions.

Clear communication reduces repeated calls, prevents misunderstandings, and limits the need to revisit decisions later. A brief explanation early can prevent multiple follow-up conversations, saving time as the claim progresses. Adjusters explain findings in plain language, provide updates when timelines change, and document key conversations to ensure continuity.

Communication also shapes how stakeholders experience the claim. When communication is consistent, stakeholders feel informed and more confident in the process. When communication is unclear or inconsistent, questions multiply, expectations diverge, and additional conversations become necessary. Structured communication breaks this cycle and keeps the claim organized.

Strong communication does not eliminate challenges, but it helps manage them efficiently. It reduces rework, minimizes repeated explanations, and supports smoother progress. Silence in a claim creates more work than communication ever will.

Managing Expectations

Expectations shape how a claim is experienced by everyone involved. Policyholders may expect immediate resolution. Contractors may anticipate quick approvals. Engineers may require additional review time. Internal teams may expect documentation within specific timelines. Each stakeholder approaches the claim from a different perspective, and these expectations do not always align.

The adjuster operates at the intersection of internal and external conversations. Managing expectations requires aligning both sides so the claim progresses with a shared understanding rather than competing assumptions. This includes providing realistic timelines, explaining what is under review, and outlining the remaining steps.

Unmanaged expectations lead to reactive communication. Policyholders request frequent updates, contractors seek early approvals, and internal teams ask for clarification. These overlapping conversations increase workload and pressure. Proactive management breaks this cycle.

Managing expectations does not mean promising outcomes. It means explaining the process. When expectations are aligned early, communication becomes more focused, follow-up questions decline, and the claim advances more efficiently.

REAL WORLD
Aligning a Multi-Stakeholder Claim

A wind loss is reported after a severe storm. The policyholder expects immediate approval for roof replacement. A contractor submits an estimate on the same day and requests authorization to begin work. At the same time, the carrier requests additional documentation, and an engineering review is under consideration due to conflicting damage indicators.

Each stakeholder has different expectations. The policyholder anticipates a quick resolution. The contractor expects approval. The carrier requires further evaluation. Without coordination, these conversations can quickly create confusion and frustration.

The adjuster sets the direction by outlining the claim's sequence. The policyholder is informed that the inspection is complete, the estimate is under review, and engineering input may be required before the coverage determination is finalized. The contractor is advised that the review is underway and that authorization will be issued upon completion of the evaluation. The carrier is updated on the inspection findings and the need for additional review.

By outlining the process and next steps, the adjuster sets clear expectations. Stakeholders understand that the evaluation is ongoing rather than delayed. Follow-up questions decrease, and the claim progresses in an organized manner.

Documentation That Guides the Claim

Documentation serves as the operational record of the claim. The file captures evaluations, decision reasoning, and next steps. Well-structured documentation keeps the claim moving with continuity.

Effective documentation connects events across time. It records timelines, captures key conversations, and identifies pending actions. This continuity allows the claim to progress without relying on memory or repeated explanation. Anyone reviewing the file can understand what has happened and what comes next.

In complex claims environments, this continuity is critical. Multiple stakeholders may review the file at different points. Supervisors, engineers, desk adjusters, and attorneys rely on documentation to understand prior decisions. When documentation clearly reflects reasoning and next steps, the claim maintains consistency even as participants change.

Clear documentation reduces friction, supports efficient handling, and reinforces direction. It captures progress, preserves continuity, and helps maintain alignment as conditions evolve. Documentation is not record-keeping. It is claim control.

Balancing Technical Skill and Leadership

Technical knowledge is essential in adjusting. Accurate inspections, sound policy interpretation, and clear scope development form the foundation of every claim, ensuring proper evaluation and fact-based decisions. However, technical expertise alone is not enough. Modern adjusters combine technical skill with communication, documentation, and expectation management. Findings must be clearly explained, thoroughly documented, and linked to next steps.

When leadership and technical skill align, claims progress smoothly. Stakeholders understand decisions and reasoning, timelines become clearer, and communication remains reliable. This disciplined approach supports efficiency and professionalism. This balance defines modern adjusting: technical skill provides the foundation, while leadership ensures claims move forward with alignment and reliability.

REAL WORLD

Auto Claim: Rapid Decision-Making Under Pressure

An adjuster handled a multi-vehicle accident with conflicting driver accounts and limited initial documentation. Each party expected a quick determination of liability, while additional information was still being gathered.

The adjuster documented available statements, identified information gaps, and explained that the claim remained under review pending further evaluation. Communication focused on the process rather than immediate conclusions.

Through structured documentation and consistent communication, the adjuster maintained clarity while the investigation progressed. This approach helped manage expectations, reduce escalation, and support a defensible outcome in a fast-paced environment.

Leadership Through Consistency

Consistency is a defining quality in claim leadership. In high-volume environments, consistent communication, documentation, and decision-making reduce the need to reinvent processes, allowing adjusters to work efficiently and maintain professionalism.

Consistency creates predictability. Structured updates, clear explanations, and defined next steps help stakeholders understand claim progress, reducing repeated questions and reactive conversations. Consistency also reduces decision fatigue. When communication and workflow are consistent, adjusters can focus on claim-specific issues rather than process decisions.

Consistency supports credibility. Steady communication and documentation build stakeholder confidence. Over time, consistency improves efficiency, reduces friction, and reinforces the adjuster's role as a reliable guide.

Stepping Into the Claim Leader Role

Becoming a claim leader does not require a complete overhaul. It involves strengthening guidance throughout the claim lifecycle. Small improvements in communication, documentation, and expectation management can have a significant impact.

Adjusters who take on this role bring clarity to complexity by providing early direction, maintaining consistency, communicating professionally, and documenting thoroughly. These actions prevent confusion, reduce escalation, and support steady progress.

The modern claims environment requires this level of leadership. High claim volume, complexity, and expectations demand more than technical evaluation. Adjusters must guide the process, align stakeholders, and maintain structure throughout. The adjuster is no longer simply processing the claim. The adjuster is leading it.

Practical Claim Leadership Actions

Turning Leadership into Action Across Every Stage of the Claim

Stepping into the claim leader role requires intentional, repeatable actions. Claim leadership is demonstrated through structure, communication, and consistency. These practices help adjusters guide claims from uncertainty to resolution while maintaining clarity, alignment, and professionalism.

START STRONG — SET DIRECTION EARLY

Begin the claim by outlining the process. Explain what will happen first, what information is needed, and when the next update will occur. Establishing direction during the first contact reduces uncertainty and prevents reactive communication later. Early clarity helps policyholders understand the path forward and stabilizes expectations.

KEY ACTIONS:

Outline inspection timing
Explain documentation needs
Identify the next step
Set update expectations

GO-TO LINES:

"Here's what will happen next."
"The first step is completing the inspection."
"After that, I'll review the findings and follow up."
"You can expect an update by [timeframe]."

KEEP THE CLAIM MOVING — COMMUNICATE NEXT STEPS

After each major interaction, confirm what has been completed and what happens next. This keeps stakeholders aligned and prevents confusion. Clear next steps build momentum and reduce the need for repeated questions.

KEY ACTIONS:

Confirm what was completed
Identify what is under review
State next action
Provide update timing

GO-TO LINES:

"At this point, the inspection is complete."
"The estimate is currently under review."
"The next step is..."
"I'll follow up once that review is finished."

BUILD DEFENSIBILITY — DOCUMENT REASONING

Documentation should explain both observations and decisions. Record findings, reasoning, and follow-up actions. Clear documentation strengthens defensibility and supports continuity when multiple stakeholders are involved.

KEY ACTIONS:

Record observations
Explain conclusions
Document communication
Identify follow-up actions

GO-TO LINES:

"Based on the inspection..."
"The evaluation indicates..."
"Additional review is being requested..."
"Next steps include..."

MAINTAIN STABILITY — PROVIDE CONSISTENT UPDATES

Even when the evaluation is ongoing, provide status updates. Consistent communication builds confidence and reduces escalation. Silence often creates uncertainty, while structured updates maintain alignment.

KEY ACTIONS:

Confirm evaluation status
Communicate delays early
Reinforce next step
Maintain update cadence

GO-TO LINES:

"Evaluation is still underway."
"I wanted to provide a status update."
"There are no changes yet, but review continues."
"I'll update you as soon as I receive additional information."

ALIGN EXPECTATIONS — SET REALISTIC TIMELINES

Avoid overly optimistic timelines. Explain review steps, coordination needs, and possible variables. Realistic expectations reduce frustration and support smoother claim progression.

KEY ACTIONS:

Explain the review process
Identify dependencies
Avoid premature commitments
Update timelines when needed

GO-TO LINES:

"This may require additional review."
"Timing will depend on..."
"I want to set realistic expectations."
"Once review is complete, we can move forward."

CLOSE WITH DIRECTION — END EVERY CONVERSATION CLEARLY

Each interaction should end with clarity. Confirm what happens next and when communication will occur. This reinforces structure and keeps the claim moving forward.

KEY ACTIONS:

Confirm next step
Set update timing
Clarify responsibilities
Reinforce expectations

GO-TO LINES:

"The next step will be..."
"You can expect an update..."
"I'll reach out once..."
"That keeps us moving forward."

CLAIM LEADERSHIP
SUMMARY

Key Takeaway

The modern adjuster leads the claim from the first conversation forward. Policyholders often enter the process with uncertainty, incomplete information, and emotional stress. Establishing clarity early builds trust, aligns expectations, and creates structure. Leadership begins at first contact and continues through each step of the claim.

In Practice

When opening a claim, focus first on direction. Explain what will happen next, outline the process, and set communication expectations. Early structure stabilizes the claim, reduces repeated questions, and supports efficient handling.

Questions for Reflection

1. What expectations do I set during my first conversation with a policyholder?
2. Do I clearly explain what happens next?
3. How do I establish direction when information is still developing?

Claim Leadership Principle

The adjuster who establishes direction early creates clarity, builds trust, and stabilizes the claim.

CHAPTER 2

When Catastrophe Strikes at Scale

Event Spotlight — Hurricane Ida

Hurricane Ida caused widespread destruction across Louisiana before moving into the Northeast, producing catastrophe-related wind and flood losses across multiple regions. Areas not historically considered high-risk experienced severe flooding, overwhelmed response systems, and created unexpected claim concentrations. Infrastructure challenges delayed inspections, and policyholders sought immediate answers as conditions continued to evolve.

Claims surged across multiple states at once, increasing the complexity of deployment and communication. Adjusters were assigned heavy workloads, multiple claim types, and rapidly changing conditions. Many were required to prioritize, triage, and make decisions with incomplete information while maintaining consistency across files, reinforcing the need for disciplined judgment under pressure rather than reactive decision-making.

Industry estimates placed insured losses above $36 billion, positioning Hurricane Ida among the most significant catastrophe events in recent history. Scale changed the nature of adjusting, shifting the focus from individual claim handling to volume management and structured decision-making. The challenge was no longer simply handling a claim; it became maintaining clarity, consistency, and quality across multiple claims simultaneously.

CHAPTER FOCUS

Catastrophe adjusting at scale requires structured leadership, disciplined decision-making, and consistent communication under pressure.

The Shift From Individual Claims to Mass Impact

Catastrophe events fundamentally change claims adjusting. Individual claims become part of a large-scale response involving hundreds or thousands of losses. Weather events, wildfires, floods, and regional disasters require adjusters to work in high-volume, rapidly changing environments. The nature of the work shifts, not just its volume.

In routine claims handling, adjusters work at a predictable pace. Catastrophe events eliminate this predictability. Claims arrive at once, property access may be restricted, policyholders may be displaced, infrastructure can be damaged, and communication networks may be unreliable. Adjusters must provide structure amid this instability, using clarity as a stabilizing force rather than relying on routine.

The scale of catastrophe claims alters decision-making. Adjusters must balance multiple priorities, move between claims, and ensure efficient communication and clear documentation as conditions evolve. They become part of a coordinated response rather than isolated claim handlers.

This shift broadens the adjuster's role. Technical evaluation remains vital, but coordination, organization, and communication are equally important. Adjusters help stabilize high-volume responses, not just assess damage.

Operating in High-Volume Environments

High claim volume defines catastrophe adjusting. Adjusters may handle dozens of claims in a short period, requiring a different approach. Without organization, tracking becomes difficult, communication turns reactive, and timelines slip. In some environments, adjusters may also be expected to bring specialized knowledge or certifications—particularly in mitigation, environmental conditions, or complex loss evaluation—reflecting the increasing complexity of modern claims handling.

Effective operation in high-volume environments requires deliberate organization. Adjusters should group claims by location, accessibility, or severity and establish defined workflows to maintain efficiency and reliability. This approach reduces mental load and supports alignment across files.

Communication shifts in high-volume settings. Policyholders often request updates simultaneously, so adjusters must balance responsiveness with workload. Setting expectations early is critical. When policyholders understand that inspections are scheduled based on routing, severity, or access, follow-up inquiries decrease. Clear initial communication reduces later pressure.

Documentation becomes even more critical as volume increases. Clear notes preserve context as adjusters move quickly between claims. Consistent documentation supports continuity and enables smooth transitions across the claim process.

High volume does not diminish the need for quality—it increases the need for discipline. Structured processes support both efficiency and accuracy, allowing adjusters to manage scale while maintaining clarity.

Rapid Deployment and Changing Conditions

Catastrophe events often require rapid deployment. Adjusters may travel to unfamiliar areas, work from temporary locations, and adapt to changing conditions. These factors introduce logistical challenges that impact claims handling.

Access to affected areas may be limited by road closures, safety concerns, or weather. Utilities may be disrupted, and policyholders may be absent. Adjusters must adapt while maintaining professionalism and structure. Flexibility is essential, as plans may change throughout the day.

Preparation reduces disruption. Organizing routes, confirming appointments, and verifying access before travel all help maintain efficiency. Even with planning, conditions can change quickly, so adjusters must be ready to shift priorities while maintaining communication and direction.

Communication is especially important during rapid deployment. Policyholders may be anxious for updates, particularly if inspections are delayed. Clear explanations help manage expectations, prevent frustration, and maintain trust.

Adjusters in catastrophe environments must balance speed with clarity. Acting quickly is necessary, but maintaining structure ensures consistency across claims.

Deployment Readiness and Availability

Catastrophe adjusting often requires rapid deployment with limited notice. Adjusters may be placed on standby and expected to respond quickly as events develop. Availability, mobility, and readiness become part of the role.

Maintaining updated availability, preparing for travel, and responding promptly to deployment requests support operational efficiency. Clear communication with carriers or firms regarding availability helps ensure assignments are managed effectively during high-demand periods.

Catastrophe adjusting often involves working within established carrier or independent adjusting firm networks. Maintaining updated profiles and consistent communication supports assignment opportunities and operational alignment during high-demand periods.

Adjusting roles may vary between field deployment and desk-based environments. While the setting may differ, the need for clear documentation, structured communication, and professional judgment remains consistent. Availability and responsiveness often influence assignment opportunities, particularly in catastrophe environments where rapid deployment is required.

Debris Removal and Site Conditions

Catastrophe events, particularly hurricanes, often generate significant debris, including damaged roofing materials, structural components, vegetation, and personal property. Debris removal may begin before or between inspections and can quickly alter site conditions. Adjusters should document conditions as observed at the time of inspection, recognizing that debris removal, emergency repairs, and mitigation efforts may alter the property. Photographs and clear notes help preserve an accurate record of the loss before conditions change.

Debris removal may also involve multiple parties, including contractors, municipal services, and specialized vendors. Coordination and clear documentation help maintain alignment as site conditions evolve. Clear communication supports claim clarity when conditions change rapidly during recovery efforts.

Prioritization in Catastrophe Claims

Catastrophe claims vary in urgency. Some involve total losses or displacement, while others are less severe. Adjusters must prioritize effectively to manage volume responsibly.

Prioritization starts with severity. Claims with safety concerns or significant displacement require prompt attention. Accessibility also affects scheduling, and grouping nearby properties improves efficiency while addressing urgent claims.

Clear prioritization ensures critical claims receive timely attention and maintains fairness across the inventory. Without it, scheduling becomes reactive and difficult to manage.

Communicating prioritization is essential. When policyholders understand scheduling is based on severity, displacement, or access, expectations become more realistic. Transparency supports professionalism and alignment. Effective prioritization allows adjusters to manage scale while maintaining clarity.

Communication During Catastrophe Events

Communication during catastrophe events is essential but challenging. Policyholders face significant disruption and seek clear expectations for timelines, inspections, and next steps. Adjusters must provide information while managing heavy workloads.

Clear, structured communication stabilizes the process. Providing an early overview reduces uncertainty. Explaining expected timelines, even if approximate, helps policyholders know what to expect.

Consistency is critical. Mixed messages or unclear updates cause confusion. Maintaining steady communication, confirming appointments, providing status updates, and documenting conversations help manage volume and prevent repeated inquiries.

Communication extends beyond policyholders. Adjusters coordinate with carriers, contractors, engineers, and internal teams. Clear updates maintain alignment, which becomes more important as claim volume increases. Professional communication supports efficiency, trust, and overall claim progression.

Mitigation and Environmental Considerations

Catastrophe events often involve immediate mitigation needs, particularly in water-related losses. Emergency drying, mold prevention, and containment efforts may begin before or between inspections. These activities can significantly affect site conditions and the scope of the loss.

Adjusters should document conditions as observed and note any ongoing or completed mitigation efforts. Understanding the role of mitigation helps support accurate evaluation and clear communication with policyholders and contractors. Coordination with mitigation providers ensures alignment as the claim develops. Mitigation timelines, documentation, and scope may also influence coverage discussions and claim progression.

Supplements

In catastrophe environments such as hurricanes and severe wind events, supplemental claim activity often increases as conditions stabilize and additional damage is identified. Initial inspections may be limited by access, safety concerns, or time constraints, and subsequent evaluations frequently introduce new scope considerations. Contractors, engineers, and policyholders may present revised estimates as repair efforts begin and hidden damage becomes more apparent.

Adjusters must approach supplements in these environments with structure and consistency. Each revision should be evaluated against original documentation, with clear reasoning recorded to explain how scope decisions evolve. In catastrophe claims, supplements are not exceptions—they are part of the claim lifecycle and require the same level of discipline as the initial evaluation.

Supplements, revised scope, and evolving findings are not disruptions to the claim process; they are part of it. Consistency in how these changes are handled determines whether the claim remains aligned or becomes fragmented.

REAL WORLD
Managing a Catastrophe Deployment

A major hailstorm strikes a metropolitan area, generating hundreds of claims quickly. Adjusters are deployed, inspection schedules fill immediately, policyholders expect fast responses, contractors submit estimates, and some properties are inaccessible due to debris and repairs.

The adjuster receives a large assignment across multiple neighborhoods. Inspections are grouped by location, reducing travel time and increasing efficiency. Policyholders are informed that scheduling is based on geographic routing and severity, which helps manage expectations.

On the first day, several properties are inaccessible. The adjuster clearly communicates with affected policyholders about rescheduling due to access limitations, preventing confusion and reducing follow-up calls. Documentation is updated after each inspection to maintain continuity.

Contractors request immediate approvals. The adjuster explains that estimates will be reviewed after inspections, aligning expectations and preventing premature authorization requests.

By grouping inspections, communicating early, and maintaining consistent documentation, the adjuster manages high-volume deployment with structure. Technical evaluation remains important, but organization and communication stabilize the response. Claims progress efficiently, and stakeholders understand the process despite the scale of the event.

Documentation Under Time Pressure

Catastrophe adjusting often involves tight timelines. Inspections and reports must be completed quickly, but documentation must remain clear and thorough despite these pressures.

Documentation under time pressure requires discipline. Recording observations immediately after inspections prevents omissions and supports accuracy. Consistent documentation formats help maintain efficiency when moving between claims and allow adjusters to transition smoothly between files.

Clear documentation also supports collaboration. Catastrophe claims may be reassigned or reviewed by multiple stakeholders. A well-documented file ensures continuity and allows others to understand the claim without repeating work.

Incomplete documentation causes delays, increases workload, and slows resolution. Maintaining documentation standards helps prevent these issues. Even in high-volume environments, documentation remains a core component of claim leadership. The adjuster is no longer managing individual claims. The adjuster is leading a coordinated response.

Practical Claim Leadership Actions

Leading at Scale During Catastrophe Events

Catastrophe events create high-volume, fast-moving claim environments where organization can quickly break down. Adjusters must establish direction early, communicate reliably, and maintain organization across multiple files. Without a defined approach, confusion increases, and timelines expand. Claim leadership during catastrophe events focuses on stabilizing the process while managing volume.

ESTABLISH DIRECTION — SET THE CATASTROPHE WORKFLOW EARLY

Large-scale events create uncertainty for policyholders and stakeholders. Providing direction early helps stabilize claims and reduce reactive communication. Even when information is still developing, outlining the catastrophe workflow supports alignment and sets realistic expectations.

KEY ACTIONS:

Explain catastrophe response workflow
Set inspection expectations
Identify routing or scheduling approach
Establish communication timeline

GO-TO LINES:

"Due to the event volume, inspections are being scheduled by area."
"Here's how the catastrophe process will work."
"We're currently scheduling inspections based on routing."
"You can expect communication once your inspection is completed."

MANAGE VOLUME — ORGANIZE CLAIMS FOR EFFICIENCY

High-volume deployments require strong organization. Grouping claims, tracking status, and maintaining consistent notes keep work from drifting. This reduces mental load and supports continuity across files.

KEY ACTIONS:

Group claims by location
Track claim status clearly
Document next steps after each inspection
Maintain consistent note structure

GO-TO LINES:

"Your claim is currently scheduled within the next routing area."
"I'm working through inspections in this area today."
"Your claim is in the next review group."
"I'll update you once your claim reaches the next stage."

STABILIZE COMMUNICATION — PROVIDE PREDICTABLE UPDATES

High claim volume increases communication pressure. Consistent updates help reduce confusion and prevent repeated inquiries. Even brief updates reinforce structure and maintain alignment.

KEY ACTIONS:

Provide initial assignment contact
Confirm inspection completion
Identify the next step after inspection
Maintain update cadence

GO-TO LINES:

"I wanted to confirm your claim is in progress."
"Your inspection has now been completed."
"The next step is estimate review."
"I'll follow up once that review is finished."

SET EXPECTATIONS — EXPLAIN CATASTROPHE TIMELINES

Policyholders often expect immediate resolution after catastrophe events. Clear communication about volume, routing, and review timelines helps prevent frustration and misunderstanding.

KEY ACTIONS:

Explain catastrophe claim volume
Set realistic inspection timelines
Clarify review process
Reconfirm expectations as conditions change

GO-TO LINES:

"Due to the volume, inspections are occurring in phases."
"Timing will depend on routing and accessibility."
"After inspection, the estimate will be reviewed."
"I want to set realistic expectations for the next steps."

MAINTAIN CONTINUITY — DOCUMENT UNDER TIME PRESSURE

Documentation becomes more important during catastrophe events. Adjusters move quickly between claims, and clear notes preserve context and support continuity.

KEY ACTIONS:

Document inspection findings immediately
Record next steps clearly
Capture communication summaries
Maintain consistent documentation format

GO-TO LINES:

"Inspection completed — review pending."
"Documentation submitted for evaluation."
"Follow-up scheduled after review."
"Next action identified for claim progression."

CLOSE WITH DIRECTION — END EACH INTERACTION CLEARLY

Each catastrophe interaction should end with clarity. Confirming next steps helps reduce uncertainty and keeps claims moving forward despite volume.

KEY ACTIONS:

Confirm next step
Set update timing
Reinforce workflow
Clarify responsibilities

GO-TO LINES:

"The next step will be estimate review."
"You can expect an update once the review is complete."
"I'll follow up after the next phase."
"That keeps your claim moving forward."

These practical leadership actions help adjusters maintain structure, communication, and consistency during catastrophe events. Even at scale, clear direction stabilizes the process and supports efficient claim progression.

CLAIM LEADERSHIP SUMMARY

Key Takeaway

Catastrophe events change the scale of adjusting. When claims surge across regions simultaneously, the adjuster's role expands from handling individual files to managing volume reliably and in alignment. Disciplined decision-making, prioritization, and effective communication become essential to maintaining quality across multiple claims.

In Practice

During catastrophe deployments, focus on applying a reliable approach across all claims. Prioritize inspections, communicate realistic timelines, and document decisions clearly. Maintaining organization across volume reduces confusion and supports reliable outcomes.

Questions for Reflection

1. How do I prioritize claims when volume increases?
2. Do I maintain consistent communication across multiple files?
3. What structure helps me manage large claim volume effectively?

Claim Leadership Principle

Consistency across many claims is the foundation of catastrophe claim leadership.

CHAPTER 3

Litigation Is No Longer Rare

Event Spotlight — Texas Hail Litigation Surge

Following multiple severe hail events across Texas, disputes increased over the scope of damage, repair methods, and valuation. Claims that were historically resolved through inspection and negotiation began moving into the legal channels at a higher rate. This shift created longer claim cycles and increased documentation requirements for adjusters and carriers.

Carriers reported rising legal costs and heightened scrutiny of claim handling decisions. Billions in insured losses were associated with hail events during this period, but the operational impact extended beyond financial exposure. Adjusters increasingly worked in environments where documentation, communication, and consistency were closely scrutinized.

Adjusters were no longer simply evaluating damage and issuing findings. Their written notes, inspection approach, and communication tone became part of the broader litigation landscape. The claim file itself increasingly served as a record that could influence legal outcomes, making each entry part of the claim's long-term record—often reviewed long after the claim itself is closed.

CHAPTER FOCUS

Modern adjusters must recognize that every claim has the potential to go to litigation. Clear documentation, consistent communication, and a professional tone are essential from the beginning of the claim.

The Changing Landscape of Claims

Litigation is now a routine aspect of claims handling rather than an exception. Litigation-aware handling is another form of claim leadership. Discipline and structured communication help move the claim forward even when disputes arise. Greater policy awareness, public access to information, legal advertising, and financial pressures have driven this shift. Adjusters must now expect claims to be reviewed, challenged, or escalated more frequently.

While not every claim leads to litigation, this environment requires a more disciplined approach. Adjusters can no longer rely on informal documentation or unstructured communication. Each claim should be managed with the expectation that decisions and communications may be reviewed later, reinforcing the need for alignment and reliability from the outset.

Litigation risk requires thorough inspections, effective communication, and documentation that clearly explains decision-making. These are professional standards that ensure claims are understandable and well supported, regardless of whether litigation occurs.

Litigation awareness focuses on maintaining alignment rather than anticipating conflict. Disciplined practices reduce confusion and strengthen the claim file from the beginning. In practice, the strength of the file often determines whether the claim holds up during review. Litigation does not begin when a claim is challenged; it begins with how the claim is handled from the start.

Documentation as a Defensive Foundation

Documentation is critical when litigation is possible. The claim file provides a written record of events, evaluations, and decisions. Thorough documentation allows the claim to be understood without relying on memory or interpretation.

Effective documentation captures observations, timelines, and communications. It explains decision-making and tracks when information was requested, received, and applied. These details ensure the claim reflects a disciplined evaluation process.

Incomplete documentation increases uncertainty and may require additional clarification, slowing progress and raising avoidable questions. Reliable documentation prevents these issues. Treating documentation as a defensive foundation shifts note-taking from a post-claim task to an ongoing process that supports transparency, alignment, and professionalism. A well-documented file does not just support a claim—it protects it.

Communication That Reduces Escalation

Communication often determines whether a claim escalates. Misunderstandings, unclear explanations, or inconsistent updates can cause frustration and prompt policyholders to seek outside opinions or escalate concerns. Clear communication helps prevent escalation. By explaining findings, timelines, and next steps, adjusters provide transparency and help stakeholders understand decisions and expectations. Most escalations are not caused by the decision itself, but by how it is communicated. Consistent communication reduces confusion.

Tone is also important. Professional, respectful communication supports constructive conversations, even during disagreements. Explaining reasoning, rather than just conclusions, keeps the focus on the claim. Documenting key conversations reinforces clarity and consistency. While communication cannot eliminate disagreements, it helps manage them, keeps the claim structured, and reduces escalation.

The Importance of Consistency

Reliability is essential when litigation risk exists. Aligned inspections, documentation, and communication demonstrate that the claim was handled professionally, supporting both understanding and defensibility. Inconsistent approaches create uncertainty and raise questions about how the claim developed. A predictable process helps prevent these issues.

Structured workflows support consistency. Standardized documentation, regular communication, and clear next steps stabilize the claim, reduce variation, and strengthen the file. Consistency allows different stakeholders to interact with the same claim without changing the outcome. Consistency demonstrates professionalism and a disciplined approach. Over time, it improves claim quality and builds stakeholder confidence.

Handling Disagreements Professionally

Disagreements are normal in claims handling. Differences in scope, valuation, or interpretation require professional communication and clear documentation, not reactive responses. Adjusters should focus on explanation rather than opposition. Clearly describing observations, reasoning, and supporting information maintains constructive dialogue and keeps discussions centered on the claim.

During disagreements, documentation becomes even more important. Recording discussions, requests, and next steps preserves clarity and ensures the claim progresses despite differing perspectives. Professional handling of disagreements reduces escalation, keeps the claim structured and fact-focused, and supports resolution while maintaining professionalism.

In some situations, disagreements may require internal review or escalation. Claim managers, supervisors, or technical specialists may be consulted to ensure consistent handling. Documenting the reason for review, the information considered, and the guidance received supports clarity. Internal coordination strengthens the claim by ensuring decisions are aligned and professionally supported.

Understanding the Role of Third Parties

Modern claims often involve third parties such as contractors, public adjusters, consultants, engineers, and legal professionals. Each brings different perspectives and objectives, making clear communication, reliable documentation, and disciplined handling essential for alignment.

With third parties involved, adjusters must maintain organization in all interactions. Document requests clearly, record responses accurately, and communicate updates consistently so all participants share the same understanding. Without this discipline, misinterpretation can develop quickly.

Professionalism is especially important with multiple stakeholders. Clear explanations keep discussions focused on the claim, while consistent communication helps prevent conflicting interpretations. Third-party involvement does not always lead to litigation, but it does increase the need for disciplined claim handling. Organized documentation, neutral communication, and consistent updates maintain clarity and alignment, even when perspectives differ.

Early Direction Prevents Later Challenges

Many disputes begin with early misunderstandings. Unclear expectations, incomplete explanations, or inconsistent timelines can create confusion that grows over time, especially in complex or high-volume claims. Establishing direction early helps prevent these challenges. Explaining the process, outlining timelines, and identifying next steps help stakeholders understand claim progression, reduce uncertainty, and support alignment.

Early direction also helps manage expectations. When policyholders understand inspections, documentation review, and communication, frustration decreases. Stakeholders are better prepared, and the claim progresses with a shared understanding. Adjusters who establish direction early tend to experience fewer escalations because questions are addressed before confusion develops. When direction is delayed, escalation fills the gap.

Writing With Precision

Precision in documentation is essential when litigation is possible or when multiple stakeholders are involved. Notes should accurately reflect observations and be supported by clear reasoning. Precise language improves clarity, strengthens defensibility, and supports consistency across the claim.

Ambiguous wording creates confusion and invites differing interpretations. Vague statements or unclear conclusions often lead to additional questions later. Writing with precision ensures the claim file reflects professional judgment and disciplined decision-making. Imprecise language does not just create confusion; it creates exposure.

Adjusters should also document changes in evaluation as claims evolve. When findings change, documentation should explain what changed, why it changed, and how decisions developed over time. This demonstrates a structured and thoughtful approach. Clear, well-organized documentation maintains continuity and ensures the claim remains understandable throughout the process.

Maintaining Objectivity

Objectivity is essential in claims handling. Adjusters must base evaluations on facts, observations, and policy terms rather than assumptions or external pressure. This supports fairness, consistency, and defensible decisions.

Objectivity strengthens documentation. Clearly distinguishing between observation, evaluation, and conclusion helps ensure decisions are understood. A logical progression from facts to conclusions supports alignment and reduces disputes.

Objectivity also helps manage disagreements. Focusing discussions on documented facts and structured evaluation keeps conversations constructive, reduces escalation, and supports resolution based on the claim file. Adjusters who maintain objectivity demonstrate professionalism and consistency, strengthening both the claim and its defensibility.

Litigation Awareness as Professional Practice

Litigation awareness is not about being defensive, but about recognizing that claims may be reviewed. Documentation and communication should consistently reflect professionalism, encouraging clear records and thoughtful explanations throughout the claim.

These practices strengthen claim handling and accountability. Adjusters who maintain litigation awareness keep thorough notes, reliable documentation, and clear explanations for key decisions. Accurate records and disciplined updates improve efficiency, reduce misunderstandings, and support defensibility if the claim is reviewed.

This approach benefits all claims, not only those that escalate. Clear documentation and effective communication reduce confusion, improve alignment, and help stakeholders understand how decisions are reached. When the claim file reflects disciplined handling, conversations remain focused and the process moves forward smoothly.

Litigation Claims Require Disciplined Handling

When litigation risk increases or representation is involved, claim handling must become more formalized. Communication should be precise, documentation detailed, and internal coordination strengthened to maintain alignment and reliability.

When representation is asserted, adjusters should confirm it and verify that all required documentation has been submitted. Letters of representation, contracts, or authorization forms clarify communication channels and identify all participants. Documenting representation and communication preferences supports consistency.

When coverage questions arise, a reservation of rights communication may also be issued. These communications clarify that the evaluation is ongoing and that coverage determinations are subject to policy terms and investigation. Documentation should clearly reflect the reason for the reservation, the information under review, and the next steps.

Adjusters should avoid informal discussions and rely on clear, documented communication. Explanations must remain factual and neutral, without speculation. Disciplined communication reduces misinterpretation and supports defensibility. Internal coordination may increase, involving supervisors, claim managers, or legal teams. Clear notes and reliable updates help maintain alignment.

Handling litigation-aware claims requires a measured, disciplined approach that supports professionalism and reduces escalation.

Public Adjusters and Attorneys Involve Different Handling Approaches

Public adjuster involvement and attorney representation affect claim handling differently. Both require coordination, but the communication approach and formality vary depending on the representation.

Public adjusters typically participate in scope discussions, document reviews, and claim evaluations. Communication remains collaborative and focused on inspection findings, estimates, and supporting documentation. Adjusters should maintain clear communication and reliable documentation throughout the process.

Attorney involvement often requires a more formal approach, with communication shifting to written correspondence and detailed documentation. Internal coordination may increase, and discussions should remain grounded in documented findings and disciplined responses. Neutral, factual communication supports defensibility.

Recognizing these differences helps adjusters adapt their approach. Clarity, professionalism, and consistency help maintain alignment in both situations.

Policyholder Interaction Changes with Representation

Policyholder interactions vary depending on representation. When a public adjuster is involved, adjusters may continue to communicate directly with the policyholder while coordinating with the representative. Discussions remain focused on inspections, documentation, and claim progression.

Attorney representation often changes the communication structure. Depending on carrier guidelines and the scope of representation, communication may be directed through counsel rather than the policyholder. Updates and explanations should be provided in a formal, structured manner to maintain clarity and consistency.

Adjusters should confirm representation and follow established communication protocols. When communication is routed through counsel, thorough documentation is essential. Recording requests, responses, and timelines ensures alignment and clarity throughout the process.

REAL WORLD EXAMPLE: Documentation Preventing Escalation

An adjuster managed a residential property claim for roof damage after a severe storm. The initial inspection found limited damage, resulting in a partial repair estimate. The policyholder later submitted a contractor's estimate for full replacement and began considering legal representation.

The adjuster's documentation included photographs, measurements, weather verification, and detailed evaluation notes. The file also reflected the communication timeline, including inspection dates, explanations, and documentation reviewed.

Upon receipt of the contractor's estimate, the adjuster documented the scope differences, requested a follow-up review, and informed the policyholder that the new information would be evaluated. The conversation and next steps were documented clearly.

This approach maintained alignment by reflecting the original evaluation, new information, and the ongoing review process. Disciplined communication and documentation allowed the claim to progress without escalation and kept all parties aligned.

Leading Claims in a Litigation-Aware Environment

Adjusters now operate in an environment where litigation is increasingly common. This requires a disciplined approach to claim handling.

Thorough documentation, reliable communication, and a professional tone support the claim, reduce misunderstandings, and maintain alignment when perspectives differ.

Representation affects claim handling. Public adjuster involvement supports a collaborative evaluation with organized documentation, while attorney representation often requires more formal communication and increased internal coordination. Understanding these differences helps adjusters adapt while maintaining alignment.

Adjuster leadership is demonstrated through consistency. Providing clear direction helps ensure stakeholders understand the process, expectations remain realistic, and decisions are supported by documented reasoning. This reduces confusion and keeps the claim organized.

Leading claims in a litigation-aware environment strengthens the overall process. It ensures decisions are documented, communication remains neutral, and professionalism is maintained throughout. These practices support both efficiency and defensibility.

Litigation may or may not occur, but structured handling consistently strengthens the claim. Adjusters who lead with clarity, consistency, and disciplined communication help ensure that claims progress with stability, professionalism, and accountability. The modern adjuster does not react to litigation. They prevent it through disciplined handling from the start.

Practical Claim Leadership Actions

Litigation Is No Longer Rare

Modern claims environments require adjusters to consider defensibility from the beginning. Clear documentation, disciplined communication, and consistent decision-making help reduce dispute risk and support professional credibility.

DOCUMENT FOR DEFENSIBILITY

Clear documentation supports claim clarity and helps explain how decisions were reached. The file should reflect reasoning, communication, and next steps.

KEY ACTIONS:

Record observations clearly and objectively
Explain decision reasoning
Document stakeholder communication
Identify follow-up actions and pending items

GO-TO LINES:

"Based on the inspection findings…"
"The evaluation indicates…"
"Additional documentation is being reviewed."
"Next steps include follow-up after review."
"This decision is based on the information available at this time."

COMMUNICATE CAREFULLY

Professional communication reduces escalation and misinterpretation. Tone and clarity are particularly important in complex or disputed claims.

KEY ACTIONS:

Use neutral, professional language
Avoid assumptions or speculative statements
Confirm understanding when discussing decisions
Document key conversations promptly

GO-TO LINES:

"I want to explain how this determination was made."
"Here is what the inspection showed."

"Let me clarify the next step in the process."
"I want to make sure we are aligned moving forward."
"This is still under review, and I will update you."

MAINTAIN CONSISTENCY

Inconsistent messaging increases dispute risk. Alignment between documentation and communication strengthens clarity.

KEY ACTIONS:

Align written and verbal communication
Maintain structured updates
Clarify changes in decisions when needed
Reconfirm timelines and expectations

GO-TO LINES:

"There are no changes to the current evaluation."
"The claim remains under review."
"I want to confirm the timeline we discussed."
"This update aligns with the previous communication."
"I'll continue to provide updates as information develops."

CLARIFY THE CLAIM PROCESS

Clear expectations help prevent misunderstanding and reduce escalation.

KEY ACTIONS:

Explain review steps and evaluation process
Identify pending inspections or expert input
Clarify documentation requirements
Provide clear next-step direction

GO-TO LINES:

"The next step is completing the review."
"Additional input is being requested."
"We are waiting for documentation to continue evaluation."
"Once review is complete, I will follow up."
"This helps ensure the claim is evaluated thoroughly."

WHEN ATTORNEYS ARE INVOLVED

Attorney involvement changes communication dynamics. Adjusters should shift to structured, neutral communication and clearly document representation. Maintaining professionalism and consistency helps support defensibility and reduces misinterpretation.

KEY ACTIONS:

Confirm representation and communication channel
Redirect claim communication through counsel when appropriate
Avoid informal explanations or speculative discussion
Document attorney requests and responses
Maintain neutral, fact-based communication

GO-TO LINES:

"I understand you are now represented. I will direct communication accordingly."
"Please have your representative forward any documentation."
"I will review the information provided and follow up."
"All communication will be documented in the claim file."
"This remains under review based on the information submitted."
"We will respond after evaluating the documentation received."

These practices help maintain defensibility and professionalism throughout the claim.

CLAIM LEADERSHIP SUMMARY

Key Takeaway

Litigation is no longer a rare outcome in claims handling. Documentation, communication, and decision-making are increasingly reviewed through a legal lens. Adjusters must approach each claim with clarity, consistency, and professional discipline, recognizing that the claim file may later serve as the record of the handling process.

In Practice

Document observations clearly, explain decisions professionally, and maintain consistent communication throughout the claim. Avoid assumptions and ensure notes reflect both findings and rationale. When representation is involved, maintain neutral communication and document all interactions. A well-structured file supports defensible decisions and reduces the need for escalation.

Questions for Reflection

1. Do my claim notes clearly explain my observations and decisions?
2. Would my communication remain clear if reviewed later?
3. Am I documenting the reasoning behind my conclusions?
4. Would a third-party reviewer understand how this claim progressed?

Claim Leadership Principle

A clear file today becomes a defensible claim tomorrow.

CHAPTER 4

High-Pressure Claims and Decision Fatigue

Event Spotlight — Fort McMurray Wildfire (Canada)

The Fort McMurray wildfire forced the evacuation of an entire city and destroyed thousands of structures. Adjusters entered an environment marked by total-loss claims, emotional distress, and overwhelming volume. Policyholders were displaced for extended periods, and claim complexity increased as recovery timelines lengthened.

Industry estimates put insured losses above $3.5 billion, making the event one of the most expensive disasters in Canadian history. Adjusters conducted back-to-back inspections and handled emotionally intense conversations across numerous files. Coverage discussions often occurred while policyholders were still processing the scale of their losses.

The pressure did not stem from a single claim but from ongoing decision-making across many claims. Fatigue became an operational risk as workloads increased and timelines tightened. Maintaining consistency required discipline amid sustained demand, where the volume of decisions—not just the complexity of claims—began to affect performance over time.

CHAPTER FOCUS

Decision fatigue undermines claim quality, communication clarity, and leadership presence. Managing pressure is now a core adjusting skill.

The Reality of Constant Decision-Making

Adjusting relies on continuous decision-making. From claim assignment, adjusters determine priorities, required information, inspection timing, documentation standards, and communication methods. These decisions persist throughout the claim process, often without interruption.

In high-pressure environments, decision volume rises sharply. Adjusters often handle multiple claims while responding to inquiries, reviewing documents, coordinating inspections, and interpreting coverage. This ongoing decision-making creates cognitive strain, shifting the focus from individual choices to maintaining clarity amid constant demands.

Decision fatigue arises when sustained mental effort reduces the quality of judgment. Adjusters may feel exhausted, less confident, or slower in assessments. Small decisions become more difficult, communication becomes reactive, and documentation may lack detail. These are natural responses to prolonged pressure, not indicators of ability.

Recognizing decision fatigue enables adjusters to apply disciplined practices that support alignment. Without it, reliability in communication, documentation, and decision-making can decline, affecting claim outcomes. Decision fatigue also increases the risk of missed documentation, reduced communication effectiveness, and variable decisions across claims. In practice, the risk is not only making the wrong decision, but also making too many decisions without a defined approach.

High-Pressure Claims Environments

Certain claims, such as catastrophes, large losses, multi-party disputes, and litigation-aware files, are inherently more complex due to incomplete information and multiple stakeholders. Adjusters must remain focused despite these uncertainties.

High-pressure claims often follow a non-linear process. Pending reports, delayed inspections, and evolving coverage interpretations require adjusters to balance speed and accuracy while maintaining clear communication.

High-pressure claims increase communication demands both externally with stakeholders and internally among claims teams and supervisors. Policyholders request updates, contractors seek approvals, and internal teams require documentation. Supervisors, desk adjusters, and internal teams may also request status updates, documentation, and file reviews as the claim develops. Adjusters must balance these internal and external expectations simultaneously.

Urgency intensifies decision-making. Same-day updates, rapid inspection scheduling, and quick documentation turnaround create overlapping timelines. Adjusters must address immediate needs while maintaining accuracy and reliability across multiple claims. This environment increases cognitive load and reinforces the need for defined workflows. When urgency is constant, a disciplined approach is what sustains reliability.

Defined workflows reduce strain by minimizing repetitive decisions, allowing adjusters to focus on evaluation rather than constant reorganization. During catastrophe deployments, managing dozens of active claims increases decision volume and mental demand.

The Impact of Decision Fatigue on Claims Handling

Decision fatigue often develops gradually. Adjusters may delay decisions, revisit resolved issues, or feel uncertain about next steps. Documentation and communication may become less detailed, slowing progress and increasing the need for follow-up.

Fatigue can also hinder prioritization. Limited mental capacity makes it harder to identify urgent claims, leading to frequent shifts in focus and reduced efficiency. These effects reflect sustained demand, not poor performance. Recognizing them allows for proactive adjustment through disciplined practices.

Awareness of decision fatigue encourages reliance on workflows rather than constant reevaluation. Disciplined documentation, reliable communication, and clear prioritization reduce the burden of repeated decisions. Without a defined approach, fatigue does not just slow claims—it destabilizes them.

Claim Inventory Management Under Pressure

High-pressure deployments require adjusters to manage multiple active claims simultaneously. Without organized file management, critical tasks may be delayed, and decision fatigue can increase. A clear claim inventory helps maintain alignment across files and reduces cognitive strain.

Segmenting claims by status improves efficiency. Files may be grouped as inspection pending, documentation pending, coverage review, or follow-up required. This approach reduces repeated reassessment and supports steady progression.

Tracking active claims strengthens prioritization. Displaced policyholders, safety concerns, and time-sensitive losses can be identified quickly. Organized file management ensures urgent claims receive attention while progress continues across all assignments.

Many adjusters rely on task management systems to support this process. A consistent tracking method helps monitor inspections, follow-ups, documentation, and pending decisions across multiple files. Whether using digital tools, carrier platforms, or dedicated planners, disciplined tracking reduces mental load, improves reliability, and stabilizes workload. When the claim inventory is clear, decision-making becomes more efficient.

Prioritization Under Pressure

High-pressure environments demand effective prioritization. Adjusters must identify urgent claims while appropriately scheduling others. Without a defined approach, attention becomes reactive, increasing the risk of delays or oversight.

Establishing clear prioritization criteria reduces strain and improves decision quality. Factors such as severity, safety, displacement, accessibility, and time sensitivity provide a structured basis for action. Consistent application makes prioritization predictable and helps communicate timelines to stakeholders.

Documenting priorities strengthens organization. Tracking urgent, pending, and scheduled claims reduces the need for constant reassessment. This structure allows adjusters to focus on evaluation and communication, improving efficiency and reducing fatigue. Clear prioritization protects both the claim and the adjuster's capacity to manage it.

Segmenting Workload to Reduce Decision Fatigue

Decision fatigue increases when adjusters shift continuously between unrelated tasks. Segmenting workload reduces this strain by grouping similar activities. Adjusters may group inspections by location, complete documentation in dedicated intervals, and schedule communication updates at consistent times. This reduces repetitive decision-making and improves efficiency.

Batching tasks supports alignment. Completing documentation immediately after inspections, scheduling follow-ups together, and reviewing coverage decisions in focused blocks helps adjusters maintain direction. A segmented workflow reduces cognitive load. Disciplined pacing improves reliability, supports professional judgment, and stabilizes claim handling during high-volume deployments.

Managing Multiple Claims Simultaneously

Adjusters often manage multiple claims at once, especially during catastrophes or high-volume periods. Each claim requires evaluation, communication, documentation, and follow-up. Without organization, switching between claims increases cognitive demand and decision fatigue.

Organizing claims helps manage this challenge. Grouping claims by location, severity, or status reduces the mental effort required to transition between files. This approach allows adjusters to maintain focus and move efficiently between claims. Organized tracking systems also ensure time-sensitive claims receive appropriate attention.

Reliable workflows across claims support alignment. When each claim follows a defined process, adjusters transition more easily, reducing the need to reorient and maintaining steady handling.

Managing multiple claims effectively requires discipline and organization. Clear organization, repeatable workflows, and documented next steps reduce cognitive load and support steady progress. These practices help adjusters maintain alignment, improve efficiency, and manage multiple claims professionally.

Collaborative Claim Handling and Shared Judgment

High-pressure claims often involve complex coverage questions, scope differences, and evolving information. Adjusters do not need to make every decision in isolation. Consulting supervisors, peers, or technical specialists supports clarity and strengthens decision-making.

Collaborative handling does not reduce adjuster ownership. Instead, it expands perspective and reduces the risk of rushed conclusions. Discussing complex files allows adjusters to confirm interpretations, identify missing information, and maintain consistency.

Shared awareness also supports alignment. When supervisors or team leads understand the claim status, decisions can be coordinated, and expectations remain realistic. This reduces rework and prevents conflicting directions. Professional collaboration strengthens claim handling. Structured consultation, shared understanding, and aligned communication reduce decision fatigue and support consistent leadership across claims.

Communication During Cognitive Strain

Decision fatigue and heavy workload can shorten, delay, or reduce the detail of communication. This can create confusion and increase the need for follow-up. Disciplined communication helps manage these challenges. Regular updates, clear next steps, and documented conversations reduce the need for repeated explanations. Clear messaging aligns stakeholders, minimizes interruptions, and preserves focus.

Scheduling communication intervals allows for focused evaluation while maintaining responsiveness. Policyholders receive predictable updates, and adjusters sustain alignment and organization, supporting efficiency and professionalism. A professional tone is essential under pressure. Calm, respectful communication stabilizes conversations and prevents escalation. Clear messaging reinforces confidence and sustains momentum, while disciplined habits reduce confusion.

REAL WORLD
Sustained Decision-Making in a Workers' Compensation Claim

An adjuster managed a workers' compensation claim involving ongoing medical treatment and extended time away from work. The injured employee required continued care, and multiple providers were involved.

The adjuster maintained thorough documentation of medical updates, communicated reliably with all parties, and clarified next steps as treatment progressed. Questions regarding timelines and outcomes were addressed through clear explanations of the process.

By maintaining organization and consistent communication, the adjuster supported claim continuity and reduced confusion over time. This approach helped guide the claim through a complex, long-term process. This reflects how decision fatigue can develop not only from volume but also from sustained duration.

Documentation as a Stability Anchor

Documentation provides stability during high-pressure periods. Clear notes help adjusters transition between files without losing context, reducing cognitive strain, and supporting continuity. Well-structured documentation clarifies claim status, decisions made, and pending actions.

Recording observations immediately after inspections maintains accuracy and reduces reliance on memory. Documenting next steps clarifies follow-up actions, prevents communication gaps, and reduces the need to reassess information later. Documentation supports continuity when returning to a claim. Clear notes provide direction, reinforce timelines, and maintain consistency, reducing decision fatigue and improving efficiency. Adjusters can quickly re-engage without having to reconstruct the claim.

Using documentation as a stability anchor allows adjusters to maintain clarity even as workload increases. Organized notes, consistent updates, and clearly identified next steps help stabilize the claim process and support disciplined claim handling under pressure.

Structuring Decisions to Reduce Cognitive Load

A disciplined approach is highly effective for managing decision fatigue. Reliable workflows reduce the need for repetitive decisions, lowering cognitive strain and supporting consistency across claims. Standard inspection practices promote uniform observations. Communication routines clarify update timing, and organized documentation preserves continuity. These practices reduce mental effort and improve understanding.

Breaking decisions into stages also helps. Adjusters can move sequentially through inspection, documentation, communication, and follow-up, allowing each step to be managed without overwhelming the process. Disciplined decision-making does not remove flexibility—it provides a foundation that supports reliability even as conditions change.

Maintaining Professional Judgment

Decision fatigue can undermine confidence, especially in high-volume or complex environments. Adjusters may question conclusions or delay decisions. Maintaining professional judgment requires alignment, organization, and disciplined documentation, allowing reliance on the file rather than memory.

Documenting decision-making reinforces confidence and reliability. Recording observations, relevant facts, and conclusions creates a defined evaluation path. This allows adjusters to review their reasoning and reduces the need for repeated reassessment.

A structured evaluation process strengthens professional judgment. Systematic review of observations, policy considerations, pending items, and next steps supports reliability and prevents reactive decisions. Clear, repeatable processes reinforce sound judgment. Professional judgment depends on disciplined handling and organized documentation. Consistent evaluation and realistic pacing support confidence, efficiency, and strong claim handling.

Recognizing the Signs of Decision Fatigue

Recognizing decision fatigue enables an early response. Common signs include difficulty prioritizing, delayed decisions, reduced documentation, uncertainty, mental exhaustion, repeated re-checking, and hesitation with routine tasks. Identifying these signals allows adjusters to reset their approach. Reviewing priorities, organizing claims, clarifying next steps, and relying on documentation restores direction and stabilizes workflow, reducing cognitive strain.

Briefly reorganizing workload improves decision-making. Identifying priorities, confirming pending actions, and updating timelines reestablishes control. A disciplined plan reduces pressure and supports reliable performance during demanding periods. Decision fatigue is a normal part of high-pressure claims work. Recognizing it allows for a proactive response. Reestablishing organization, clarifying priorities, and documenting decisions sustain professionalism, reliability, and performance.

Leadership Through Disciplined Decision-Making

Adjusters lead claims by establishing alignment, especially amid evolving information and high workload. Disciplined decision-making supports communication, documentation, and prioritization, allowing claims to progress with direction rather than react to uncertainty.

Leadership in high-pressure environments is demonstrated through organization and discipline. A defined evaluation process stabilizes claims, while stakeholders benefit from predictable communication, clear explanations, and steady handling. This approach reduces confusion and maintains alignment. Disciplined decision-making also improves efficiency. Clear documentation of observations, reasoning, and next steps reduces rework, lowers cognitive load, and allows focus on new developments. Reliable workflows support pacing and overall performance.

Adjusters make constant decisions, often across multiple claims. Implementing a defined process—reviewing facts, documenting reasoning, clarifying priorities, and identifying next steps—reduces decision fatigue and supports confidence. This disciplined approach reinforces professional leadership and ensures claims progress with direction and control.

Decision fatigue is a normal part of high-pressure claims handling. Disciplined prioritization, predictable communication, and thorough documentation help adjusters sustain alignment under sustained workload. Adjusters who lead through organization reduce cognitive strain, improve efficiency, and move claims forward with confidence.

REAL WORLD
Decision Fatigue in High-Volume Deployment

An adjuster managed more than sixty active claims following a severe wind event. Inspections, contractor estimates, and policyholder inquiries occurred simultaneously. As the workload increased, communication became reactive, and documentation lagged behind inspections.

Recognizing the strain, the adjuster implemented a clear prioritization approach. Displaced policyholders were addressed first, inspections were grouped by location, and update intervals were scheduled. Documentation was completed immediately after each inspection, and the next steps were recorded consistently.

Disciplined communication reduced repeated inquiries, and reliable documentation improved continuity when transitioning between claims. By reestablishing organization, the adjuster stabilized the workload, improved performance, and sustained steady claim progression.

This example illustrates how disciplined decision-making manages cognitive load. When adjusters prioritize, document, and communicate effectively, decision fatigue decreases and claims remain organized.

Practical Claim Leadership Actions

High-Pressure Claims and Decision Fatigue

High-pressure claims require adjusters to manage workload, decision-making, and communication with discipline. Tight timelines, complex losses, and multiple stakeholders can create cognitive strain, leading to reduced clarity. Structured approaches help maintain consistency, reduce errors, and support sound professional judgment.

SLOW DOWN CRITICAL DECISIONS

Pressure can lead to rushed conclusions, especially when timelines are compressed or stakeholders are seeking immediate answers. Slowing down key decisions allows adjusters to evaluate available information and maintain clarity.

KEY ACTIONS:

Review available information before making decisions
Document reasoning for key conclusions
Identify unknowns or pending information
Confirm next step before finalizing direction

GO-TO LINES:

"I'm reviewing the information before making a determination."
"This decision requires additional evaluation."
"There are still items under review."
"I want to confirm next steps before moving forward."

MAINTAIN EXTERNAL COMMUNICATION DISCIPLINE

Stress can influence tone, pacing, and clarity. Structured communication helps maintain professionalism even in demanding situations. Calm, consistent messaging stabilizes the claim and prevents unnecessary escalation.

KEY ACTIONS:

Use calm, structured messaging
Confirm decisions clearly
Provide consistent updates
Avoid reactive or rushed responses

GO-TO LINES:

"Here is the current status of the claim."
"I want to provide a clear update."
"There are no changes yet, but review continues."
"I'll follow up once the evaluation is complete."

MANAGE INTERNAL COMMUNICATION AND ESCALATION

High-pressure claims require coordination with supervisors, desk adjusters, and internal teams. Clear internal communication helps maintain alignment, reduces rework, and supports consistent claim handling.

KEY ACTIONS:

Provide clear status updates to internal stakeholders
Document internal requests and guidance
Confirm priorities when multiple requests are received
Escalate complex issues when needed

GO-TO LINES:

"Here is the current status of the claim."
"This file may require additional review."
"I want to confirm priority on this claim."
"I'm coordinating internally before moving forward."

USE DOCUMENTATION TO REDUCE MENTAL LOAD

Clear documentation supports decision-making and reduces cognitive strain. Organized notes allow adjusters to track progress and maintain continuity across multiple claims.

KEY ACTIONS:

Record observations promptly
Identify pending actions and follow-ups
Track timeline updates clearly
Maintain organized file notes

GO-TO LINES:

"Documentation has been updated following inspection."
"Next steps have been recorded in the file."
"The claim remains under review."
"Follow-up is scheduled."

RECOGNIZE WORKLOAD IMPACT

High claim volume can affect pacing and clarity. Recognizing workload pressure allows adjusters to maintain structure and prioritize effectively.

KEY ACTIONS:

Prioritize complex or time-sensitive claims
Set realistic timelines
Communicate delays early
Maintain structured workflow across files

GO-TO LINES:

"I'm prioritizing based on urgency and severity."
"Your claim remains scheduled."
"I want to set realistic expectations for timing."
"The claim is progressing and remains active."

These practices help adjusters maintain clarity, professionalism, and consistent decision-making in high-pressure environments. Structured communication, disciplined documentation, and thoughtful pacing reduce decision fatigue and support sound professional judgment. Adjusters who lead with structure maintain direction, even as workload and complexity increase.

CLAIM LEADERSHIP SUMMARY

Key Takeaway

High-pressure claims require sustained decision-making across multiple files, conversations, and timelines. As workload increases, fatigue can affect judgment, communication, and reliability. Adjusters who recognize decision fatigue and apply disciplined handling are better positioned to sustain professional judgment under pressure.

In Practice

Break decisions into defined steps and avoid rushing conclusions as workload increases. Apply reliable documentation practices, maintain an organized claim inventory, and confirm key details before finalizing findings. Disciplined task management and consistent file tracking preserve accuracy during sustained demand and support defensible claim handling.

Questions for Reflection

1. Do I notice changes in my decision-making as my workload increases?
2. What structure helps me maintain consistency across multiple claims?
3. How do I slow down enough to ensure clarity when working under pressure?

Claim Leadership Principle

Structure reduces fatigue. Discipline preserves judgment. Clarity sustains leadership under pressure.

CHAPTER 5

The Expanding Role of the Modern Adjuster

Event Spotlight — Francis Scott Key Bridge Collapse

A cargo ship collision caused the collapse of a major bridge, triggering complex liability exposure involving infrastructure damage, marine risk, business interruption, and multiple stakeholders. The event extended beyond a single line of coverage and required cross-disciplinary coordination. The scope of the claim continued to evolve as investigations progressed.

Early industry estimates suggested insured losses could reach several billion dollars. Engineers, legal teams, investigators, carriers, and claims professionals worked in parallel to assess the impact and determine responsibility. Adjusters worked in a collaborative environment where communication and coordination were central to progress.

The claim extended beyond physical damage to include operational disruption and financial exposure. Adjusters were required to interpret evolving information while maintaining clarity for stakeholders. The role expanded from inspection to structured leadership in a multi-party claims environment, where coordination—not control—determined whether the claim progressed efficiently.

CHAPTER FOCUS

The modern adjuster operates in complex, multi-party claims environments. Leadership, coordination, and clarity are essential to advancing complex claims.

The Expanding Role of the Modern Adjuster

The adjuster's role has expanded beyond technical tasks to encompass broader professional responsibilities. Adjusters now guide communication, manage expectations, coordinate stakeholders, and maintain direction throughout the claim, leading the process rather than simply processing information.

This shift reflects the increasing complexity of claims, including more catastrophes, litigation, and multi-party involvement. Policyholders face disruption and uncertainty, while contractors, consultants, and internal stakeholders participate. Adjusters must provide structure and clarity as decisions are made with evolving information. Modern claims handling is also dependent on structured systems that govern how information is stored, tracked, and accessed. These systems are not simply tools—they are where consistency is enforced across the claim lifecycle.

As the claims environment continues to evolve, adjusters are adopting new tools and methods. Remote inspections, drone-assisted evaluations, and digital documentation are increasingly common, particularly in large or complex claims. These technologies improve efficiency and access but do not replace the adjuster's responsibilities. Adjusters must continue to interpret information, communicate effectively, and maintain structure throughout the claim. While technology supports the process, professional judgment and leadership remain central to effective claim handling. Technology may accelerate the process, but it does not replace the need for clarity.

Adjusters now assume leadership through coordination, communication, and professional judgment rather than authority. They guide claims by maintaining organization and ensuring information is understood, reflecting the realities of modern claims handling.

The Modern Claims Operating System

Modern claims handling operates as an integrated information system. Adjusters do not work within isolated tasks or separate roles; they operate within a structured flow of information that is captured, interpreted, and organized across multiple environments. The effectiveness of a claim depends on how consistently this system is maintained under pressure.

Field Adjusting: Information Capture and Field Readiness Layer

Field adjusting represents the direct information capture layer of the claims system. Adjusters evaluate damage at the source, documenting conditions as they exist in real time. This includes inspections, photographic evidence, environmental conditions, and on-site observations.

In addition to documentation, field adjusting requires physical and operational readiness. Adjusters must navigate active loss environments that may include unstable structures, weather exposure, debris, restricted access, or ongoing hazards. As a result, appropriate field equipment and protective gear, including personal protective equipment (PPE), become part of the operational foundation of the role.

Field readiness may include safety gear, inspection tools, measuring devices, communication equipment, and documentation resources. These items support the adjuster's ability to safely access the loss environment while maintaining accurate, consistent documentation.

In this environment, accuracy depends on disciplined observation, preparation, and structured documentation. The adjuster translates physical conditions into organized records that can be used throughout the claim lifecycle. Even though decisions may begin in the field, they must be recorded in a manner that ensures continuity beyond the inspection.

Field adjusting also requires coordination with stakeholders on site, including contractors, policyholders, engineers, and other professionals. The adjuster's role is not only to observe conditions but also to ensure those observations are captured in a structured format that remains usable throughout all stages of the claim.

Desk Adjusting: Information Interpretation Layer

Desk adjusting represents the interpretation layer of the claims system. Rather than directly observing conditions, adjusters analyze inspection reports, photographs, estimates, correspondence, and third-party documentation to determine the direction of the claim.

In this environment, clarity depends on synthesis. The adjuster must interpret multiple sources of information and convert them into a coherent claim narrative. Each piece of documentation becomes part of a broader evaluation process that requires consistency, reasoning, and structured judgment.

Because the adjuster is not physically present at the loss site, communication and documentation become the primary tools for maintaining alignment. Every decision must be traceable through the file, ensuring continuity across all stages of the claim.

Desk adjusting is not a simplified version of field work. It is a different form of cognitive workload that requires sustained attention, structured thinking, and disciplined evaluation under conditions of limited direct visibility.

Systems, Software, and Tools: Information Infrastructure Layer

Modern claims handling is supported by structured systems, software, and digital tools that serve as the infrastructure of the claims process. These systems organize, store, and track information across the lifecycle of a claim.

Claim management platforms, estimating tools, documentation systems, and communication logs allow adjusters to maintain consistency in how information is recorded and accessed. These tools ensure that observations, decisions, and communication are not only captured but also organized to support continuity and collaboration.

In field adjusting, systems support the transition from physical observation to structured reporting. Inspection notes, photographs, and damage assessments are uploaded into centralized platforms, preserving the integrity of on-site findings.

In desk adjusting, these systems become the primary environment for evaluation. Adjusters rely on structured data, documented communication, and organized files to guide decisions and maintain claim progression.

Across both environments, systems reduce fragmentation. They create consistency, improve traceability, and ensure that all stakeholders are working from the same information. When used effectively, these tools do not replace judgment; they reinforce it by maintaining structure and clarity.

A Unified Operating System

Field adjusting captures information, desk adjusting interprets information, and systems organize information. Together, these three layers form the operating structure through which modern claims are evaluated, communicated, and resolved.

The adjuster's effectiveness depends not on a single environment but on the ability to maintain clarity as information moves through each layer. When this system is structured, claims progress consistently, communication remains aligned, and decisions remain defensible even under pressure.

Modern claims handling is therefore not defined by location or role, but by the discipline with which information is captured, interpreted, and managed across the entire system.

From Technical Evaluator to Claim Guide

Traditional adjusting focused on technical evaluation, including inspection, documentation review, and estimate preparation. While still important, these tasks alone are no longer sufficient. Modern claims require adjusters to guide the process from start to resolution by explaining timelines, clarifying next steps, and maintaining alignment among participants. As central coordinators, adjusters prevent confusion and maintain structure.

Leading the claim also requires anticipating how decisions affect stakeholders. Explaining the evaluation process, outlining documentation needs, and providing timely updates create clarity and support steady progress. The adjuster is no longer responsible only for what is decided, but for how those decisions are understood. This shift expands technical expertise rather than replacing it. Technical evaluation remains essential, but it now operates within a broader leadership role that integrates inspection, communication, and coordination.

Managing Expectations Throughout the Claim

Expectation management is now critical to adjusting. Policyholders often have limited familiarity with the process and may expect immediate answers. Unclear timelines or requirements can lead to frustration. Adjusters manage expectations by providing early clarity. Explaining the process, outlining timelines, and identifying required documentation help stakeholders understand expectations and reduce uncertainty.

Expectation management continues throughout the claim. Regular updates, explanations, and outlining next steps help maintain alignment and make communication more productive. Managing expectations requires consistency, not lengthy explanations. Structured communication from adjusters reduces confusion and supports a smoother claim process. Clear expectations reduce repeated conversations and stabilize the claim.

Coordinating Multiple Stakeholders

Modern claims often involve multiple participants—contractors, public adjusters, consultants, engineers, attorneys, and internal teams. Each brings different perspectives, timelines, and objectives. Without coordination, communication can fragment, and the claim can lose direction. Effective coordination maintains alignment among all participants.

The adjuster coordinates these interactions by clarifying information requests, documenting responses, and providing reliable updates. Organized information keeps stakeholders aligned and prevents conflicting interpretations, allowing the claim to progress with direction. Coordination ensures that multiple perspectives do not become multiple versions of the claim.

Professionalism is essential in multi-party environments. Differences in opinion may arise over scope, cause, timelines, or responsibility. Clear, neutral communication and reliable documentation prevent misunderstanding and keep information aligned.

Coordination does not require controlling every interaction. It requires maintaining direction. By identifying next steps, clarifying responsibilities, and documenting communication, adjusters keep discussions focused on the claim. This leadership sustains alignment and prevents multiple perspectives from creating confusion.

REAL WORLD
Coordinating Multiple Stakeholders

An adjuster managed a commercial property claim for roof damage and interior water intrusion after a windstorm. The policyholder hired a contractor for a repair estimate, the carrier requested an engineering evaluation, and a public adjuster later submitted an expanded scope that differed from both.

Each participant provided information at different times, fragmenting communication. The policyholder requested updates, the contractor sought approval, and the engineer requested more documentation. Without coordination, timelines diverged, and expectations became unclear.

The adjuster established direction by identifying next steps and clarifying responsibilities. The engineering inspection timeline was shared with all participants, the contractor's estimate was documented for review, and the policyholder received a clear explanation of the evaluation process. Communication was recorded in the claim file, and follow-up actions were scheduled.

By coordinating communication and documenting updates, the adjuster maintained alignment across stakeholders. Differences in scope were reviewed systematically, expectations remained realistic, and the claim progressed with direction. This example reflects the modern adjuster's role in guiding communication, coordinating participants, and maintaining momentum throughout the claim.

Communication as a Core Professional Skill

Communication is central to the adjuster's role. Adjusters explain findings, discuss timelines, respond to questions, and guide stakeholders through the process. Clear communication prevents misunderstandings, reduces escalation, and sustains alignment.

Effective communication focuses on explanation and direction. Describing observations, outlining next steps, and providing reliable updates help stakeholders understand claim progression. Transparency reduces uncertainty and supports cooperation, even when timelines shift or additional evaluation is required.

Tone is equally important. Professional, calm, and respectful communication sustains constructive dialogue. Even during disagreements, disciplined messaging keeps the focus on facts and documented findings, reinforcing professionalism and preventing escalation. How information is delivered often determines how it is received.

Documentation reinforces communication. Recording key conversations, summarizing updates, and identifying next steps ensure consistency. When the claim file clearly reflects communication, stakeholders can track the claim's progression. Communication is now a core professional responsibility that supports clarity, alignment, and effective claim handling.

The Human Side of Claim Progress

Claims progress not only through process, but through the actions of people. Internal teams, external stakeholders, and policyholders all influence the speed and effectiveness of each claim.

Clear, professional, and consistent communication encourages stakeholders to respond promptly and prioritize the claim. Contractors provide timely estimates, engineers complete evaluations efficiently, and internal teams process documentation more smoothly. These outcomes depend not only on process but also on the adjuster's communication style, clarity, and reliability.

Internal alignment is equally important. When supervisors, desk adjusters, and support teams understand the claim status and trust the adjuster's communication, coordination improves. Clear updates, organized documentation, and consistent professionalism enable teams to respond efficiently and support claim progress.

The adjuster's approach directly influences claim momentum. Structured communication, a professional tone, and reliable follow-through support alignment among all participants. When stakeholders feel informed and confident in the process, cooperation increases, and delays decrease. Momentum in a claim is often driven by clarity, not urgency.

Balancing Speed and Accuracy

Modern claims environments emphasize speed, with policyholders expecting prompt responses and carriers seeking efficiency. However, careful evaluation is needed to ensure accuracy and defensibility. Balancing speed and accuracy is essential to maintain efficiency and professional standards.

Adjusters manage this balance by structuring claims from the outset. Early inspections, clear documentation, and consistent communication keep claims moving without sacrificing accuracy. When stakeholders understand timelines and next steps, progress continues even as evaluation proceeds.

Rushing decisions without sufficient information can lead to complications and necessitate revision. Delayed decisions without communication can lead to frustration. Adjusters must maintain steady progress while preserving alignment. Speed without discipline creates rework; a defined approach sustains it.

Documentation as Leadership

Documentation is often viewed as administrative, but in modern claims, it serves a leadership function. Clear notes preserve continuity, support communication, and maintain direction. Disciplined documentation guides stakeholders and reinforces reliable handling.

Documenting observations, timelines, communication, and decisions ensures the claim remains understandable. This clarity benefits all participants, allowing stakeholders to follow progression and understand reasoning.

Documentation also supports consistency. Clearly recording decisions and documenting updates as information evolves allows the claim to progress with structure, reduces repeated evaluation, and maintains continuity. Documentation is not just a record of the claim—it is how the claim is guided.

Problem-Solving in Dynamic Conditions

Modern claims rarely follow a predictable path. Weather, access challenges, documentation delays, and stakeholder disagreements can affect progress. Adjusters must adapt while maintaining alignment and organization.

Problem-solving includes identifying alternative timelines, clarifying documentation requirements, coordinating access, and adjusting communication. These actions sustain momentum and prevent the claim from stalling.

Effective problem-solving focuses on identifying needs and determining how to meet them. Adjusters evaluate available information, identify gaps, and establish next steps. Rather than reacting, they move the process forward with direction. A defined approach to problem-solving keeps the claim progressing even as conditions change.

Professional Judgment in Complex Claims

Professional judgment is increasingly important in complex claims. Adjusters interpret information, evaluate documentation, assess timelines, and determine next steps, often with incomplete information.

Professional judgment is strengthened by documentation and disciplined review. Recording observations, identifying facts, and explaining conclusions maintain transparency and support alignment.

Judgment also means recognizing when more information is needed. Adjusters must balance action with evaluation. Moving too quickly can create challenges, while delays without communication cause frustration. Professional judgment maintains this balance and supports consistent claim handling.

Establishing Direction Without Control

Adjusters often lead claims without formal authority by coordinating stakeholders, guiding communication, and sustaining momentum. This form of leadership relies on alignment rather than control.

A defined process helps claims progress even when stakeholders have differing priorities. Clear timelines, documented decisions, defined next steps, and predictable communication support alignment. Alignment, not authority, is what moves the claim forward.

The Modern Adjuster as Claim Leader

The adjuster's expanding role reflects modern claims handling. Technical evaluation remains essential but is now combined with coordination, communication, and professional judgment. Adjusters guide the claim through disciplined handling and reliable leadership.

This leadership stabilizes complex claims. Clear communication, reliable documentation, and organized workflows reduce confusion and maintain alignment as conditions change.

The modern adjuster leads by maintaining direction. Communication supports understanding, documentation reinforces reliability, and disciplined decision-making moves the claim forward. These practices improve efficiency, strengthen professionalism, and support defensible outcomes.

The adjuster is no longer only evaluating damage. The role now requires establishing clear, consistent direction from first contact through resolution. As the role has expanded, the expectation is no longer participation in the process, but ownership of how the claim moves forward.

Practical Claim Leadership Actions

The Expanding Role of the Modern Adjuster

The modern adjuster balances technical expertise with leadership responsibilities. In addition to evaluating losses, adjusters guide communication, manage expectations, and maintain direction throughout the claim. These actions help ensure consistency and clarity in complex environments.

LEAD THE CLAIM PROCESS

Adjusters guide communication and direction from the first interaction through resolution. Establishing structure early helps prevent confusion and supports steady progress.

KEY ACTIONS:

Establish claim structure early
Communicate expectations clearly
Identify next steps consistently
Maintain direction throughout the claim

GO-TO LINES:

"Here's how the claim will move forward."
"The next step is completing the inspection."
"I'll outline what to expect."
"I'll continue guiding the process as we move forward."

INTEGRATE TECHNICAL AND LEADERSHIP SKILLS

Technical findings must be clearly explained and connected to decisions. Leadership strengthens how technical expertise is applied within the claim.

KEY ACTIONS:

Explain inspection findings clearly
Connect findings to coverage or scope decisions
Document reasoning thoroughly
Clarify next actions for stakeholders

GO-TO LINES:

"Based on the inspection findings…"
"This evaluation supports the following scope…"
"Here is how this impacts the claim."
"The next step following this review will be…"

MANAGE STAKEHOLDER COORDINATION

Modern claims often involve contractors, engineers, policyholders, and internal teams. Coordinated communication helps maintain alignment.

KEY ACTIONS:

Align communication across stakeholders
Confirm responsibilities clearly

Document coordination efforts
Maintain a consistent update schedule

GO-TO LINES:

"I want to keep everyone aligned on next steps."
"Here is the current status of the review."
"We are coordinating information from all parties."
"I'm coordinating internally and will update you on next steps."
"I'll provide an update once the review is complete."

BUILD ALIGNMENT TO MOVE THE CLAIM FORWARD

Claims progress more efficiently when stakeholders are aligned. Clear communication, a professional tone, and consistent follow-through encourage timely responses and cooperation from internal and external parties.

KEY ACTIONS:

Communicate clearly and consistently with all stakeholders
Maintain a professional, calm tone across interactions
Follow through on commitments and update timelines
Reinforce next steps to keep all parties aligned

GO-TO LINES:

"I want to keep everyone aligned as we move forward."
"Here's where we are and what happens next."
"I'll follow through on this and update you."
"This keeps the claim moving in the right direction."

MAINTAIN PROFESSIONAL CONSISTENCY

Leadership is demonstrated through reliability and structured communication. Consistency supports clarity and improves claim outcomes.

KEY ACTIONS:

Provide structured updates
Maintain documentation clarity
Set realistic expectations
Close conversations with direction

GO-TO LINES:

"I'll provide the next update by..."
"There are no changes at this time, but review continues."
"This keeps the claim progressing."
"The next step will be..."

These practices help adjusters operate effectively within the expanded leadership role of modern claims. By combining technical expertise with structured communication, stakeholder coordination, and consistent direction, adjusters guide claims with clarity and professionalism.

CLAIM LEADERSHIP SUMMARY

Key Takeaway

The role of the modern adjuster continues to expand beyond inspection and documentation. Complex claims now involve multiple stakeholders, evolving information, and coordinated decision-making. Adjusters increasingly serve as central points of clarity, guiding communication, managing expectations, and maintaining direction throughout the claim.

In Practice

When working on complex claims, focus on both coordination and evaluation. Clarify roles, communicate updates consistently, and document developing information. Structured communication and organized documentation help align stakeholders, reduce confusion, and keep the claim progressing with clarity.

Questions for Reflection

1. Do I help clarify roles and expectations during complex claims?
2. How do I maintain communication across multiple stakeholders?
3. What structure do I use to track evolving information?

Claim Leadership Principle

The modern adjuster brings clarity to complexity and direction to the claim.

PRELUDE

Leading Through Complexity at Scale

Modern catastrophe claims require leadership that extends beyond individual files. Adjusters operate in fast-moving environments where volume increases, stakeholders multiply, and conditions evolve quickly. In these situations, clarity becomes harder to maintain, and structure becomes more important. Leadership at scale is not defined by control but by the ability to stabilize the process while managing complexity.

Large-scale events create competing priorities. Policyholders seek immediate answers, carriers require accurate evaluation, and field conditions may continue to change. Adjusters must balance these demands while maintaining organization across multiple claims. This requires disciplined communication, consistent workflow management, and the ability to set direction even as information continues to develop.

Leading through complexity at scale reflects the broader leadership perspective outlined in the Mosaic Way. As conditions shift, adjusters must adapt communication, maintain composure, and move between roles. They may serve as evaluators, coordinators, communicators, and decision guides within the same deployment. The ability to shift while maintaining clarity supports stability throughout the claim process.

This section examines real-world catastrophe environments where complexity is unavoidable. The focus is not on controlling every variable but on guiding claims through structured communication, consistent documentation, and clear direction. Leadership at scale helps prevent confusion, reduce escalation, and maintain momentum across high-volume deployments.

PART II

Catastrophe Claims and Real World Complexity

Catastrophe claims are significantly more complex than standard property evaluations. Large-scale events impact entire communities, disrupt infrastructure, and generate widespread demand. Adjusters often work with incomplete information, limited access, and uncertain recovery timelines. Policyholders may be displaced, utilities may be unavailable, and damage conditions may continue to change. Claims begin amid instability and urgency, requiring immediate professional leadership.

Catastrophe events generate high claim volume, urgency, and rapidly changing conditions. Adjusters may handle multiple claims in a short period, often with limited access to properties. Inspections can be delayed by safety issues, debris, or infrastructure damage, while limited contractor and mitigation resources further complicate recovery. Adjusters must prioritize inspections, manage communication, and maintain documentation under pressure. Defined processes are essential for maintaining alignment and preventing confusion.

In catastrophe environments, decisions are often made with incomplete information. Damage conditions may change between inspections, and additional losses may emerge. Adjusters should document observations thoroughly and communicate updates promptly. Recording inspection times, noting limitations, and tracking evolving conditions support continuity and alignment, especially in prolonged or multi-stakeholder claims. Organization enables adjusters to move claims forward effectively as conditions change.

Managing expectations is critical in catastrophe claims. Policyholders may face displacement, business interruption, or financial uncertainty, often with immediate questions about repairs, temporary housing, and recovery timelines. Adjusters should explain coverage, outline next steps, and communicate potential delays. Predictable communication stabilizes the process. Establishing and updating expectations early reduces misunderstandings and supports steady progression.

In many catastrophe scenarios, the adjuster becomes a central point of coordination. Multiple stakeholders, including policyholders, contractors, carriers, engineers, and technical specialists, look to the adjuster for direction as recovery begins. Internal coordination is equally important, as supervisors, desk adjusters, and support teams require timely updates and documentation across claims. Without disciplined communication, information can become fragmented. The adjuster's role includes organizing observations, documenting updates, and maintaining alignment among participants. Reliable communication and organized documentation keep the claim moving forward.

The fast pace of catastrophe claims requires adjusters to balance urgency with prioritization. Not all claims can be addressed simultaneously, and decisions must be made about which claims require immediate attention and which can be scheduled. Initial inspections focus on immediate damage and claim stabilization, while follow-up inspections refine the scope as more information emerges. Documenting each stage maintains clarity and supports sound decisions. Adjusters must advance claims efficiently while maintaining thorough, organized documentation.

This section explores catastrophe claims across a range of real-world scenarios, including wildfires, hurricanes, flooding events, infrastructure failures, and aviation losses. Each chapter highlights how scale, disruption, and evolving information reshape the adjuster's role. These scenarios demonstrate how adjusters maintain direction while operating in complex, rapidly changing environments.

Catastrophe claims require more than technical accuracy. They demand leadership that provides stability and direction amid rapidly changing conditions. Through organized documentation, reliable communication, and disciplined decision-making, adjusters guide claims from initial response through recovery. This leadership is essential for effective catastrophe handling in today's claims environment.

CHAPTER 6

Wildfires and Total Loss Communities

Event Spotlight — Camp Fire (California)

The Camp Fire swept through Paradise, California, destroying entire neighborhoods in hours. Thousands of homes, businesses, and public structures were lost, leaving communities without infrastructure, utilities, or immediate recovery options. Adjusters encountered policyholders who had been fully displaced and faced significant emotional and financial uncertainty.

Industry estimates place insured losses above $12 billion, making this one of the most destructive wildfires in U.S. history. The scale of the loss shifted the focus of adjusting from repair evaluation to rebuilding coordination. Policyholders needed guidance on coverage, including additional living expenses, debris removal considerations, and reconstruction timelines, while internal teams required clear documentation, alignment, and structured claim handling.

Total-loss communities fundamentally change the claims process. Adjusters move beyond damage assessment to help set the course for recovery. Discussions quickly shift from inspection to long-term planning, structured guidance, and coordinated decision-making, with early clarity directly influencing the pace of recovery.

CHAPTER FOCUS

Wildfire total-loss events require adjusters to lead discussions about rebuilding, expectations, and timelines. The claim process becomes a pathway to recovery rather than a documentation task. Adjusters provide clarity in an environment defined by loss, uncertainty, and urgency, guiding both the process and the people involved.

Wildfires and Total Loss Communities

Wildfire claims are more complex than typical property losses. The primary challenge is not damage evaluation, but guiding recovery after a complete loss. Adjusters often work in communities where multiple homes and infrastructure are destroyed, and access is limited. This scale alters both the pace and expectations of claims handling.

Total-loss communities require a different approach. While inspection, documentation, and estimate preparation remain essential, conditions such as displacement, unclear property boundaries, unavailable utilities, and ongoing debris removal add complexity. Adjusters must establish direction in these evolving environments.

Wildfire claims carry a significant emotional impact. Policyholders often face sudden displacement and uncertainty, making effective communication essential. Clearly explaining processes, timelines, and next steps helps maintain stability during disruption.

The adjuster's role extends beyond evaluation to providing steady, professional direction. In total-loss environments, coordination is the foundation for both the claim and recovery processes.

Structured handling is essential in total loss environments. Adjusters must balance speed and accuracy, communicate consistently, and maintain documentation despite changing conditions.

The Scale of Community-Level Loss

Wildfires often impact entire neighborhoods, affecting streets, homes, and surrounding structures. Adjusters must manage multiple total-loss claims within the same area rather than isolated losses. Widespread destruction can limit access due to road closures, safety restrictions, and debris removal.

Infrastructure challenges, such as unavailable utilities, damaged signage, and missing landmarks, further complicate claims. These factors require careful documentation and verification. Community-level wildfire losses require strong organization. Tracking claims by location, documenting access conditions, and maintaining consistent workflows help manage complexity. When loss occurs at scale, organization is the only way to maintain clarity across claims.

Confirming Total Loss Conditions

Many wildfire claims involve complete destruction, with debris fields, unstable ground, and few reference points. Confirming total loss requires careful evaluation and disciplined documentation. Even when loss is obvious, adjusters must ensure clarity in the file.

Photographs, detailed notes, and mapping information establish a clear record of loss. Documenting landmarks, access routes, and structural indicators supports claim continuity. Property identification can be challenging when address markers are destroyed, and boundaries are unclear. Adjusters may need to use mapping tools, aerial imagery, or prior records, or coordinate with policyholders and officials. Careful verification prevents misidentification.

Confirming total loss requires more than visual assessment. Structured documentation of location, conditions, and observations provides stability and ensures claims begin accurately. Accuracy at the start prevents complications later in the claim.

Personal Property and Inventory Challenges

Personal property documentation is a significant aspect of total loss wildfire claims. Policyholders may need to reconstruct inventories from memory, records, or prior documentation, making the process both time-consuming and emotionally demanding.

Adjusters should clearly explain documentation expectations and support organized inventory development. Outlining categories, methods, and timelines reduces confusion. Reliable communication and defined expectations support progress and alignment. A clear approach helps transform an overwhelming task into a manageable process.

Displacement and Policyholder Communication

Wildfire losses often result in displacement. Policyholders may be in temporary housing or coordinating remotely. Communication must adapt as contact information and priorities change.

Adjusters may be unable to meet onsite, so communication often occurs virtually. Clear explanations of the claim process are especially important. Early clarity stabilizes expectations and supports alignment.

Policyholders may have urgent questions about timelines and next steps. Structured updates reduce uncertainty. Predictable communication helps policyholders navigate recovery. When stability is lost, communication becomes the primary source of direction.

Arson, Fraud, and Origin Considerations

Certain claims involve questions regarding the cause of loss. Fire-related claims may require origin and cause investigations, expert analysis, and coordination with external agencies. Adjusters should document conditions objectively and avoid speculation. These claims often involve increased scrutiny and legal involvement. Maintaining clear documentation and neutrality is essential. Objectivity protects both the claim and the adjuster, especially when conclusions may be reviewed or challenged.

REAL WORLD
Total Loss and Displacement

An adjuster managed multiple total loss claims after a wildfire destroyed an entire residential area. Policyholders were displaced, unable to access properties due to safety restrictions and debris removal, and many communicated remotely.

One policyholder requested immediate information on rebuilding timelines, living expenses, and property documentation. At the same time, internal teams required coverage verification, documentation, and file updates for multiple claims in the area.

The adjuster established a defined process by explaining the claim workflow, outlining coverage, and identifying next steps. Scheduled updates maintained communication, and documentation reflected site conditions and evolving information. The adjuster supported the policyholder through documentation requirements while coordinating internally to maintain alignment.

By establishing direction, maintaining steady communication, and documenting thoroughly, the adjuster stabilized a complex situation. This example demonstrates how disciplined leadership supports alignment and steady progress in total-loss environments.

Debris Removal and Access Limitations

Debris removal is often a significant factor in wildfire claims, and site conditions can change rapidly as cleanup operations begin. Adjusters may inspect properties before debris removal, during staged removal, or after clearance is complete. Each phase presents different information, and documentation must capture these evolving conditions. Without structured notes, important context may be lost as the site changes.

Before debris removal, access may be restricted for safety. Local authorities may limit entry because of unstable debris or hazards. Adjusters must follow local guidance and coordinate inspections.

Documentation should focus on site conditions, landmarks, and visible indicators of loss. Early documentation is critical because conditions can change quickly. What is visible early may not be visible later, making initial documentation essential.

After debris removal, additional information may become available. Foundation outlines, utilities, driveways, and structural remnants may become visible. These details can help confirm property identification and provide clarity. Follow-up inspections may be required to document these developments. Staged evaluations should be clearly documented to reflect how the claim environment evolved.

Adjusters should record inspection timing, access conditions, and site limitations. Documenting the extent of debris removal and access restrictions ensures the claim file reflects observed conditions and inspection context.

Debris removal rapidly alters the claim environment. Structured documentation helps adjusters maintain consistency and supports continuity from the initial inspection through resolution. In some cases, debris removal may be coordinated through local or state programs, which may require additional verification and documentation.

Community Coordination and Volume

Wildfires often generate a high volume of claims within a concentrated geographic area. Entire neighborhoods or communities may be affected simultaneously. Adjusters may handle multiple total loss claims in close proximity, each requiring documentation, communication, and follow-up. This volume increases urgency and requires disciplined organization.

Grouping inspections by location improves efficiency and reduces travel time. A defined scheduling approach allows adjusters to document multiple claims reliably, easing transitions and supporting alignment across files. As volume increases, reliability becomes critical to maintaining control of the claim environment.

Communication demands increase during wildfire events, with multiple policyholders seeking updates simultaneously. Adjusters must manage communication and documentation carefully. Disciplined practices—such as confirming next steps and providing regular updates—help manage demand and maintain alignment.

High claim volume requires disciplined handling. Organization, reliable documentation, and coordinated communication sustain alignment across claims. These practices bring stability and support communities through complex recovery. Internal teams may also require ongoing updates, documentation, and coordination across multiple claims, increasing overall demands.

Documentation in Total Loss Scenarios

Documentation is essential even in total-loss situations. In large wildfires, properties may be destroyed, and conditions can change rapidly. Clear notes, photographs, and timelines help ensure the claim remains understandable. Early documentation is especially important because sites can change quickly.

Recording site conditions, access limitations, and inspection timing provides critical context. Notes should document when the inspection occurred, what conditions were present, and any restrictions that affected the evaluation. This helps stakeholders understand how the claim developed and why certain steps occurred in sequence. Consistent documentation supports clarity and continuity throughout the life of the claim.

Adjusters should document communication carefully, including conversations, requested information, and next steps. This is especially important when policyholders are displaced or communication is remote. Clear documentation ensures all parties understand the claim's progression.

Documentation provides stability in total loss scenarios. Structured notes guide the claim, support continuity, reinforce professionalism, and ensure clarity and consistency. In environments where conditions change quickly, documentation becomes the anchor that holds the claim together.

Managing Expectations in Large-Scale Events

Wildfires affecting multiple communities can cause unavoidable delays. High claim volume, access limitations, safety restrictions, and debris removal all impact timelines. Managing expectations is essential to maintain alignment and prevent confusion.

Adjusters manage expectations by explaining the process early. Outlining the inspection order, documentation requirements, and potential delays provides clarity. Realistic timelines help stakeholders understand that recovery occurs in stages. Early transparency reduces uncertainty.

Regular updates help maintain alignment. Even when progress depends on external factors, communication stabilizes the process. Confirming status, next steps, and timelines prevents assumptions and reduces frustration.

Managing expectations in wildfire claims requires transparency and consistency. Clear communication guides the claim through changing conditions. Structure and realistic direction help stabilize situations and support steady progress. Recovery timelines for total loss communities may extend for months or longer, depending on rebuilding conditions and resource availability. Clear expectations reduce uncertainty and help sustain cooperation over long timelines.

Applying Policy Language and Managing Expectations

Wildfire claims often require adjusters to explain both limitations and next steps. Coverage depends on policy limits, scope definitions, and applicable provisions, which may not align with policyholder or third-party expectations, particularly in total loss environments.

Adjusters should rely on policy language to guide these conversations. Clear explanations of coverage, limitations, and next steps help maintain alignment and reduce misunderstanding. Policy language provides structure, supporting consistent and professional communication.

Adjusters must also manage third-party expectations. Contractors, public adjusters, and other representatives may propose scopes or timelines that differ from policy requirements. Adjusters should acknowledge these perspectives while maintaining alignment with documented findings and policy provisions. Structured communication keeps discussions focused on the claim rather than competing interpretations.

Delivering difficult information requires professionalism and precision. Adjusters should avoid speculation and communicate decisions based on documented findings and policy language. Reliable, policy-based explanations keep conversations focused and productive.

Managing expectations through clear policy explanations supports claim progression. Even when outcomes differ from initial expectations, disciplined communication sustains momentum and reduces escalation. This approach reinforces the adjuster's role as a steady source of direction in complex claims environments.

Subrogation and Recovery Considerations

In some claims, responsibility may extend beyond the insured loss and involve third-party liability. Subrogation allows the carrier to pursue recovery from responsible parties after payment is issued. Identifying subrogation potential early is critical, particularly in large-loss or multi-party environments.

Infrastructure failures, fires, and equipment-related losses may involve contractors, manufacturers, or service providers. Adjusters should document conditions carefully, preserve relevant information, and avoid actions that could limit recovery opportunities. Early coordination with internal teams, engineers, or legal representatives supports a structured evaluation.

Delays in identifying subrogation potential or incomplete documentation may reduce recovery opportunities and complicate the claim. Maintaining awareness of potential third-party involvement supports both claim handling and long-term claim outcomes.

Working Within Changing Conditions

Wildfire claims evolve rapidly as access restrictions change, debris removal progresses, and new information emerges. Adjusters must adapt while maintaining direction. Without clear documentation and communication, shifting conditions can create confusion and disrupt continuity.

Documenting changes preserves continuity. Recording follow-up inspections, updated site conditions, and newly available information ensures the claim file reflects how the evaluation developed. These notes help stakeholders understand why timelines shift and how decisions evolve. Disciplined documentation prevents gaps as conditions change.

Adjusters may need to revise timelines as access improves or further evaluation becomes possible. Communicating updates sustains alignment and keeps expectations realistic. Reliable updates reinforce professionalism and keep the claim moving forward.

Working in changing conditions requires flexibility and discipline. Adjusters who document developments, communicate updates, and maintain organized workflows stabilize claims and preserve continuity. A disciplined approach keeps the claim steady even when the environment is not.

The Human Side of Total Loss Communities

Wildfires affect entire communities, not just individual properties. Policyholders may face displacement, uncertainty, and long-term rebuilding decisions, creating urgency and emotional strain. Adjusters must remain professional while recognizing the scale of impact.

Clear communication provides stability during disruption. Explaining the claim process, outlining next steps, and confirming timelines reduce uncertainty. Regular, reliable updates offer direction and help maintain trust.

Maintaining a professional tone is essential in total-loss communities. Calm, respectful communication keeps interactions constructive. Adjusters provide objectivity and steady direction as the claim moves forward.

The human impact of wildfire losses underscores the need for disciplined handling. Adjusters provide stability through alignment, reliability, and professional communication, supporting claims through complex recovery. In total-loss environments, professionalism and alignment become stabilizing forces.

Leading Claims in Total Loss Communities

Wildfire claims require adjusters to guide complex, evolving situations. Community-level losses, access limitations, displacement, and high claim volume all impact handling. Adjuster leadership is especially important as stakeholders seek direction during recovery.

Disciplined documentation, reliable communication, and organized workflows help manage complexity. These practices support alignment across multiple claims, especially when conditions and timelines are uncertain.

The adjuster's expanding role is particularly evident in wildfire claims. Adjusters coordinate stakeholders, manage expectations, and sustain momentum across multiple properties and participants. This leadership stabilizes the claim environment and supports steady progression toward resolution.

In total-loss communities, adjusters provide stability. Through alignment, organization, and professionalism, they support claims through challenging environments. Their leadership brings order to disruption and supports community recovery. Leadership at this level is not about control, it is about providing direction when everything else is uncertain.

Practical Claim Leadership Actions

Wildfires and Total Loss Communities

Wildfire events affecting total loss communities create high emotional intensity, extended timelines, and complex coordination. Adjusters must establish structure early, communicate clearly, and maintain organization across multiple total-loss claims. These actions help stabilize the process for policyholders navigating significant disruption.

ESTABLISH STABILITY EARLY

Policyholders in total loss communities often face immediate displacement and uncertainty. Providing structure early helps reduce confusion and support alignment.

KEY ACTIONS:

Explain the total loss claim process clearly
Outline immediate next steps
Clarify the temporary living expense process
Set expectations for communication timing

GO-TO LINES:

"I want to walk you through what happens next."
"Here's how the total loss process works."
"The first step is..."
"I'll keep you updated as we move forward."

COMMUNICATE WITH CLARITY AND EMPATHY

Wildfire losses often involve emotional conversations. Clear, calm communication helps stabilize the claim while maintaining professionalism.

KEY ACTIONS:

Acknowledge the scope of loss professionally
Use clear, straightforward language
Avoid speculation about timelines
Confirm next steps at the end of each conversation

GO-TO LINES:

"I understand this is a difficult situation."
"Let me explain the process clearly."

"Here is what we know at this stage."
"The next step will be..."

SET REALISTIC REBUILD EXPECTATIONS

Wildfire rebuilding timelines are often extended due to permitting, contractor demand, and infrastructure delays. Early expectation management prevents frustration.

KEY ACTIONS:

Explain rebuild timeline realities
Clarify permitting and contractor delays
Set expectations for estimate development
Reconfirm expectations as conditions evolve

GO-TO LINES:

"Rebuilding timelines may take longer due to demand."
"Permitting and contractor availability will affect timing."
"I want to set realistic expectations early."
"We'll continue to update timelines as conditions change."

APPLY POLICY CLEARLY AND SET BOUNDARIES *(NEW — CRITICAL ADD)*

Wildfire claims often require adjusters to communicate coverage limitations and align expectations with policy provisions. Clear, policy-based explanations help maintain direction and reduce conflict.

KEY ACTIONS:

Explain coverage and limitations clearly
Reference policy language when appropriate
Avoid speculative or informal interpretations
Maintain consistency between documentation and communication

GO-TO LINES:

"This is what the policy allows in this situation."
"Here's how coverage applies based on the policy."
"This portion is outside the current scope of coverage."
"I want to keep this aligned with the policy requirements."

GUIDE PERSONAL PROPERTY DOCUMENTATION

Total loss claims often require policyholders to reconstruct personal property inventories without physical reference. This process can be time-consuming and emotionally difficult.

KEY ACTIONS:

Explain personal property documentation expectations
Provide structured guidance for inventory development
Break documentation into manageable steps
Set realistic timelines for completion

GO-TO LINES:

"We'll work through personal property documentation step by step."
"You don't have to complete everything at once."
"I'll guide you through what's needed."
"We'll build this process together over time."

ORGANIZE TOTAL LOSS DOCUMENTATION

Total loss claims require clear documentation to support coverage, valuation, and communication.

KEY ACTIONS:

Document total loss determination clearly
Record communication regarding coverage

Track policy limit discussions
Identify pending documentation needs

GO-TO LINES:

"This file reflects the total loss determination."
"Here's how coverage applies to this loss."
"Documentation is being updated."
"Next steps include…"

MANAGE HIGH-VOLUME TOTAL LOSS CLAIMS

Wildfire events often involve multiple simultaneous total loss claims. Structured workflow supports consistency.

KEY ACTIONS:

Track claim status clearly
Prioritize time-sensitive items
Maintain consistent note structure
Document next steps for each file

GO-TO LINES:

"I'm managing multiple claims in this area."
"Your claim remains active and progressing."
"I'm prioritizing based on urgency."
"I'll continue to move this forward."

COORDINATE STAKEHOLDERS CLEARLY

Wildfire claims often involve contractors, policyholders, internal teams, and support services. Clear coordination helps maintain alignment.

KEY ACTIONS:

Clarify stakeholder roles
Confirm communication channels
Document coordination efforts
Maintain update schedule

GO-TO LINES:

"I want to keep everyone aligned on next steps."
"I'm coordinating internally and will update you."
"We are working across multiple parties."
"I'll provide an update once the review is complete."

These practices help adjusters maintain clarity, professionalism, and structure when managing wildfire claims in total-loss communities. By combining empathy with disciplined communication, clear policy, organized documentation, and consistent direction, adjusters provide stability in high-impact environments and help guide recovery.

CLAIM LEADERSHIP
SUMMARY

Key Takeaway

Wildfires that cause total loss fundamentally change the claims process. Policyholders face complete displacement and long-term recovery, not just repairs. Adjusters must provide clear guidance on rebuilding, timelines, and expectations, ensuring policy clarity and direction during periods of uncertainty.

In Practice

When managing total loss claims, explain the next steps early and set realistic expectations. Address coverage, additional living expenses, and the rebuilding process, using policy language to guide discussions. Structured communication helps policyholders understand the process, even when outcomes differ from initial expectations.

Questions for Reflection

1. Do I clearly explain the next steps in total-loss claims?
2. How do I help policyholders understand rebuilding timelines?
3. Am I applying policy language clearly when expectations differ?
4. Am I providing structure during conversations about long-term recovery?

Claim Leadership Principle

Total loss claims require guidance beyond the inspection. Clear direction, consistent communication, and policy-based decisions help stabilize the claim and support recovery.

CHAPTER 7

Hurricanes and Widespread Property Damage

Event Spotlight — Hurricane Katrina

Following Hurricane Katrina, catastrophe-related wind and flood damage impacted multiple Gulf Coast states. Entire neighborhoods experienced structural destruction, storm surge impact, and long-term displacement. Adjusters managed simultaneous property, contents, and additional living expenses claims across widespread geographic areas.

Industry estimates placed insured losses above $60 billion, making it one of the costliest hurricanes in United States history. The event introduced large-scale disputes involving wind versus flood causation, coverage interpretation, and extended rebuilding timelines. Adjusters were required to document complex losses while navigating evolving information.

Widespread damage changes the claim environment. Contractors become limited, repair timelines extend, and policyholder expectations must be carefully managed. The adjuster becomes a central point of clarity in a rapidly changing recovery process, where early documentation and communication influence how the claim develops over time.

CHAPTER FOCUS

Hurricane claims require disciplined evaluation, clear communication, and reliable documentation. Adjusters must manage expectations while maintaining accuracy across widespread damage.

Hurricanes and Widespread Property Damage

Hurricane claims differ from localized losses because they affect entire regions rather than individual structures. The primary challenge is managing layered damage, high claim volumes, and competing scope interpretations. Wind damage, water intrusion, storm surge, and prolonged exposure can affect thousands of properties simultaneously. This scale requires adjusters to manage high volume, shifting conditions, and increased communication demands.

Widespread property damage demands a different approach. Adjusters must prioritize inspections, coordinate travel, and manage expectations across large areas. Flooding, debris, and infrastructure disruption may limit access. Policyholders may be displaced, utilities may be unavailable, and damage may continue to develop after the storm.

These conditions require a disciplined response. In regional events, organization becomes the foundation for managing both volume and complexity.

Hurricane claims often involve layered damage, with wind, rain, and water exposure occurring in sequence. Determining the full scope requires thorough documentation and evaluation. As conditions may change between inspections, adjusters must clearly document observations to maintain continuity throughout the claim process.

Handling hurricane claims requires organization, consistency, and professional judgment. Adjusters must guide claims through widespread disruption, extending their role beyond inspection. Clarity across multiple claims keeps the entire process stable.

The Scale of Regional Impact

Hurricanes can affect entire cities, coastal regions, and inland areas simultaneously, resulting in a high volume of claims in a short time. Adjusters may be responsible for many properties across large distances, making planning and prioritization essential.

Travel conditions often complicate inspections. Flooded roads, debris, and limited fuel can restrict access. Adjusters must adapt to changing conditions and prioritize safety, adjusting inspection schedules as access improves.

Infrastructure disruptions, such as power outages, communication issues, and temporary housing, can alter how adjusters interact with policyholders. Flexibility, supported by structured processes, is necessary. The regional scale of hurricane damage requires adjusters to stay organized. Grouping inspections by location, documenting access issues, and tracking claim status help manage complexity. When geography expands, organization becomes critical to maintaining control of the claim environment.

Layered Damage and Evolving Conditions

Hurricane damage develops in stages. Wind can damage roofs, leading to water intrusion. Prolonged rain and subsequent flooding or storm surge further complicate evaluation due to these layered conditions.

Adjusters should document observations thoroughly. Identifying visible damage, recording water intrusion, and noting structural impacts support accurate evaluation. Photographs and detailed notes preserve continuity as the claim progresses.

Conditions may change after the initial inspection. Additional water damage can emerge as structures dry, and temporary repairs may alter site conditions. Follow-up inspections and thorough documentation are essential to track these changes.

Evaluating layered damage requires patience and a disciplined approach. Adjusters should assess claims as conditions evolve rather than relying on a single inspection. Layered damage requires layered documentation to preserve continuity over time.

Pre-Existing Damage and Prior Claims

Hurricane claims frequently involve properties with previous storm damage. Roofs, exterior components, and structural elements may show wear, unrepaired damage, or a history of prior claims. Distinguishing between pre-existing conditions and new storm-related damage requires careful documentation and evaluation.

Adjusters should clearly document current conditions and note any visible prior damage or wear. When appropriate, claim history and prior repairs should be reviewed to support an accurate evaluation. Clear communication helps explain how current findings relate to the current claim.

A disciplined, objective approach is required in these situations. Structured documentation and consistent communication help maintain clarity when damage results from multiple events and overlapping conditions. Clear separation of past and present damage is essential to maintaining claim accuracy.

Prioritizing Inspections After the Storm

After a hurricane, demand for inspections rises sharply. Adjusters must identify which claims need immediate attention and which can be scheduled later, using clear prioritization criteria.

Safety concerns often guide prioritization. Properties with structural instability, roof failure, or active water intrusion require prompt inspection. Accessibility issues, such as flooding or restricted areas, may delay evaluation.

Establishing inspection routes improves efficiency. Grouping claims geographically reduces travel time and supports consistency, helping manage high claim volumes.

Clear communication about scheduling helps manage expectations. Informing policyholders when inspections are likely to occur reduces uncertainty. Prioritization is essential in hurricane claims. Structured planning ensures clarity and efficiency. Clear prioritization supports both fairness and operational efficiency across large claim inventories.

Communication Across High Claim Volume

Hurricanes create significant communication demands. Policyholders may request updates, report new damage, or seek guidance as conditions change. Contractors, mitigation teams, and internal stakeholders also require coordination.

As adjusters manage inspections and documentation across multiple claims, communication management becomes essential. A disciplined approach helps manage this volume. Providing reliable updates, confirming next steps, and documenting key conversations reduces repeated inquiries. When stakeholders understand claim status, uncertainty decreases and follow-up requests become more focused.

Establishing communication windows or defined update intervals allows adjusters to focus on inspections while remaining responsive. Policyholders receive predictable updates, and communication remains organized and efficient. This approach reduces interruptions and sustains alignment under pressure.

Maintaining a professional tone is crucial during hurricane events. Policyholders may face disruption, property damage, and uncertainty. Calm, respectful, and clear communication stabilizes interactions. Even brief updates reinforce direction and reduce confusion. Consistent communication reduces both confusion and unnecessary escalation across multiple claims.

Temporary Repairs and Ongoing Damage

Temporary repairs are common after hurricanes. Policyholders may tarp roofs, board openings, remove wet materials, or start emergency mitigation before or between inspections. As site conditions can change quickly, adjusters must document these developments to maintain continuity.

During inspections, adjusters should thoroughly document temporary repairs. Recording completed work, visible damage, and ongoing mitigation preserves continuity. Photographs, detailed notes, and timelines provide context for changes in property condition and support accurate evaluation and reliable claim handling.

Ongoing damage can develop after the storm, including worsening water intrusion, material deterioration, and mold growth. Additional inspections may be required. Tracking changes over time ensures that decisions reflect current conditions and supports steady claim progression.

Temporary repairs and evolving damage require adjusters to remain flexible while maintaining organization. Disciplined documentation, predictable communication, and staged evaluations help manage changing conditions and ensure claims progress with professionalism.

Mitigation and Subcontractor Coordination

Mitigation providers and subcontractors often play a critical role in hurricane claims, especially when water intrusion and ongoing damage require immediate action. Emergency drying, debris removal, tarping, and temporary stabilization may begin before or between inspections and often involve multiple crews or specialized vendors.

These activities can significantly alter site conditions. Materials may be removed, damaged areas may be modified, and access points may shift as work progresses. Adjusters must document both observed damage and any mitigation or subcontractor activity to maintain continuity in the claim file.

Adjusters should coordinate effectively with mitigation providers and subcontractors by identifying completed work, confirming ongoing activity, and documenting how these efforts relate to the loss. Clear communication helps ensure that mitigation supports the claim process and remains aligned with documented findings and policy provisions.

Structured coordination reduces confusion. When roles, timelines, and site conditions are clearly documented, all parties remain aligned. This approach supports efficient claim progression and reinforces the adjuster's role in maintaining direction within complex, multi-party environments.

In widespread hurricane events, demand for services such as tree removal, debris clearing, and emergency mitigation increases significantly. Limited availability of qualified providers may result in variations in pricing, scope, and timelines. These conditions can create challenges for both policyholders and adjusters as work progresses.

Adjusters should remain focused on documenting observed conditions, confirming completed work, and maintaining alignment with policy provisions. Clear communication helps manage expectations when costs, timelines, or scope differ from initial assumptions. Structured documentation and consistent communication support transparency and help guide the claim through these conditions.

Access Challenges and Safety Considerations

Access to damaged areas may be limited after hurricanes due to flooding, debris, downed power lines, and structural hazards. Blocked roads, restricted entry, and unsafe or uninhabitable properties can affect inspections. Adjusters must prioritize safety, often requiring staged inspections instead of immediate evaluation.

Adjusters should follow local guidance and restrictions, including emergency directives, utility advisories, and community access limitations, which may delay inspections. Documenting access constraints explains scheduling decisions and supports transparency. Clear documentation maintains alignment when timelines shift due to safety concerns.

Safety considerations may limit the scope of the inspection. Some areas may be unsafe due to collapse risk, water damage, or unstable debris. Adjusters should record these limitations and document what was safely observed, ensuring the claim file reflects both completed evaluations and encountered constraints.

Adjusters who prioritize safety and document conditions demonstrate professionalism and disciplined claim handling. Structured notes, clear explanations, and staged evaluations maintain continuity and allow claims to progress responsibly while protecting all parties.

Extended power outages are also common after hurricanes and can significantly affect habitability. Loss of electricity may impact refrigeration, climate control, and basic living conditions, leading policyholders to seek guidance on temporary living arrangements. In some cases, evacuation or temporary relocation may be necessary.

Adjusters should document the reported conditions and explain how additional living expenses are evaluated in accordance with the policy provisions. Clear communication helps set expectations regarding coverage, duration, and required documentation. Providing structured guidance supports policyholders while maintaining alignment with policy requirements.

Field Conditions and Adjuster Deployment Reality

Hurricane deployments create challenging working conditions for field adjusters. Travel may involve long distances, limited fuel availability, and restricted access to affected areas. In some cases, lodging may be unavailable, requiring adjusters to operate with limited resources while maintaining professional responsibilities. These conditions affect inspection scheduling, communication timing, and overall claim pacing. Adjusters must balance field constraints with claim expectations, maintaining organization and clarity despite operational challenges.

Defined workflows and disciplined communication help manage these conditions. Clear documentation of access limitations, delays, and field conditions supports transparency and maintains alignment with policyholders and internal teams. Field conditions are a defining aspect of hurricane claims. Adjusters who maintain organization and professionalism under these constraints support reliable claim handling.

Documentation in Widespread Events

Documentation is especially important during hurricane events. High claim volume, changing conditions, and multiple inspections require disciplined recordkeeping. Organized notes and photographs provide continuity and make it easier to track claim development.

Recording inspection timing, site conditions, and observed damage ensures claims remain understandable. Notes should detail when inspections occurred, present conditions, and any evaluation limitations. Documenting communication captures expectations, updates, and next steps, supporting alignment.

When multiple inspections occur, documentation tracks changes over time. Temporary repairs, additional damage, or improved access may alter observations. Recording these developments creates a clear record of claim progression and supports reliable decision-making.

Using documentation as a central reference helps manage complexity during widespread hurricane events. Organized notes reduce the need for repeated information searches and support efficient handling. Disciplined documentation improves communication, reinforces alignment, and supports claims as conditions evolve.

Managing Expectations During Recovery

Hurricane recovery often takes time. High claim volume, limited contractor availability, infrastructure disruption, and access issues can delay timelines. Policyholders may expect immediate resolution, but staged evaluation is often necessary. Managing expectations is essential for clarity and to prevent confusion.

Adjusters manage expectations by explaining the claim process early. Outlining the inspection order, documentation requirements, and potential delays provides structure. Offering estimated timelines, even if subject to change, helps stakeholders understand recovery progress. Early transparency reduces uncertainty and supports alignment.

Regular updates maintain clarity as conditions evolve. Even when progress depends on external factors, communication stabilizes the claim. Confirming status, outlining next steps, and clarifying timeline changes prevent assumptions. Policyholders benefit from consistent, predictable updates.

Managing expectations supports smoother claim handling. Clear communication reduces frustration, improves cooperation, and maintains direction. Providing realistic timelines and consistent updates helps guide claims through complex recovery.

Applying Policy Language and Managing Expectations

Hurricane claims often require adjusters to explain both coverage and limitations. Damage may have multiple causes, and coverage depends on policy provisions, scope definitions, and endorsements. These factors may not match policyholder or third-party expectations.

Adjusters should rely on policy language to guide these conversations. Clear explanations of coverage, limitations, and next steps maintain alignment and reduce misunderstanding. Policy language supports consistent and professional communication.

Third-party expectations must be managed carefully. Contractors, mitigation teams, and public adjusters may propose scopes or timelines that differ from policy requirements. Adjusters should acknowledge these views while maintaining alignment with documented findings and policy. Policy provisions should guide all discussions. Disciplined communication keeps conversations focused on the claim.

Delivering difficult information requires professionalism and precision. Adjusters should avoid speculation and base decisions on documented findings and policy language. Reliable, policy-based explanations maintain focus and reduce escalation.

Managing expectations through clear policy explanations supports the progression of claims. Even when outcomes differ from initial expectations, structured communication sustains momentum and reinforces the adjuster's role in complex claims environments. Hurricane claims may also involve higher deductibles, coverage limitations, or policy changes that affect loss evaluation.

REAL WORLD
Coverage Alignment in a Layered Hurricane Claim

An adjuster handled a hurricane claim involving roof damage, water intrusion, and interior damage following a storm. A contractor submitted a scope of work that included a full roof replacement and extensive interior repairs, while the policyholder expected immediate approval for all proposed work.

The adjuster documented wind damage, identified areas of water intrusion, and identified conditions requiring further evaluation. During the review, the adjuster explained how the policy applied to the observed damage, clarified coverage considerations, and outlined the next steps in the evaluation process.

The contractor's scope was acknowledged, but the adjuster maintained alignment with documented findings and policy provisions. The policyholder was informed that portions of the claim required additional review and that coverage would be determined based on the policy and inspection results.

Through disciplined communication and consistent updates, the adjuster clarified expectations and advanced the claim. By relying on policy language and documented observations, the adjuster maintained alignment, reduced misunderstanding, and supported a defensible claim outcome.

Coordinating Multiple Participants

Hurricane claims often involve multiple participants, including contractors, mitigation teams, engineers, roofing specialists, and internal stakeholders. Each may operate on different timelines and offer different perspectives. Without coordination, communication can become fragmented, slowing claim progression.

Adjusters maintain direction by documenting requests, recording responses, and clarifying next steps. Identifying responsibilities and confirming follow-up actions keeps participants aligned and ensures information flows through the claim efficiently.

Clear communication keeps discussions focused on the claim. Neutral, disciplined messaging prevents conflicting interpretations. Reliable documentation creates a shared reference point, and coordinated execution supports efficient claim progression.

Managing multiple participants requires organization and reliability. Adjusters who guide communication, reduce confusion, and sustain alignment demonstrate professional claim leadership. Coordination is central to this role.

Leading Claims After Widespread Damage

Hurricane claims require adjusters to operate amid large-scale disruption. Regional damage, layered site conditions, and high communication volume shape claim handling. With multiple active claims and evolving information, leadership is essential to maintain direction.

Thorough documentation, reliable communication, and organized prioritization help manage these conditions. These practices create stability even as timelines shift and information changes. Organization enables adjusters to transition between claims while maintaining momentum.

The adjuster's expanding role is especially evident in hurricane claims. Adjusters guide stakeholders, manage expectations, coordinate participants, and sustain direction. This leadership stabilizes the claim environment and supports steady resolution.

In widespread damage events, adjusters provide direction. Through organization, alignment, and professional judgment, they lead claims through complexity. A disciplined approach brings order to disruption and supports reliable claim handling in high-volume environments.

Regulatory Timelines and Claim Status Requirements

In modern claims environments, timelines are not only operational—they are also regulatory. Most states require adjusters and carriers to acknowledge claims, initiate investigations, provide periodic status updates, and communicate claim determinations within defined timeframes. These requirements shape how the claim must be managed from the outset.

Adjusters who understand and apply these timelines strengthen compliance and claim clarity. When timelines are tracked and communication aligns with regulatory expectations, the claim process becomes more structured and predictable for all parties involved.

Timelines vary by jurisdiction, but expectations are consistent. Claims must be acknowledged promptly. Investigations must begin without unnecessary delay. Status updates must be provided while the claim remains under review. Determinations must be communicated within the required period or, if additional time is needed, be accompanied by a clear explanation.

In practice, this means adjusters must actively track key dates and align their workflow accordingly. Waiting until a deadline approaches increases risk. Leading the claim requires anticipating those timelines and communicating before they become pressure points.

Clear documentation supports this process. Each contact, update, and decision should reflect both claim progress and adherence to required timeframes. When documentation and communication align with regulatory expectations, the file becomes more defensible and easier to manage, even in complex or high-volume environments.

Communication tied to timelines should remain structured and professional. Providing updates before they are requested reduces escalation and reinforces control over the process. Policyholders are less likely to become frustrated when they understand that the claim is progressing within defined and required timeframes.

Adjusters may communicate this by clearly reinforcing status and expectations. Statements such as "The claim is still under review, and I will provide an update within the required timeframe" or "We are continuing the investigation and will follow up with additional information" help maintain alignment while meeting regulatory obligations.

When timelines cannot be met due to complexity, volume, or the need for additional investigation, communication becomes even more important. Providing a clear explanation, documenting the reason for the delay, and setting the next expected update date maintains credibility and reduces the risk of misunderstanding.

Regulatory timelines are not separate from claim leadership; they are integral to it. Adjusters who integrate these requirements into their daily workflow bring structure, consistency, and accountability to the claim. This approach supports compliance, strengthens defensibility, and helps ensure that claims move forward in a controlled, professional manner.

Practical Claim Leadership Actions

Hurricanes and Widespread Property Damage

Hurricane events often produce widespread property damage across large geographic areas. Adjusters must manage high claim volume, evolving damage conditions, and multiple stakeholders. Establishing structure early, applying policy clarity, and maintaining consistent communication help stabilize the claim process and prevent confusion.

ESTABLISH CLAIM DIRECTION EARLY

Widespread damage creates uncertainty. Early structure helps guide the claim and reduce reactive communication.

KEY ACTIONS:

Explain the inspection process and possible delays
Set expectations for access and safety conditions
Identify documentation needs
Establish communication timeline

GO-TO LINES:

"Here's how the inspection process will work."
"Access may be limited due to current conditions."
"The first step is completing the inspection."
"I'll provide updates as we move forward."

MANAGE EVOLVING DAMAGE CONDITIONS

Hurricane losses may involve hidden damage, supplemental findings, and changing scope.

KEY ACTIONS:

Communicate possibility of additional damage
Document initial findings clearly
Identify pending inspection items
Revisit scope as new information emerges

GO-TO LINES:

"Additional damage may become visible over time."
"This is what we observed during the initial inspection."
"Some areas will require further evaluation."
"We'll reassess as conditions develop."

MAINTAIN CONSISTENT COMMUNICATION

High-volume hurricane claims increase the risk of confusion. Structured updates help maintain alignment.

KEY ACTIONS:

Provide initial status update
Confirm inspection completion
Identify next evaluation step
Maintain update cadence

GO-TO LINES:

"Here is the current status of your claim."
"The inspection has been completed."

"The next step is…"
"I'll follow up with an update."

SET REALISTIC TIMELINE EXPECTATIONS

Hurricanes often create delays in access, contractor availability, and material availability.

KEY ACTIONS:

Explain inspection scheduling realities
Set expectations for estimate review
Clarify supplement process
Reconfirm timelines as conditions change

GO-TO LINES:

"Inspection timing may be affected by access conditions."
"Review timelines may take longer due to volume."
"Supplements may be needed as additional damage is identified."
"I'll update you as timelines change."

APPLY POLICY CLEARLY AND SET BOUNDARIES

Hurricane claims often involve multiple causes of loss and differing scope interpretations. Clear policy-based communication helps maintain alignment and reduce disputes.

KEY ACTIONS:

Explain coverage based on observed damage
Clarify limitations tied to policy provisions
Avoid speculative or informal interpretations
Maintain consistency between documentation and communication

GO-TO LINES:

"This is how the policy applies to the observed damage."
"Coverage is based on the inspection findings."
"Some items may require additional review."
"I want to keep this aligned with policy requirements."

COORDINATE STAKEHOLDERS CLEARLY

Hurricane claims often involve contractors, mitigation teams, engineers, and internal teams working simultaneously.

KEY ACTIONS:

Clarify roles and responsibilities
Confirm communication channels
Document coordination efforts
Maintain a consistent update schedule

GO-TO LINES:

"I want to keep everyone aligned on next steps."
"I'm coordinating across all parties involved."
"We are reviewing information from multiple sources."
"I'll provide an update once the review is complete."

ORGANIZE HIGH-VOLUME CLAIMS

A structured workflow helps prevent claims from drifting during widespread events.

KEY ACTIONS:

Track claim status clearly
Document next steps
Prioritize time-sensitive claims
Maintain consistent note structure

GO-TO LINES:

"I'm managing multiple claims in this area."
"Your claim remains active and progressing."
"I'm prioritizing based on urgency."
"Next steps are documented and scheduled."

REGULATORY TIMELINES AND CLAIM STATUS REQUIREMENTS

Modern claims leadership requires awareness of state-specific regulatory timelines. These timelines set expectations for acknowledgment, investigation, status updates, and claim determination. Adjusters who align communication and workflow with these requirements strengthen compliance, reduce risk, and support professional credibility.

Timelines vary by state, but most jurisdictions require timely acknowledgment of the claim, prompt investigation, periodic status updates, and communication of claim decisions within defined timeframes. These requirements are not administrative details; they shape how the claim must be managed.

Adjusters should incorporate these timelines into their workflow from the outset of the claim. This includes documenting key dates, tracking required responses, and proactively communicating status updates before deadlines approach.

KEY ACTIONS:

Identify applicable state regulations at the start of the claim
Track acknowledgment, inspection, and determination deadlines
Provide required status updates within regulatory timeframes
Document all communications tied to compliance requirements
Escalate files that may approach or exceed timeline thresholds

GO-TO LINES:

"I want to keep you updated as we continue through the review process."

"Your claim is still under evaluation, and I will provide an update within the required timeframe."

"We are continuing the investigation and will follow up with additional information."

"This review is ongoing, and I'll provide a status update as required."

"I want to ensure this claim is handled within all required timelines."

Maintaining awareness of regulatory timelines supports consistency and defensibility. When adjusters align their communication, documentation, and decision-making with these requirements, they reinforce structure, reduce uncertainty, and ensure the claim progresses in a compliant, professional manner.

These practices help adjusters maintain alignment and momentum when managing hurricane-related claims. By combining disciplined communication, clear policy explanations, thorough documentation, and coordinated effort, adjusters move claims forward through evolving conditions and support efficient, professional handling.

CLAIM LEADERSHIP SUMMARY

Key Takeaway

Hurricane events create widespread damage across large geographic areas, increasing claim volume and extending recovery timelines. Limited contractor availability, infrastructure challenges, and evolving conditions require adjusters to manage expectations while maintaining accuracy. Clear communication, policy-based decisions, and structured evaluation are essential to stabilizing the claim environment.

In Practice

When handling hurricane claims, set realistic timelines and explain potential delays early. Document damage carefully, communicate consistently, and use policy language to guide scope and coverage discussions. Avoid overcommitting on repair expectations. Providing clarity during widespread disruption helps reduce confusion, align stakeholders, and support consistent claim handling.

Questions for Reflection

1. Do I set realistic expectations during widespread damage events?
2. How do I communicate potential delays in inspections or repairs?
3. Am I applying policy language clearly when scope or coverage differs?
4. Am I maintaining consistent documentation across multiple claims?

Claim Leadership Principle

Clear expectations, consistent communication, and policy-based decisions help stabilize claims during widespread disruption.

CHAPTER 8

Flood Events and Coverage Disputes

Event Spotlight — Major Flood Events and Coverage Complexity

Severe flooding across multiple regions has caused extensive property damage, business interruption losses, and infrastructure disruption. Events such as the Midwest Floods of 2019, Hurricane Harvey, and the 2022 Pakistan Floods demonstrate how quickly water can enter structures, affecting interiors, equipment, and contents at scale. In each of these events, policyholders experienced significant losses while navigating complex recovery environments.

Billions in insured and uninsured losses were associated with these disasters. Coverage disputes arose over surface water, storm surge, sewer backup, and policy exclusions. In events like Hurricane Harvey, distinguishing between flood and wind-driven damage added complexity. Adjusters were required to interpret and explain technical policy language while managing emotionally charged conversations with policyholders facing immediate disruption.

Flood claims in large-scale events consistently create tension between the severity of damage and the scope of coverage. Policyholders witness visible, often overwhelming losses, while coverage interpretation may be constrained by policy provisions. This gap between expectations and policy reality must be managed carefully. The adjuster's role is to communicate clearly, maintain professionalism, and guide the claim with consistency and structure.

In many of these events, policyholders also rely on disaster relief programs such as the Federal Emergency Management Agency, making timely claim documentation and clear coverage communication critical for accessing broader recovery support.

Across global events, including large-scale flooding in regions such as South Asia and the United States, the same patterns emerge. Rapid-onset damage, evolving site conditions, and widespread impact increase both claim volume and complexity. Early communication, disciplined documentation, and clear explanation of the evaluation process directly influence how coverage discussions unfold and whether claims remain aligned or escalate.

CHAPTER FOCUS

Flood claims require strong communication and clear documentation. Adjusters must balance policy interpretation with professional clarity and consistency, especially in environments where large-scale events heighten both expectations and scrutiny.

Flood Events and Coverage Disputes

Flood claims are often complex, involving more than physical damage. The primary challenge is applying coverage limitations while managing expectations that may not align with the policy. Although the loss may be visible, questions about coverage, causation, and timing add complexity. Water may enter a structure from multiple sources, including rainfall, surface water, storm surge, or plumbing issues—requiring thorough documentation and clear communication.

Flood events frequently impact large geographic areas, affecting multiple properties at once. Conditions can change rapidly as water levels rise or recede, and access becomes limited. Damage may continue to develop after the initial event. Adjusters must evaluate these conditions while maintaining a disciplined approach. In flood events, alignment distinguishes visible damage from understood loss.

Coverage discussions are common because policyholders may not fully understand how different water sources are handled. Questions about timing, origin, and extent of damage often arise. These conversations require precision and professionalism. Adjusters should thoroughly document observations and clearly communicate the evaluation process.

Handling flood claims requires disciplined documentation, reliable communication, and careful evaluation. Adjusters must guide the claim while remaining objective. A defined approach ensures that complex coverage discussions remain grounded in documented facts.

Reservation of Rights and Coverage Clarity

Flood claims may involve uncertainty regarding coverage, particularly when multiple potential causes of loss are present or when policy limitations apply. In these situations, a reservation of rights may be issued to allow the claim investigation to continue while preserving the policy terms.

Adjusters should recognize that a reservation of rights is a standard part of handling complex coverage situations. It does not determine the claim outcome but clarifies that the evaluation is ongoing and subject to policy provisions. Clear communication explains this process and maintains transparency.

When discussing coverage, adjusters should focus on documenting observations and explaining the evaluation process. Avoid speculation and rely on policy language to ensure consistency and professionalism. Structured communication maintains alignment, even when coverage questions are unresolved.

Reservation-of-rights situations require a disciplined approach. Clear documentation, consistent messaging, and a professional tone reduce confusion and support defensible claim handling. This approach reinforces the adjuster's role in maintaining direction during complex coverage discussions. Clarity in these moments prevents uncertainty from escalating.

REAL WORLD
Coverage Uncertainty in a Flood Claim

An adjuster handled a residential claim following a regional flood, during which water entered the home due to heavy rainfall and rising groundwater. The policyholder reported extensive interior damage to flooring, drywall, and personal property, and expected full coverage for the loss.

During inspection, the adjuster documented water lines, exterior conditions, and the impact on the surrounding property. Standing water had entered at ground level, with additional moisture observed in adjacent areas. The policyholder noted that water may have entered through multiple pathways.

Since the source and cause of water required further evaluation, the claim remained under review. A reservation of rights was issued to continue the investigation while preserving policy provisions. The adjuster explained that coverage determination would depend on documented findings and policy language.

The policyholder initially expressed concern about delays and uncertainty. The adjuster clearly explained the evaluation process, identified the required information, and outlined next steps. Updates were provided as conditions were reviewed and new information became available.

By documenting observations carefully and maintaining clear, policy-based communication, the adjuster guided the claim through uncertainty. This approach reduced misunderstandings, supported a defensible evaluation, and upheld professionalism in a coverage-sensitive situation.

The Nature of Flood-Related Damage

Flood damage often affects structures differently than other types of loss. Water typically enters at ground level, spreads across flooring, and penetrates walls, insulation, cabinetry, and contents. The full extent of damage may not be apparent during the initial inspection. Moisture can remain in materials, and deterioration may continue after the event. These conditions require careful, disciplined evaluation from the outset.

Adjusters must document observed conditions thoroughly. Recording water lines, affected materials, visible staining, and damaged contents establishes a clear baseline. Photographs and detailed notes preserve continuity and support later comparison. Early documentation is critical, as drying and material removal can quickly alter site conditions.

Flood damage may extend beyond the initial entry point. Water can migrate through adjoining rooms, seep beneath flooring, and affect adjacent areas. Documenting how water moved through the structure clarifies the extent of loss. Recording transitions between affected and unaffected areas supports a consistent evaluation. Water movement must be documented as clearly as the damage itself.

Conditions often change after an inspection. As moisture is addressed, drying, material removal, and new findings may emerge. Follow-up inspections can reveal hidden damage. Clear documentation at each stage tracks claim development and ensures decisions reflect evolving conditions. Disciplined notes preserve continuity throughout the claim.

Determining the Source of Water

Identifying the water source is critical in flood-related claims. Water may originate from rainfall, surface water intrusion, storm surge, overflow, or internal sources. Understanding the origin guides evaluation and supports consistent claim handling. Careful observation and disciplined documentation are required.

Adjusters document observations of exterior conditions, water lines, surrounding terrain, and environmental impacts. These details clarify how water entered the structure. Recording drainage patterns, water-depth indicators, and adjacent property conditions further enhances clarity. Observations should be documented objectively, without speculation.

Multiple water sources may contribute to flood events. Heavy rain, wind-driven water, rising water levels, and drainage overflow can occur simultaneously. Adjusters must document visible conditions without making assumptions. Notes should reflect observed facts, inspection limitations, and any conditions needing further evaluation.

Clear documentation of water source considerations preserves objectivity. Structured observations, consistent notes, and neutral language support defensible claims handling. Accurate source identification is central to both evaluation and clarity of coverage.

Subrogation Considerations in Flood Claims

Flood-related claims may involve third-party liability, particularly when water intrusion is caused by drainage systems, construction issues, or equipment failure. Identifying subrogation potential early helps preserve recovery opportunities and supports structured claim handling.

Adjusters should document site conditions carefully, including surrounding property conditions, drainage patterns, and any external factors that may contribute. Photographs, timelines, and objective notes help clarify whether responsibility extends beyond the insured loss.

Early awareness of subrogation potential allows for coordination with internal teams or specialists. Maintaining clear documentation and avoiding actions that could alter site conditions without proper record-keeping supports both claim evaluation and potential recovery efforts. Thorough documentation preserves the integrity of the claim and supports recovery pathways.

Coverage Questions and Claim Discussions

Flood claims often prompt coverage-related questions. Policyholders may seek clarification on damage evaluation, water impact documentation, and factors influencing claim review. These conversations often begin early and may continue as new information emerges. Clear communication is essential to maintain alignment.

Adjusters should explain the process rather than speculate on outcomes. Describing how observations are documented, conditions are evaluated, and information is reviewed maintains clarity. When stakeholders understand the steps, expectations remain grounded in the process.

Avoiding assumptions is especially important in flood claims. Water source, duration, and extent of damage require careful documentation and evaluation. Adjusters should document conditions, identify next steps, and communicate which information remains under review.

Clear communication reduces confusion and maintains professionalism. When policyholders understand how their claims are evaluated, conversations remain constructive. Structured messaging supports alignment and guides the claim through complex flood-related conditions. Clear process explanations prevent confusion from driving the conversation.

Partial Denials and Coverage Limitations

Flood claims may result in partial denials or coverage limitations depending on policy provisions, endorsements, and the documented cause of loss. While damage may be extensive, coverage may apply only to certain portions of the claim. These situations require clear, structured communication.

Adjusters should focus on explaining how the claim is being evaluated and how policy provisions and applicable endorsements apply to the observed conditions. When portions of a claim are not covered, communication should remain professional, consistent, and grounded in the policy. Clear explanations help reduce confusion and maintain alignment, even when outcomes differ from expectations.

Written communication may also be required to document coverage decisions. These communications should reflect documented observations, policy language, and the evaluation process. Consistency between documentation and communication supports clarity and defensible claim handling.

Mold, Fungi, and Secondary Conditions

Flood-related damage may create conditions that allow mold, fungi, or other secondary issues to develop over time. These conditions are often influenced by the duration of water exposure, environmental factors, and mitigation efforts.

Adjusters should document observed conditions without speculation and note any factors that may contribute to ongoing damage. Clear documentation of timing, moisture exposure, and site conditions helps support the evaluation process.

When discussing these conditions, adjusters should focus on explaining the evaluation process and how policy provisions and applicable endorsements apply. Disciplined communication maintains understanding, particularly as conditions evolve after the initial inspection.

Timing and Water Exposure

Flood damage can develop over time. Water may remain in a structure for extended periods before receding, especially during large-scale events. Prolonged exposure increases the extent of impact. Materials may absorb moisture, flooring may swell, and walls may deteriorate as conditions change. These factors make timing a key component of claim evaluation.

Adjusters should document timing whenever possible. Recording when the event occurred, when water was first observed, and when the inspection took place provides essential context. This information helps explain material conditions at the time of inspection and supports a consistent evaluation.

Changes between inspections should also be documented. Drying, removal of affected materials, and additional findings may alter site conditions. Recording these developments helps track the progression of the damage. Consistent documentation ensures the claim reflects evolving conditions rather than a single point in time.

Understanding timing helps explain how damage developed and why conditions appear as observed. This clarity supports communication, strengthens documentation, and helps ensure flood claims are handled consistently and professionally.

Access Limitations During Flood Events

Flood events often create significant access challenges. Standing water, debris, unstable flooring, and electrical hazards may delay inspection. Roads may be blocked, structures may be unsafe to enter, and conditions may change as water levels rise or recede. Adjusters must prioritize safety while maintaining claim progression. These conditions often require staged inspections instead of immediate evaluation.

Access limitations should be documented clearly. Recording water levels, restricted areas, and safety concerns helps explain inspection timing and scope. Notes should reflect what could be safely observed and what requires follow-up. This documentation provides transparency and helps stakeholders understand why the evaluation occurred in stages.

Follow-up inspections may be required once water recedes and conditions improve. Additional damage may become visible as water is removed and materials are exposed. These staged evaluations require structured documentation to track claim development. Recording inspection timing and updated observations helps maintain continuity.

Adjusters who document access limitations help maintain understanding. Clear notes, reliable updates, and staged evaluations support disciplined claim handling. This approach allows flood claims to progress safely while preserving professionalism and alignment.

Communication During Coverage Sensitivity

Flood claims often involve sensitive discussions. Policyholders may have questions regarding coverage considerations, evaluation timing, and next steps, often while conditions are still developing. Clear, disciplined communication supports professionalism and reduces confusion.

Adjusters should focus on explaining observations and the evaluation process. Describing what was observed, what remains under review, and what steps will follow helps maintain understanding. Providing reliable updates reduces uncertainty and keeps stakeholders aligned. This approach keeps communication grounded in documented information.

Tone is particularly important during coverage-sensitive discussions. Policyholders may be navigating uncertainty as they manage property damage and recovery decisions. Professional, calm, and respectful communication helps maintain constructive conversations. Clear explanations guide the claim and preserve objectivity.

Documenting communication also supports clarity. Recording discussions, requesting information, and identifying next steps ensure consistency as the claim develops. Structured documentation reinforces communication and helps ensure that flood claims progress with transparency and professionalism.

Documentation in Coverage-Sensitive Claims

Documentation is especially important when coverage questions may arise. Flood-related claims often involve evolving conditions, multiple observations, and staged inspections. Clear notes, photographs, and timelines help ensure the claim remains understandable from start to resolution. Strong documentation provides structure and supports consistent claim handling.

Recording observations without interpretation helps maintain objectivity. Notes should reflect what was observed, where water impact was visible, and what conditions were present at the time of inspection. Avoiding speculative language helps ensure that documentation remains neutral and defensible. This disciplined approach supports professional handling in coverage-sensitive environments.

Documenting communication is equally important. Recording policyholder questions, adjuster responses, and identifying next steps helps maintain alignment. These notes provide continuity and reduce the risk of misunderstanding as the claim develops. Consistent documentation reinforces clarity across multiple interactions.

Strong documentation supports stability in flood claims. As conditions evolve and additional information becomes available, structured notes help track development. Clear documentation ensures the claim progresses with transparency, consistency, and professional judgment.

Managing Large-Scale Flood Events

Flood events often affect multiple properties within a region. Entire neighborhoods or communities may experience similar conditions simultaneously. Adjusters may handle multiple claims simultaneously, each requiring evaluation, communication, and documentation. This volume increases urgency and demands disciplined organization.

Grouping inspections by location improves efficiency and reduces transition time between claims. A defined scheduling approach allows adjusters to evaluate multiple properties while maintaining reliable documentation practices. Predictable workflows reduce cognitive strain and support alignment across files.

Communication demand may also increase during large-scale flood events. Policyholders often request updates as water levels change, drying progresses, or new information becomes available. Disciplined communication practices—such as scheduled update intervals and clearly defined next steps—help manage demand without sacrificing alignment.

Large-scale flood events require disciplined handling. Organization, reliable documentation, and coordinated communication sustain alignment across multiple claims. By applying these practices, adjusters provide stability in complex environments and support effective claim progression.

Maintaining Objectivity in Disputed Situations

Coverage discussions in flood claims can create differing perspectives. Policyholders, contractors, and other stakeholders may interpret conditions differently as information develops. Adjusters must maintain objectivity throughout the claim. Clear documentation and disciplined communication help ensure that the evaluation remains grounded in observed conditions rather than assumptions.

Focusing on facts sustains professionalism. Recording water lines, affected materials, inspection timing, and environmental conditions creates a reliable record. Explaining the evaluation process—not just the conclusions—helps stakeholders understand how decisions are made. This approach keeps the claim organized and reduces misunderstandings.

Objectivity also helps manage disagreements. When documentation is clear, and observations are recorded reliably, conversations remain focused on the claim rather than interpretation. Clear notes provide a shared reference point, reducing escalation and supporting constructive dialogue as the claim progresses.

Maintaining objectivity is essential in flood claims. Evolving conditions, coverage sensitivity, and multiple perspectives require disciplined handling. Adjusters who document thoroughly and communicate reliably ensure claims remain transparent and professionally managed.

Leading Claims in Flood Environments

Flood events require adjusters to manage evolving conditions, coverage sensitivity, and regional impact. Water exposure may change over time, inspections may occur in stages, and documentation must carefully track developments. These claims require disciplined evaluation and reliable communication from initial response through resolution.

The adjuster's leadership is reflected in maintaining direction. Recording observations, explaining the evaluation process, and documenting changes help guide the claim. Thorough documentation preserves continuity, while reliable communication sustains alignment. These practices support efficiency in complex environments.

Flood claims often involve complexity beyond visible damage. Moisture migration, staged drying, and evolving site conditions require careful evaluation. By maintaining objectivity and organization, adjusters ensure the claim progresses in a clear direction. This leadership stabilizes coverage-sensitive situations and supports professional handling.

In flood events and coverage discussions, the adjuster provides direction. Through clear documentation and professional communication, claims are guided through changing conditions. A disciplined approach brings stability to evolving environments and supports reliable progression. Speed without discipline creates rework.

Disaster Relief Coordination and Regulatory Alignment

Flood events often trigger broader disaster response efforts that extend beyond the scope of an insurance claim. In large-scale events, policyholders may seek assistance from governmental and non-governmental disaster relief organizations. These programs operate alongside the insurance process and often rely on timely claim documentation and communication.

In the United States, agencies such as the Federal Emergency Management Agency (FEMA) provide disaster assistance when an event is declared a federal disaster. Internationally, organizations such as the Red Cross and the United Nations Office for the Coordination of Humanitarian Affairs coordinate relief efforts in regions affected by earthquakes, flooding, wildfires, and other large-scale disasters.

These programs often require documentation from the claims process, including coverage letters, partial denial letters, and proof of loss, to qualify for certain types of aid. Delays or unclear communication during the claims process can directly affect a policyholder's ability to access disaster relief resources, extending recovery timelines during already critical periods.

Adjusters should remain mindful that their role extends beyond claim evaluation in these environments. Timely communication, clear documentation, and structured updates support not only the claim but also the policyholder's broader recovery process and access to external assistance.

Regulatory timelines remain critical during disasters. While some jurisdictions may implement emergency provisions or temporary adjustments, requirements for acknowledgment, investigation, and communication still apply. Maintaining awareness of these timelines ensures compliance and supports coordinated recovery efforts across multiple systems.

At large-scale events, aligning insurance processes with disaster relief systems is essential. Adjusters who communicate clearly, document consistently, and issue timely written decisions help ensure that policyholders can move forward with their claims and any applicable relief programs. In these situations, timeliness is not only a regulatory expectation—it directly influences recovery outcomes.

Practical Claim Leadership Actions

Flood Events and Coverage Disputes

Flood claims often involve complex coverage considerations, overlapping causes of loss, and heightened scrutiny. Clear documentation, structured communication, and consistent expectation management help reduce disputes and support defensible claim handling.

CLARIFY COVERAGE EARLY

Flood-related claims often involve policy interpretation and coverage questions. Early clarity helps reduce misunderstanding.

KEY ACTIONS:

Explain the coverage review process
Clarify policy limitations and applicable endorsements where appropriate
Identify pending evaluation items
Avoid premature coverage conclusions

GO-TO LINES:

"This claim is currently under review based on policy provisions."
"Coverage will be determined after evaluation is complete."
"There are still items being reviewed."
"I'll update you as the evaluation progresses."

DOCUMENT THE CAUSE OF LOSS CAREFULLY

Flood events may involve multiple contributing factors. Clear documentation supports defensibility.

KEY ACTIONS:

Record observed damage clearly
Document site conditions
Identify contributing factors
Explain reasoning for conclusions

GO-TO LINES:

"This is what was observed during inspection."
"Conditions indicate multiple contributing factors."
"Additional review may be required."
"Findings are based on documented observations."

COMMUNICATE WITH PRECISION

Coverage discussions require careful, professional communication.

KEY ACTIONS:

Use neutral, clear language
Avoid assumptions about coverage
Confirm understanding with stakeholders
Document key conversations

GO-TO LINES:

"I want to explain how the evaluation is being conducted."
"Here is what we know at this stage."
"Some items remain under review."
"I'll clarify next steps as information develops."

MANAGE EXPECTATIONS AROUND DISPUTES

Flood claims may involve disagreement regarding the cause of loss, scope, or coverage interpretation.

KEY ACTIONS:

Explain the evaluation process clearly
Identify need for additional review
Clarify documentation requirements
Provide next-step direction

GO-TO LINES:

"Additional information is needed to continue the evaluation."
"This requires further review."
"Here is what will happen next."
"I'll provide an update once review is complete."

MAINTAIN DEFENSIBLE DOCUMENTATION

Flood claims often receive increased scrutiny. Structured documentation supports consistency and clarity.

KEY ACTIONS:

Document observations objectively
Explain decision reasoning
Track communication timeline
Identify pending follow-up actions

GO-TO LINES:

"Documentation reflects observed conditions at the time of inspection."
"This conclusion is based on documented findings."
"The claim remains under review."
"Next steps have been recorded."

DISASTER RELIEF COORDINATION AND REGULATORY ALIGNMENT

Flood events may involve coordination with disaster relief programs. Claim documentation may support access to external assistance.

KEY ACTIONS:

Recognize when disaster relief programs may apply
Provide timely coverage letters and claim documentation
Ensure written communication is clear and consistent
Maintain awareness of regulatory timelines during disaster events
Document all communications that may support external assistance
Respond within required timeframes to avoid delays in recovery processes

GO-TO LINES:

"I'll continue to provide updates as your claim moves forward."

"Documentation from this claim may also support any disaster assistance you pursue."

"You may be eligible for additional support outside of the claim, depending on the situation."

"I will provide clear documentation as the evaluation progresses."

"If you need documentation for a specific program, let me know and I will align that with the claim."

"Your claim is under review, and I will provide updates within the required timeframes."

"Written communication will outline what has been evaluated and next steps."

These practices help adjusters manage flood-related claims with clarity, professionalism, and defensibility. By combining structured documentation, precise communication, and policy-based evaluation, adjusters guide claims through coverage-sensitive environments with consistency and confidence.

CLAIM LEADERSHIP SUMMARY

Key Takeaway

Flood claims often create tension between the severity of damage and the scope of coverage. Policyholders may experience significant loss, while coverage limitations require careful explanation. Adjusters must communicate clearly, apply policy provisions and applicable endorsements, and maintain professionalism when navigating coverage-sensitive discussions.

In Practice

When handling flood claims, explain the evaluation process early and use clear, consistent language. Document observed damage carefully and distinguish between physical damage and applicable coverage. Avoid premature conclusions and rely on policy language to guide discussions. Structured communication helps reduce confusion and supports defensible claim handling.

Questions for Reflection

1. Do I explain the evaluation process clearly during flood-related claims?
2. How do I document differences between observed damage and applicable coverage?
3. Am I relying on policy language when expectations differ?
4. Am I maintaining professionalism during difficult coverage conversations?

Claim Leadership Principle

Clear, policy-based communication supports claim stability and reduces confusion in coverage-sensitive situations.

CHAPTER 9

Infrastructure Failures and Large Liability Losses

Event Spotlight — Surfside Condominium Collapse (Florida)

A residential condominium building collapsed in the early morning hours, resulting in structural failure, significant loss of life, liability exposure, and involvement of multiple stakeholders. Ninety-eight people died in one of the deadliest structural failures in recent U.S. history, causing widespread devastation for families, residents, and the surrounding community.

Investigations identified long-standing structural concerns in portions of the building, including the pool deck, which had been previously recognized. The event highlighted how infrastructure-related issues can develop over time and contribute to large-scale failures. Property damage, personal injury, and long-term displacement were central to the claim environment. The investigation required engineering analysis and coordinated communication among multiple parties.

Industry estimates indicated insured losses could reach several billion dollars across multiple policies. Carriers, attorneys, engineers, and adjusters worked together to evaluate responsibility and coverage. As information developed over time and responsibility remained unclear, structured documentation and consistent updates were essential throughout the investigation.

Infrastructure failures expand the adjuster's responsibilities beyond property evaluation. In large-scale events, the claim environment extends beyond physical damage to include human impact, legal exposure, and long-term recovery. Liability considerations, expert input, and stakeholder coordination become central to the process. Adjusters must operate within a collaborative environment, relying on technical analysis and legal review while maintaining alignment, discipline, and reliable communication throughout the evaluation. In these situations, alignment allows the claim to move forward even when responsibility is still being determined.

CHAPTER FOCUS

Large liability losses require coordination with experts and structured communication. Adjusters must manage complexity while maintaining consistency, documenting evolving information, and sustaining clear direction even when responsibility and outcomes are still being determined.

Loss of Life and Sensitive Claim Handling

Claims involving loss of life require a distinct approach compared to standard property or liability cases. Adjusters may interact with grieving families and navigate emotionally complex situations that demand professionalism, clarity, and care.

These claims are never routine. Communication should remain clear, respectful, and measured. Adjusters often speak with next of kin or multiple family members, each coping with loss while seeking information about the claim. The adjuster must maintain structure and ensure all communication remains appropriate and professional.

Documentation remains essential, though the process may differ. Information may be received through third parties, official reports, or delayed communication. Timelines may vary, and coordination may involve legal representatives, estate contacts, or other stakeholders. Adjusters must remain organized as they adapt to these circumstances.

Professional composure is critical. Adjusters must balance precision with sensitivity, ensuring information is communicated accurately without causing confusion or distress. A steady, organized approach helps stabilize the claim process during difficult situations. In these claims, professionalism is measured not only by accuracy but also by how information is delivered.

Handling claims involving loss of life requires discipline, respect, and awareness. The adjuster's role extends beyond evaluation to supporting the process with professionalism and reliability, maintaining alignment while recognizing the seriousness of the circumstances.

Infrastructure Failures and Large Liability Losses

Infrastructure-related losses complicate claims handling. Unlike individual property losses, these events often impact multiple parties, involve shared systems, and have broader operational and financial effects. Incidents such as water main breaks, structural collapses, utility failures, and roadway incidents can damage several properties at once. Adjusters must manage this complexity, coordinate stakeholders, and ensure clear documentation.

Infrastructure failures often result in significant liability exposure, with damage extending beyond a single insured location. Adjacent properties, businesses, vehicles, and public spaces may be affected, and multiple parties may report losses. This broadens the scope of the claim and underscores the need for disciplined handling.

Infrastructure failures can evolve rapidly. Ongoing water flow, structural instability, and changing access conditions require adjusters to document conditions as they develop. These dynamic environments demand organization and careful evaluation.

Handling infrastructure failures requires direction, coordination, and professional judgment. The adjuster's role includes guiding claims through complex, multi-party situations. When multiple parties are involved, maintaining direction is essential to keep the claim on track.

Infrastructure failures often involve uncertainty about who is responsible. Determining the cause may require engineering analysis, and liability is not always immediately clear. Multiple parties may be involved, and responsibility is assessed over time. Adjusters should document conditions thoroughly and communicate clearly while responsibility remains under review. These claims rarely yield immediate conclusions—technical findings, timelines, and perspectives must align before outcomes are determined.

The Nature of Infrastructure-Related Losses

Infrastructure-related losses often stem from shared systems such as water supply lines, drainage networks, structural supports, roadways, and utilities that connect multiple properties. Failures can cause widespread disruption and interconnected damage, requiring careful evaluation and precise documentation.

Water main breaks can flood streets and adjacent buildings, affecting multiple structures simultaneously. Structural failures may impact neighboring properties or shared walls, while utility interruptions can halt operations across several businesses. These events develop quickly and create layered losses. Adjusters must respond with disciplined evaluation and thorough documentation. Interconnected damage requires coordinated documentation across locations.

Unlike standard property claims, infrastructure losses often require input from engineers, legal teams, and technical experts before conclusions are reached. While adjusters may not control the outcome, they play a critical role in maintaining organization, documenting developments, and supporting reliable communication throughout the evaluation.

Adjusters should document the full scope of impact by recording affected areas, visible damage, and surrounding conditions. Photographs, location references, and timelines preserve continuity. Early documentation is essential, as cleanup, repairs, or ongoing failures may alter site conditions.

Recognizing the interconnected nature of infrastructure losses guides evaluation. Adjusters must consider how failures affect multiple areas and how conditions evolve. Disciplined documentation and clear communication sustain alignment across complex, multi-location claims.

Real-World
Multi-Party Liability Following a Water Main Failure

An adjuster handled a claim arising from a municipal water main failure that flooded several properties, including homes and businesses. Each affected party reported damage and expected prompt resolution, while responsibility remained undetermined.

The municipality, contractors, and property owners offered differing perspectives on the cause. An engineering review was required to determine contributing factors, and liability remained under evaluation.

The adjuster documented site conditions, recorded the event timeline, and communicated that the claim was under review pending further investigation. Updates focused on the evaluation process rather than immediate conclusions.

Through structured documentation and consistent communication, the adjuster maintained alignment among stakeholders. This approach managed expectations, reduced confusion, and guided the claim through a complex, multi-party liability environment.

Multiple Parties and Expanding Scope

Infrastructure failures often involve multiple stakeholders, including property owners, tenants, municipalities, contractors, engineers, and utility providers. Each may provide information, report damage, or request updates. This environment increases urgency and requires disciplined coordination.

Communication must remain organized. Requests and responses should be documented clearly and recorded reliably. Identifying responsibilities and confirming next steps helps prevent confusion and sustains alignment across stakeholders.

The scope of damage may expand over time as additional parties report losses and secondary impacts emerge. Water migration, structural shifts, or operational disruptions can affect surrounding areas. Adjusters must monitor these developments closely to maintain direction.

Managing multiple participants requires organization and reliability. Clear documentation keeps information aligned as the claim evolves. Disciplined handling enables adjusters to guide complex infrastructure losses while maintaining professionalism and direction.

Early Documentation in Dynamic Conditions

Infrastructure failures often develop rapidly and may still be unfolding during initial inspection. Ongoing water flow, structural instability, and utility interruptions create urgency. Adjusters must document conditions thoroughly and establish a baseline before the environment changes.

Recording site conditions, active damage, and surrounding impact creates a critical reference point. Photographs should capture water flow, affected areas, and visible progression of damage. Notes should include inspection timing, observed conditions, and ongoing activity. Early documentation is essential, as cleanup, shutdowns, or repairs may quickly alter the scene.

Access may be limited during early stages due to safety concerns, restricted zones, or emergency operations. Adjusters should document these limitations clearly, noting what was safely observed and what requires follow-up. Recording access constraints defines the evaluation scope and supports transparency.

Early documentation establishes the claim baseline. As conditions stabilize and additional inspections occur, these records provide continuity. Disciplined documentation enables adjusters to track developments and maintain alignment as losses evolve.

REAL-WORLD
Industrial Explosion and Workplace Liability

An adjuster handled a claim arising from an explosion at a manufacturing facility that resulted in multiple injuries and significant operational disruption. Employees required medical treatment, and the site was secured for safety and investigation.

The incident involved industrial processes and specialized materials, requiring coordination with engineers, safety investigators, and regulatory agencies. Questions about cause, safety procedures, and responsibility emerged early, while the evaluation continued.

Multiple stakeholders requested updates, including company representatives, injured parties, and external investigators. The adjuster maintained structured documentation, recorded the timeline of events, and communicated that the claim remained under review pending further analysis.

By focusing on documentation and consistent communication, the adjuster supported alignment across parties and helped guide the claim through a complex, high-exposure liability environment.

Liability Considerations and Professional Neutrality

Large infrastructure losses often involve complex liability considerations, with failures potentially involving municipalities, contractors, property owners, or utility providers. Determining responsibility may require investigation across multiple parties. Adjusters must maintain professional neutrality while documenting conditions and evaluating damage.

The adjuster's role is to document observations and assess impact, not to determine or assign responsibility. Documentation should focus on visible conditions, timing, and the scope of damage. Notes must remain factual and avoid assumptions about cause or liability. This disciplined approach supports objectivity and professional claim handling.

Neutrality ensures the claim remains grounded in documented facts rather than assumptions.

Communication should remain neutral. Explaining observations, outlining next steps, and documenting information requests maintains professionalism. Avoiding conclusions about responsibility keeps discussions structured and focused on evaluation, helping prevent misunderstandings and supporting alignment.

REAL WORLD
Utility Failure and Community Impact

An adjuster handled a large liability claim arising from a utility failure that caused prolonged power outages in a residential area. Multiple homes experienced damage from food spoilage, equipment failure, and temporary displacement.

Residents, local officials, and service providers requested updates, while internal teams evaluated liability exposure and documentation requirements.

The adjuster maintained structured documentation of reported damages, coordinated communication among affected parties, and clarified that the evaluation was ongoing. Updates were provided consistently as new information became available.

By maintaining organization and clear communication, the adjuster ensured alignment among stakeholders. This approach managed expectations, reduced escalation, and guided a complex, community-impact claim.

Coordinating With Multiple Stakeholders

Infrastructure failures often require coordination among multiple participants, including engineers, contractors, municipal representatives, utility providers, property owners, and tenants. Stakeholders may operate on different timelines and provide varying observations. Without organization, communication can fragment and slow claim progression.

Documenting requests and responses supports continuity. Recording who provided information, when it was received, and whether follow-up is required keeps details organized as the claim develops. Clear records reduce confusion and sustain alignment among participants.

Clear communication strengthens coordination. Explaining inspection timing, identifying pending information, and confirming next steps keep stakeholders informed. Reliable messaging prevents conflicting interpretations and supports steady progress.

Managing stakeholder coordination requires discipline and organization. Adjusters who maintain thorough documentation, provide reliable updates, and clearly define responsibilities guide complex infrastructure claims effectively. This approach sustains alignment and ensures participants remain coordinated.

Expanding Damage and Secondary Impact

Infrastructure failures often cause secondary damage beyond the initial loss. Water intrusion can spread to adjacent structures, structural instability may affect neighboring properties, and utility outages can interrupt business operations. These expanding conditions increase complexity and require careful evaluation.

Adjusters must document both primary and secondary damage. Recording the initial failure location, surrounding impact, and areas affected over time establishes clarity. Photographs, notes, and timelines support understanding of loss expansion. Structured documentation guides evaluation.

Secondary impacts may develop gradually. Water migration, delayed structural movement, or operational disruption may become apparent after the initial inspection. Follow-up inspections may be needed to document these changes. Recording updated observations, tracks claim progression, and maintains continuity. Secondary damage often defines the full scope of the loss.

Access and Safety Challenges

Infrastructure failures may create hazardous, rapidly changing conditions. Flooded areas, unstable structures, active utility concerns, and restricted zones can limit access. Adjusters must prioritize safety while maintaining claim progression. An immediate inspection may not be possible, so a staged evaluation is required.

Adjusters should follow local guidance and safety advisories. Municipal restrictions, utility shutdowns, or emergency operations may affect access. Documenting these limitations explains inspection timing and scope. Notes should reflect what was safely observed and what requires follow-up. This documentation supports transparency and shared understanding.

Follow-up inspections may occur once conditions stabilize. As water recedes, structures are secured, or utilities are restored, further evaluation becomes feasible. Documenting staged inspections and updated observations preserves continuity and ensures the claim reflects evolving conditions.

Safety considerations directly affect evaluation. Documenting access limitations, hazards, and inspection timing defines the scope and supports alignment. This disciplined approach allows claims to progress responsibly while maintaining professionalism.

Communication in Multi-Party Claims

Communication becomes more complex as additional parties are involved. Property owners, tenants, municipalities, contractors, engineers, and utility representatives may all request updates or provide information. Without organization, discussions can fragment. Clear communication sustains alignment among participants.

Regular, well-defined updates reduce confusion. Explaining inspection timing, identifying pending information, and outlining next steps improve coordination. When stakeholders understand the process, collaboration improves. Predictable messaging keeps the claim organized and moving forward.

A professional tone is essential in multi-party claims. Neutral, respectful communication maintains constructive discussions, especially when perspectives differ. Clear explanations keep conversations focused on documented conditions rather than interpretation.

Documenting communication reinforces reliability. Recording conversations, requests, and follow-up actions tracks claim development. Disciplined documentation strengthens communication and preserves continuity as claims evolve.

Documentation for Large Liability Losses

Large liability exposures require precise, disciplined documentation. Infrastructure failures and multi-property impacts often involve evolving conditions and multiple stakeholders. Clear notes, photographs, and timelines ensure the claim is understandable from the outset. Strong documentation provides a foundation for complex environments.

Recording inspection timing, observed damage, and surrounding conditions establishes a reliable record. Notes should reflect when inspections occurred, what was observed, and any limitations. Documenting communication supports continuity, especially when multiple parties are involved. These details help sustain alignment as the claim develops.

Documentation should track changes between inspections. Expanding damage, additional claims, or updated information may alter the evaluation. Recording follow-up observations shows how conditions evolve. This approach ensures the claim reflects a clear progression.

Documentation also supports coordination. With multiple stakeholders, clear records maintain consistency. Organized notes reduce confusion and provide a shared reference point. Strong documentation guides large liability claims through complex, evolving conditions.

Managing Volume and Complexity

Infrastructure failures may generate numerous related claims across multiple properties. Adjusters may need to evaluate several locations within the same event, increasing complexity and requiring disciplined organization. Without organization, information can fragment across claims.

Grouping inspections by location improves efficiency and reduces transition time. A defined scheduling approach allows adjusters to evaluate multiple properties while maintaining reliable handling. Predictable workflows reduce cognitive load and support alignment across files.

Tracking claim status supports organization. Recording which claims require follow-up, are pending information, or are scheduled for inspection helps maintain progression. Defined tracking reduces redundant evaluation and improves efficiency.

Managing complexity requires discipline and reliability. Organized workflows, thorough documentation, and coordinated communication sustain alignment. These practices enable adjusters to manage multiple related claims while preserving professionalism and control.

Leading Claims in Infrastructure Losses

Infrastructure failures and large liability losses require adjusters to guide complex, multi-party situations. These claims often involve evolving conditions, expanding scope, and coordination among many stakeholders. The adjuster's leadership is essential for maintaining clarity and direction.

Structured documentation, consistent communication, and professional neutrality help manage complexity. These practices promote transparency, reduce confusion, and maintain alignment among participants. Organization stabilizes the claim as information develops.

The adjuster's expanding role is especially evident in infrastructure losses. Adjusters coordinate participants, document evolving conditions, and maintain direction across multiple properties. This leadership supports steady claim progression in dynamic environments.

Infrastructure failures and large liability losses require more than technical evaluation. They require leadership that maintains clarity when responsibility is uncertain, coordination when multiple parties are involved, and structure as information develops. Through disciplined documentation, consistent communication, and professional neutrality, adjusters bring stability to complex, evolving claims. In these environments, clarity is what allows progress even when outcomes remain uncertain.

Practical Claim Leadership Actions

Infrastructure Failures and Large Liability Losses

Infrastructure failures often involve complex liability questions, multiple stakeholders, and evolving information. These claims may include utilities, municipalities, contractors, and affected property owners. Adjusters must maintain structure, document carefully, and communicate clearly as facts develop and responsibility remains under review.

ESTABLISH CONTROL THROUGH STRUCTURE

Infrastructure failures often unfold over time. Early structure helps prevent confusion and keeps stakeholders aligned.

KEY ACTIONS:

Identify involved parties early
Outline investigation process
Clarify communication channels
Establish update expectations

GO-TO LINES:

"This claim involves multiple parties and remains under investigation."
"Here is how the evaluation process will proceed."
"We are coordinating across all involved parties."
"I will provide updates as information develops."

DOCUMENT DEVELOPING INFORMATION CAREFULLY

Facts may evolve as investigations continue. Clear documentation supports defensibility and continuity.

KEY ACTIONS:

Record observations objectively
Document timeline of events
Identify pending investigation items
Update documentation as information develops

GO-TO LINES:

"Documentation reflects conditions at the time of inspection."
"Additional findings are being reviewed."
"This remains under investigation."
"Updates will be documented as information becomes available."

MANAGE MULTI-PARTY COMMUNICATION

Infrastructure losses often involve multiple organizations and viewpoints. Structured communication helps maintain clarity.

KEY ACTIONS:

Confirm stakeholder roles
Align communication across parties
Document coordination efforts
Provide consistent updates

GO-TO LINES:

"I want to ensure all parties remain aligned."
"We are coordinating input from multiple stakeholders."

"Updates will be shared as information is confirmed."
"The evaluation process is ongoing."

HANDLE SENSITIVE AND HIGH-IMPACT SITUATIONS

Infrastructure failures may involve serious injury, loss of life, or significant community impact. These conditions require a heightened level of professionalism and awareness.

KEY ACTIONS:

Maintain a respectful and measured communication tone
Identify appropriate points of contact (family, representatives, or officials)
Avoid speculation in emotionally sensitive situations
Document communication carefully in high-impact claims

GO-TO LINES:

"I want to ensure communication remains clear and appropriate as we move forward."
"We are proceeding carefully as information is confirmed."
"I will provide updates as they become available."
"This remains under review, and we are coordinating next steps."

AVOID PREMATURE CONCLUSIONS

Liability may not be immediately clear. Adjusters must communicate carefully while the information develops.

KEY ACTIONS:

Identify unknown factors
Explain the investigation process

Avoid early liability assumptions
Reconfirm next steps

GO-TO LINES:

"Responsibility is still being evaluated."
"This requires further review before conclusions are made."
"There are multiple factors under consideration."
"Next steps will follow completion of the investigation."

MAINTAIN DIRECTION WITHOUT FULL CONTROL

Infrastructure claims often depend on engineering analysis, legal review, and external input. Adjusters may not control the outcome, but must maintain structure throughout the process.

KEY ACTIONS:

Track claim status clearly
Document next steps
Coordinate with experts and internal teams
Maintain organized file notes

GO-TO LINES:

"We are awaiting expert input to continue evaluation."
"The claim remains under review pending additional findings."
"I will update once further information is available."
"The process is moving forward as information develops."

These practices help adjusters maintain clarity and defensibility when handling infrastructure failures and large liability losses. By combining structured documentation, disciplined communication, and coordination across multiple parties, adjusters guide complex claims forward—even when responsibility remains uncertain, outcomes are still developing, and conditions involve significant human or community impact.

CLAIM LEADERSHIP SUMMARY

Key Takeaway

Infrastructure failures give rise to complex claims involving liability exposure, expert analysis, and multiple stakeholders. Information develops over time, and responsibility may not be immediately clear. Adjusters must maintain structured documentation, coordinated communication, and professional clarity throughout the claim's investigation.

In Practice

When handling infrastructure-related losses, focus on organization and communication. Coordinate with engineers, attorneys, and stakeholders while documenting updates as information evolves. Avoid premature conclusions and rely on structured communication to guide the claim while responsibility is being determined.

Questions for Reflection

1. How do I organize information in multi-party liability claims?
2. Do I maintain clear communication with experts and stakeholders?
3. Am I documenting updates as the claim develops?
4. Am I maintaining clarity when responsibility is still being evaluated?

Claim Leadership Principle

Complex liability claims require disciplined coordination, clear communication, and clarity under uncertainty.

CHAPTER 10

Aviation Losses and Multi-Party Claims

Event Spotlight — Global and U.S. Aviation Loss Events

Significant aviation losses have underscored the complexity and scale of multi-party claims. Events such as the Malaysia Airlines Flight 370 disappearance, Malaysia Airlines Flight 17 shootdown, and Ethiopian Airlines Flight 302 crash illustrate how aviation incidents can trigger an immediate, global, multi-stakeholder response. More recent, U.S.-relevant events, including the Alaska Airlines Flight 1282 incident and the Colgan Air Flight 3407 crash, further demonstrate how technical failures, operational factors, and regulatory oversight contribute to complex claim environments.

A commercial aviation incident or loss often triggers a complex claim involving hull damage, passenger liability, and third-party exposure. Across global and U.S. events, claims span jurisdictions and require coordination among airlines, manufacturers, regulators, insurers, and legal teams. Financial exposure is significant, and liability considerations evolve as investigations progress.

Aviation losses consistently involve numerous stakeholders, including passengers, operators, manufacturers, insurers, and regulatory authorities. In events such as the Malaysia Airlines Flight 17 shootdown, geopolitical factors complicate liability considerations, whereas in cases such as the Ethiopian Airlines Flight 302 crash and the Alaska Airlines Flight 1282 incident, technical and manufacturing issues influence claim development. These layers increase complexity beyond a single point of loss.

In the United States, aviation claims also operate within a structured regulatory environment, with agencies such as the National Transportation Safety Board and the Federal Aviation Administration playing central roles in investigations and oversight. These entities influence timelines, findings, and the flow of information, directly affecting claim development and communication.

Internationally, liability and compensation in aviation claims are often shaped by frameworks such as the Montreal Convention, which sets standardized rules for passenger claims across jurisdictions.

In today's environment, aviation claims are subject to immediate global scrutiny. Information, liability exposure, and stakeholder expectations evolve in real time across jurisdictions. Claims professionals must operate in a structured, highly coordinated environment where communication and documentation remain consistent despite rapidly changing conditions.

Multi-party aviation claims require disciplined communication and organized documentation. Information evolves over time, and responsibility may be shared among multiple entities. The adjuster's role becomes one of coordination and clarity, with structured communication determining how effectively the claim progresses.

CHAPTER FOCUS

Aviation losses illustrate the complexity of multi-party claims. Adjusters must manage communication, documentation, and coordination among multiple stakeholders in environments where scale, scrutiny, regulatory involvement, and jurisdictional complexity intersect.

Aviation Losses and Multi-Party Claims

Aviation losses are among the most complex claims adjusters handle. These cases often involve multiple parties, extensive documentation, and coordination with various stakeholders. Unlike single-property claims, aviation losses typically include aircraft damage, damage to surrounding property, business interruption, and potential liability exposure. Adjusters must manage these overlapping elements while maintaining clarity in environments where information develops across multiple sources.

Aviation incidents may occur at airports, private airfields, or off-site locations, and damage often extends beyond the aircraft. Hangars, equipment, vehicles, and surrounding property may also be affected, increasing evaluation complexity and requiring thorough assessment and coordination. These conditions often reflect the same multi-layered impact seen in global aviation events, where damage, liability, and operational disruption intersect.

Multi-party involvement is typical in aviation losses. Aircraft owners, operators, maintenance providers, airports, insurers, regulators, and third parties may all contribute information or report damage. This environment requires clear communication and consistent documentation. The adjuster's role includes maintaining direction across this coordinated process, ensuring that information remains aligned as the claim develops.

Handling aviation losses requires organization, professional neutrality, and thorough documentation. Clarity is essential from the outset. In aviation claims, complexity is not only technical—it is also operational and legal, and it is constantly evolving across multiple parties and jurisdictions.

The Complexity of Aviation Incidents

Aviation incidents often involve multiple types of damage at once. Aircraft structures, engines, avionics, and surrounding property may all be affected, along with hangars, ground equipment, vehicles, or airport infrastructure. These conditions require urgent, structured evaluation from the outset.

Adjusters must document both aircraft and surrounding property damage. Recording site conditions, debris patterns, impact points, and affected areas establishes a reliable baseline. Photographs and detailed notes preserve continuity, especially as recovery operations may quickly alter conditions. Early documentation is critical.

Environmental factors such as weather, terrain, runway surface, and obstacles can influence damage patterns. Recording these conditions supports objectivity and accurate interpretation. These details provide essential context for the incident.

Aviation incidents rarely follow predictable patterns. Damage may be dispersed, layered, or influenced by secondary impacts. Disciplined documentation—organized notes, photographs, and timelines—supports evaluation and preserves continuity. In these environments, understanding depends on how well conditions are documented before they change.

Multiple Parties and Shared Information

Aviation losses typically involve multiple stakeholders. Aircraft owners, operators, airport authorities, maintenance providers, insurers, and third parties may all participate. Each party may provide information, request updates, or contribute documentation. This multi-party environment increases complexity and requires disciplined coordination.

Disciplined communication is essential. Information requests should be documented clearly, and responses recorded accurately. Identifying who provided information and when preserves continuity and keeps evolving details organized.

Adjusters must track communications carefully. Multiple participants may provide overlapping or changing information as the investigation and recovery progress. Recording these exchanges prevents confusion and maintains alignment across stakeholders.

Managing shared information requires organization and reliability. Clear documentation, neutral communication, and defined next steps effectively guide aviation claims. These practices help adjusters maintain direction in complex, multi-party incidents. When multiple sources contribute information, disciplined coordination keeps the claim on track.

REAL WORLD
Early Legal and Multi-Party Coordination in an Aviation Claim

An adjuster handled an aviation-related loss involving multiple stakeholders early in the process, including legal representatives, insurers, and airport authorities. Communication quickly shifted to formal requests, coordinated timelines, and structured information sharing among parties.

The adjuster ensured the claim file remained complete and clearly organized. Inspection findings, site conditions, and stakeholder communications were thoroughly and consistently documented. All responses were grounded in verified observations and aligned with the ongoing investigation.

As information developed, updates were communicated in a structured and timely manner to all involved parties. This helped maintain alignment and reduced confusion as multiple sources contributed input and requested clarification.

By maintaining disciplined documentation and structured communication, the adjuster ensured a clear and defensible claim file. This approach maintained control in a complex, multi-party environment and allowed the claim to progress with stability and consistency.

Documentation at the Loss Site

Aviation loss sites may contain dispersed debris, damaged structures, and affected surrounding property. Conditions can change quickly as safety personnel secure the area or recovery operations begin. In many cases, sites may also be under the control of investigative authorities, limiting access and affecting how documentation is conducted. Initial documentation is therefore critical. Recording site conditions, debris distribution, impact points, and surrounding damage helps establish a clear baseline for the claim.

Photographs should capture both overall conditions and detailed observations. Wide-angle images document the general layout, while close-up photographs record specific damage. Notes should reflect the inspection timing, observed conditions, and any active recovery or investigative activity. This documentation supports continuity as the site evolves and conditions change.

Access may be restricted in certain situations. Safety concerns, site control by authorities, or an ongoing investigation may limit the scope of the inspection. Adjusters should clearly document these limitations, noting what can be observed and what requires follow-up. Recording access constraints helps define the evaluation's boundaries and supports transparency in the claim file.

Early documentation guides the claim. As debris is removed, aircraft components are relocated, or structures are secured, conditions can change rapidly. Establishing a baseline preserves the original environment and supports consistent claim handling. Initial documentation provides the reference point for all subsequent evaluation, coordination, and communication.

Liability Exposure in Aviation Claims

Aviation losses often involve significant liability considerations. Damage may affect aircraft owners, operators, airport facilities, third-party property, and nearby structures. Multiple participants may be involved, and responsibility may be evaluated separately across jurisdictions. Adjusters must maintain professional neutrality while documenting conditions in environments where liability exposure may be substantial.

Documentation should focus on observed facts. Recording the damage location, surrounding impact, and environmental conditions supports objectivity and consistency. Notes should avoid conclusions about responsibility, particularly when investigations are ongoing or involve multiple parties. This disciplined approach supports defensible claim handling.

Communication should also remain neutral. Explaining observations, identifying next steps, and documenting information requests help maintain professionalism. Avoiding assumptions about responsibility keeps discussions focused on evaluation rather than interpretation, especially in multi-party settings.

Professional neutrality supports clarity in aviation claims. Structured documentation and consistent communication help ensure the claim remains organized while responsibility is addressed through appropriate investigative and legal channels. Neutrality ensures that documentation supports evaluation without influencing conclusions.

High-Impact and Fatality Considerations

Aviation losses may involve serious injury or loss of life. These conditions introduce an additional level of complexity that extends beyond physical damage and liability assessment. Communication, documentation, and coordination must be handled with heightened professionalism, as multiple parties, including family representatives, legal counsel, and authorities, may be involved.

Adjusters must maintain a measured, disciplined approach in these environments. Communication should remain clear, respectful, and aligned with the investigation process. Information often emerges over time, and updates may be limited or controlled by investigative authorities. Consistent communication helps support alignment across all parties.

Documentation remains critical. Recording communications, identifying points of contact, and documenting the timing and scope of interactions help maintain continuity. These records support coordination and ensure the claim remains organized as conditions evolve.

Professional neutrality is especially important in high-impact aviation claims. Adjusters should avoid speculation and focus on documenting observed conditions, confirmed facts, and defined next steps. This approach promotes clarity and allows responsibility and findings to be addressed through appropriate investigative and legal channels.

Handling high-impact aviation losses requires structured coordination, disciplined communication, and consistent documentation. These practices help maintain clarity and direction in environments that are both operationally complex and human-impactful.

Coordinating With Technical Specialists

Aviation claims often involve technical specialists. Engineers, aviation maintenance professionals, investigators, and other experts may evaluate aircraft components, structural damage, and the surrounding impact. Their findings may influence claim development, clarify the extent of damage, and shape how the loss is understood over time.

Adjusters should carefully document coordination with specialists. Recording inspection timing, participants, and information received supports continuity. Notes should reflect the areas evaluated, preliminary findings when appropriate, and whether follow-up or additional analysis is expected. This helps track claim progression as technical input develops.

Communication among participants should remain disciplined. Clarifying requests, confirming the scope of evaluation, and documenting responses sustain alignment across all parties. Coordination with specialists adds complexity, making clear records essential. Organized documentation ensures that technical findings are integrated into a consistent, coherent claim narrative.

Property Damage Beyond the Aircraft

Aircraft incidents often extend beyond damage to the aircraft itself. Hangars, ground equipment, vehicles, and surrounding structures may also be affected. Adjusters must carefully evaluate these areas, as total exposure may span multiple locations and stakeholders. Recording the full extent of property damage, supported by photographs and detailed notes, establishes a reliable record and ensures all affected areas are accounted for.

Secondary damage may also develop. Fuel release, debris movement, fire, or structural instability can affect nearby property and surrounding areas. These conditions may evolve over time, requiring follow-up inspections and ongoing evaluation. Documenting these developments helps track changes and supports accurate claim handling as conditions stabilize.

Careful assessment of surrounding damage is essential in aviation losses. Disciplined documentation, consistent follow-up, and clear communication help ensure that all affected property is accurately evaluated and that the claim reflects the full scope of impact.

Communication in Multi-Party Environments

Communication becomes more complex when multiple stakeholders are involved. Participants may request updates, provide additional information, or respond at different stages of the claim. Structured communication helps manage this environment and maintain alignment across all parties. Consistent updates and clear explanations of inspection timing and next steps support clarity and reduce confusion.

A professional tone is essential. Neutral communication helps sustain constructive discussions, especially in multi-party environments where perspectives may differ. This approach supports coordination and reduces the risk of misinterpretation. Documenting communication ensures consistency. Recording conversations, requests, and responses helps track claim development and maintain continuity across interactions.

Managing Evolving Conditions

Aviation loss sites rarely remain static. Debris removal, aircraft recovery, safety restrictions, weather exposure, and additional technical inspections can alter the loss environment over time. These changes can affect documentation, scope evaluation, access to components, and coordination among involved parties. Adjusters must recognize that the scene observed during the initial inspection may differ significantly from conditions at later visits.

Follow-up inspections are critical to managing evolving conditions. Each subsequent visit should be documented with updated photographs, revised observations, and notes detailing changes since the prior inspection. Changes in aircraft position, removed components, environmental exposure, or newly identified damage should be clearly recorded to maintain continuity.

Communication about evolving conditions should also be carefully documented. Participants may provide updates on site access, component removal, or additional findings. Recording these updates helps maintain alignment and supports a consistent understanding of how the claim is developing over time.

Managing evolving conditions requires proactive documentation, disciplined follow-up, and reliable communication. These practices help adjusters maintain control of complex aviation claims and ensure that changes at the loss site are accurately reflected throughout the claim lifecycle. Without structured follow-up, evolving conditions can create gaps in understanding and disrupt claim continuity.

Organization in Complex Claims

Aviation losses generate a significant volume of documentation. Inspection reports, photographs, engineering evaluations, maintenance records, recovery documentation, and communications from multiple stakeholders must all be tracked. Without organized systems, important details may be overlooked, and continuity may be lost.

Establishing consistent workflows helps reduce complexity. Adjusters should document inspection timing, communication updates, and technical findings in a structured, repeatable manner. Maintaining chronological notes supports continuity and ensures the claim narrative remains clear as information evolves.

Grouping documentation by category improves alignment. Site documentation, technical evaluations, communication logs, and follow-up inspections can be organized separately. This approach helps adjusters quickly find relevant information and maintain a clear understanding of claim status at any point in the process.

Effective organization is essential in aviation claims. Disciplined documentation, categorized information, and reliable workflows help adjusters manage complexity while maintaining momentum.

Organization enables adjusters to manage volume without sacrificing clarity or continuity.

Leading Multi-Party Aviation Claims

Aviation losses often involve multiple stakeholders, including aircraft owners, operators, maintenance providers, engineers, recovery teams, airport authorities, insurers, and legal representatives. Each stakeholder may provide information, request updates, or influence claim development.

Disciplined documentation and reliable communication guide these complex interactions. Clarifying requests, recording responses, and documenting technical input help maintain alignment among participants. Maintaining professional neutrality ensures that communication remains objective and focused on the claim process.

The adjuster's expanding role is particularly evident in aviation claims. Adjusters coordinate inspections, monitor evolving conditions, manage communications, and organize large volumes of information. These responsibilities require professional judgment, consistency, and deliberate organization.

In aviation losses, leadership is demonstrated through direction, precision, and the ability to guide multiple parties through a complex, evolving claims environment. Structured documentation, clear communication, and consistent coordination enable adjusters to maintain control without direct authority.

Practical Claim Leadership Actions

Aviation Losses and Multi-Party Claims

Aviation losses often involve significant damage, multiple stakeholders, and detailed investigations. These claims may include aircraft owners, operators, maintenance providers, insurers, investigators, and regulatory authorities. Adjusters must maintain structure, document carefully, and communicate clearly as information develops across multiple parties and jurisdictions.

ESTABLISH INVESTIGATION STRUCTURE EARLY

Aviation losses typically involve multiple investigations and technical reviews. Early structure helps maintain alignment across all participants.

KEY ACTIONS:

Identify involved stakeholders early
Outline investigation process
Clarify communication protocol
Establish update expectations

GO-TO LINES:

"This claim involves multiple parties and remains under coordinated review."
"Here is how the investigation process will proceed."
"We are coordinating across all involved stakeholders."
"I will provide updates as information develops."

DOCUMENT DEVELOPING INFORMATION CAREFULLY

Aviation losses often involve technical findings and evolving conclusions. Clear documentation supports continuity and defensibility.

KEY ACTIONS:

Record observations clearly
Document timeline of events
Identify pending reports
Update file as findings develop

GO-TO LINES:

"Documentation reflects conditions at the time of inspection."
"Additional findings are currently under review."
"This remains part of an ongoing evaluation."
"Updates will be documented as information becomes available."

MANAGE MULTI-PARTY COMMUNICATION

Aviation claims involve multiple stakeholders, each contributing information and requiring updates. Alignment depends on clear communication.

KEY ACTIONS:

Confirm stakeholder roles
Align communication channels
Document coordination efforts
Maintain consistent updates

GO-TO LINES:

"I want to ensure all parties remain aligned."
"We are coordinating input from multiple stakeholders."

"Updates will be shared as information is confirmed."
"The evaluation process is ongoing."

COORDINATE WITH TECHNICAL SPECIALISTS

Aviation claims often require input from engineers, maintenance professionals, and investigators. Coordination must remain structured and documented.

KEY ACTIONS:

Identify involved specialists early
Document technical input and timelines
Clarify the scope of evaluations
Track follow-up requirements

GO-TO LINES:

"We are coordinating with technical specialists as part of the evaluation."
"This portion of the claim requires expert review."
"Findings will be incorporated as they are finalized."
"We will update once technical analysis is complete."

MANAGE EXPECTATIONS DURING INVESTIGATION

Aviation investigations may take time and involve multiple reviews across different parties. Clear communication helps maintain alignment while evaluation continues.

KEY ACTIONS:

Explain investigation timeline
Clarify the evaluation process
Avoid premature conclusions
Provide next-step direction

GO-TO LINES:

"This investigation involves multiple steps and will take time."
"We are working through the evaluation process methodically."
"Conclusions will follow completion of the investigation."
"I will provide direction as next steps are confirmed."

MAINTAIN PROFESSIONAL CLARITY AND NEUTRALITY

Aviation claims often involve liability considerations across multiple parties. Adjusters must remain neutral while maintaining clear and structured communication.

KEY ACTIONS:

Use clear, neutral language
Avoid speculation regarding responsibility
Document communication consistently
Maintain organized file notes

GO-TO LINES:

"Responsibility is still being evaluated."
"This remains under review at this stage."
"We are documenting all findings as they develop."
"Updates will follow as more information becomes available."

MAINTAIN DIRECTION IN COMPLEX ENVIRONMENTS

Aviation claims often depend on technical analysis, legal review, and coordination across multiple entities. Adjusters may not control outcomes, but must maintain structure throughout the process.

KEY ACTIONS:

Track claim status clearly
Document next steps
Coordinate with stakeholders and experts
Maintain organized workflows

GO-TO LINES:

"The claim remains under review pending additional findings."
"We are awaiting further information to proceed."
"The process is moving forward as information develops."
"I will update once the next stage is confirmed."

MANAGE EVOLVING LOSS CONDITIONS

Aviation loss environments may change rapidly due to recovery operations, investigation activity, and site control. Conditions observed during the initial inspection may differ from those observed later.

KEY ACTIONS:

Document initial site conditions clearly
Record changes during follow-up inspections
Track removal of debris or components
Update documentation as conditions evolve

GO-TO LINES:

"Conditions are being documented as they change."
"Follow-up inspections will capture updated findings."
"The site continues to evolve as recovery progresses."
"Documentation reflects current observed conditions."

HANDLE FATALITY AND HIGH-IMPACT CLAIMS

Aviation losses may involve serious injury or loss of life. These conditions require a heightened level of professionalism, structured communication, and careful coordination across all parties. Communication may include family representatives, legal counsel, and official authorities.

KEY ACTIONS:

Maintain a respectful and measured communication tone

Identify appropriate points of contact (family representatives, legal counsel, or authorities)

Avoid speculation in sensitive situations

Document communication carefully and consistently

Align communication with ongoing investigations and official channels

GO-TO LINES:

"We are proceeding carefully as information is confirmed."

"Communication will follow appropriate channels as the investigation continues."

"Updates will be provided as information becomes available."

"This remains under coordinated review across all involved parties."

These practices help adjusters manage aviation losses with clarity, coordination, and professional discipline. By combining structured documentation, disciplined communication, and coordination across multiple stakeholders, adjusters guide complex aviation claims forward—even as information evolves, responsibility is assessed, and multiple parties contribute to the evaluation process.

CLAIM LEADERSHIP SUMMARY

Key Takeaway

Aviation losses involve multiple stakeholders, evolving information, and coordinated evaluation across disciplines. These claims may also involve serious injury or loss of life, requiring a heightened level of professionalism and structured communication. Responsibility may be shared, and findings often develop over time. Adjusters must maintain clear communication and organized documentation to ensure clarity throughout the claim. In multi-party aviation claims, structure sustains alignment as complexity increases and information evolves.

In Practice

When working on multi-party claims, track stakeholders, document updates consistently, and communicate changes clearly. In high-impact situations, maintain a professional and measured tone while aligning communication with appropriate representatives and ongoing investigations. Avoid assumptions during evaluation and ensure all parties understand next steps. Structured coordination maintains direction and keeps the claim aligned as conditions and information develop.

Questions for Reflection

1. How do I track communication across multiple stakeholders?
2. Do I document updates as new information develops?
3. Am I maintaining clarity while responsibility is still being determined?
4. Am I maintaining professionalism in high-impact or sensitive situations?

Claim Leadership Principle

Multi-party claims require structured coordination and disciplined communication. Clarity is sustained when communication, documentation, and coordination remain consistent among all stakeholders, particularly in complex, high-impact environments. Clarity is sustained when communication, documentation, and coordination remain consistent across all stakeholders.

PRELUDE

Risk, Alignment, and Professional Judgment

As claims environments evolve, risk considerations increasingly shape the adjusting process. Litigation, coverage disputes, and complex stakeholder involvement require careful professional judgment. Decisions made during the claims process can be reviewed later, so it's important to stay aligned, consistent, and reliable.

Risks in claims handling often stem from communication breakdowns and inadequate documentation. When expectations are unclear or reasoning is undocumented, misunderstandings can arise. Clear explanations, disciplined notes, and reliable follow-through strengthen the claim and support defensibility. These practices also promote stakeholder alignment and reduce the likelihood of escalation.

Professional judgment is central to navigating these environments. Adjusters must evaluate information, communicate decisions, and move the claim forward while maintaining neutrality and professionalism. This requires balancing technical evaluation with clear, structured communication. The ability to remain measured under pressure supports both claim accuracy and process stability.

This section focuses on documentation, communication, and risk-aware decision-making. The goal is not to create rigid procedures but to support consistent, effective judgment in complex situations. When adjusters exercise disciplined judgment and maintain reliable communication, the claim process remains stable, aligned, and defensible.

PART III

Litigation, Risk, and Documentation

Modern claims handling now operates in an environment where litigation exposure, documentation quality, and communication clarity are directly connected. Claims that once resolved through inspection, estimate preparation, and negotiation now more frequently involve attorneys, expert evaluations, competing scope opinions, and extended claim timelines. As expectations rise and disputes become more common, the adjuster's responsibilities expand. The role now includes not only evaluating damage but also building a structured, defensible claim record that supports each decision made throughout the claim lifecycle.

Documentation has become the foundation of professional claims handling. Inspection notes, photographs, diagrams, measurements, timelines, and communication logs collectively form the backbone of the claim file. These records do more than capture observations. They demonstrate the reasoning behind decisions, show how information was gathered, and reflect the steps taken to advance the claim. A well-documented file allows stakeholders to understand how conclusions were reached and what information guided the handling. This clarity becomes critical when claims involve questions, escalation, or review.

Adjusters must document both the technical and procedural aspects of the claim. Technical documentation includes damage observations, inspection findings, and supporting photographs. Procedural documentation includes communication with policyholders, coordination with contractors, scheduling of inspections, and updates provided to stakeholders. Together, these elements create a complete claim narrative that reflects consistency, professionalism, and disciplined handling. When documentation is thorough, the claim file shows a clear progression from initial report through resolution.

Risk increases when claims involve multiple interpretations of damage, scope, or coverage. Policyholders, contractors, engineers, and attorneys may each present different perspectives. These differences can lead to confusion, delays, or disputes. In these situations, clarity is essential. Disciplined documentation helps track what was observed, what information was provided, and what decisions were made. Reliable communication further supports alignment. When both remain clear, misunderstandings are reduced and claim handling stays focused.

The adjuster's file often serves as the primary reference when questions arise. Participants may review inspection notes, communication history, and decision timelines to understand how the claim progressed. A well-organized file provides transparency and supports professional handling. It also preserves continuity when claims span time or involve multiple participants. Clear documentation ensures that decisions remain grounded in recorded observations rather than recollection, strengthening defensibility.

Litigation exposure underscores the importance of discipline throughout the claim process. When claims escalate, documentation may be scrutinized. Inspection timing, communication tone, follow-up actions, and decision rationale may all be examined. Adjusters must approach each claim consistently, professionally, and with attention to detail. Maintaining neutral communication, documenting updates, and recording inspection findings help demonstrate thoughtful handling. A well-documented claim reflects a structured, reasonable evaluation process.

Communication plays a critical role in reducing litigation risk. Clear explanations of next steps, timelines, and inspection findings help set expectations. Documenting these interactions ensures stakeholders understand the claim's progression. When communication remains disciplined and professional, confusion is reduced, helping prevent escalation and supporting collaborative claim handling.

Reliability throughout the claim lifecycle further strengthens documentation. Prompt inspection records, documented follow-up actions, and organized communication logs create continuity. This continuity helps adjusters track claim development and ensures no steps are overlooked. Disciplined documentation also supports efficient review by supervisors, carriers, and technical specialists. An organized file improves understanding and efficiency.

This section examines how litigation trends, documentation practices, communication, and expert coordination influence modern claims handling. The chapters that follow explore how adjusters protect the claim through disciplined documentation, prevent escalation through effective communication, reduce exposure through reliable handling, and coordinate with attorneys and technical experts. These practices help manage complexity and sustain momentum throughout the claim.

Strong claims handling today requires more than technical evaluation. It requires precision, discipline, and documentation that supports every decision. By maintaining organized records, reliable communication, and coordinated workflows, adjusters create defensible claim files that move the claim from initial report through resolution.

CHAPTER 11

The Rise of Litigation in Claims Handling

Event Spotlight — Property Litigation Expansion Following Catastrophe Events

Following major catastrophes, carriers across multiple regions reported significant increases in litigation over property claims. Disputes arose over the scope of damage, repair methodology, and valuation, particularly in areas affected by widespread storms and hail. In events such as Hurricane Irma and Hurricane Harvey, litigation rates increased substantially as claims moved beyond traditional inspection and negotiation into legal review.

Billions of dollars in insured losses were associated with these events. Hurricane Harvey resulted in over $125 billion in total damages, while Hurricane Irma generated more than $50 billion in insured losses. In some catastrophe-affected regions, particularly in states like Florida, litigation rates on property claims reached levels at which a significant percentage of claims—often cited at 10-15 percent in certain periods—entered legal dispute, compared with much lower historical norms.

The operational impact extended beyond financial exposure. Litigation lengthened claim timelines, expanded documentation requirements, and introduced additional layers of review. In today's environment, claim handling often occurs with the expectation that files may be reviewed, challenged, or litigated after initial evaluation. Adjusters found their files reviewed not only for accuracy but also for consistency, tone, and completeness.

The claim file became more than a record of damage. It became a record of decisions, communication, and professional judgment. In litigation-prone environments, documentation may be reviewed by attorneys, experts, and regulatory bodies, requiring a higher level of clarity and consistency throughout the claim lifecycle. Adjusters were required to approach each claim with the understanding that their documentation might later be scrutinized. In some markets, litigation costs and associated legal fees became a defining factor in overall claim expenses.

CHAPTER FOCUS

Litigation has become a common part of claims handling. Adjusters must approach each claim with clarity, structure, and professional discipline from the outset. Preparation for potential review is now part of standard claims handling practice.

The Rise of Litigation in Claims Handling

Litigation has become a routine consideration in claims handling. Although not every claim results in legal action, the possibility shapes how claims are evaluated, documented, and communicated. Adjusters operate with the understanding that their decisions and records may be reviewed long after initial handling, raising expectations for professionalism, clarity, and consistency. Documentation is now prepared with the awareness that it may be scrutinized beyond the immediate claim.

Several factors contribute to this trend, including heightened policy awareness, broader access to information, legal advertising, and the growing complexity of claims. Policyholders may seek additional opinions, and contractors or consultants are often engaged earlier in the process. These conditions expand communication and heighten the need for thorough, well-organized documentation.

The rise in litigation does not change the core purpose of adjusting. Adjusters still assess damage, document findings, and guide claims toward resolution. However, a more disciplined approach is required. Clear communication, reliable documentation, and organized handling ensure that claims remain understandable as they develop. Litigation awareness is now part of professional practice—not a situational response but an embedded element of modern claims handling from the outset.

Litigation Awareness in Everyday Claims

Litigation awareness does not mean treating every claim defensively. It means recognizing that claims may be reviewed later and ensuring the file clearly documents how the evaluation was conducted. Consistent, well-structured documentation reduces confusion and reinforces professionalism. Litigation awareness is part of disciplined claims management, not a reactive mindset.

Routine documentation plays a central role. Recording inspection observations, site conditions, limitations, and relevant details forms the foundation for evaluation. Records should capture both observed conditions and the reasoning behind conclusions and next steps. This level of documentation ensures clear claim progression, supports transparency, and strengthens defensibility. A complete file allows others to understand the claim long after it has been closed.

Litigation awareness also shapes communication practices. Clear explanations of findings, timelines, and next steps help align expectations and reduce the risk of misunderstanding. Documenting all communication, including updates and responses, creates a complete, reliable claim history. Consistent communication supports resolution and reduces escalation.

Integrating litigation awareness into daily claims handling reinforces professionalism. Consistent documentation, structured communication, and disciplined workflows produce claim records that reflect thorough evaluation. This approach improves claim quality and ensures decisions remain clear and defensible if reviewed later. Litigation awareness is not reactive—it is built through consistency from the outset of the claim.

Insurance Insolvency and State Takeover

In some cases, carrier insolvency or financial instability leads to state involvement through guaranty associations or regulatory oversight. When this occurs, claim handling may transition to new administrators, and processes, timelines, and authority structures may change.

These transitions introduce additional complexity. Documentation, communication history, and prior decisions may be reviewed under new standards, making continuity of the claim file essential. Adjusters in these situations must maintain clear records and reliable communication to support the claim as responsibility shifts.

When control changes, clarity becomes the adjuster's primary responsibility. The claim file serves as the central point of continuity, reinforcing the need for consistency, accuracy, and defensibility at every stage.

Communicating During Insolvency or Coverage Limit Constraints

Certain claims are subject to financial or regulatory constraints that affect how they are handled. When a carrier becomes insolvent or coverage limits restrict recovery, adjusters must communicate clearly while maintaining professionalism and structure.

These conditions often create uncertainty for policyholders. Delays, process changes, or the involvement of guaranty associations may affect timelines and expectations. Policyholders may not fully understand how these factors influence the claim.

The adjuster's role is to provide clear, factual communication regarding what is known, what is changing, and what steps will follow.

Explaining the process without speculation helps maintain alignment. When information is limited or evolving, communication should focus on confirmed details and identify when additional updates will be provided.

Maintaining a neutral, structured approach is essential. Adjusters should avoid assurances beyond documented information and ensure that all communication reflects current claim conditions. Documenting updates, timelines, and changes in handling helps preserve continuity.

Clear communication during insolvency-related situations reduces confusion, supports professionalism, and maintains direction even when external conditions affect the claim.

REAL WORLD
Claim Handling During Carrier Insolvency

An adjuster managed a property claim when the carrier entered insolvency proceedings. Communication shifted as the claim was transferred to a guaranty association, and timelines became uncertain.

The policyholder requested immediate updates and expressed concern regarding coverage and payment. The adjuster explained that the claim was transitioning through a defined process and that timelines would depend on the new handling structure and regulatory coordination.

Communication remained focused on confirmed information. The adjuster documented all updates, clarified next steps as they became available, and avoided speculation regarding outcomes or timing.

By maintaining clear, structured communication and documenting each stage of the transition, the adjuster reduced confusion and preserved continuity as responsibility shifted. This approach ensured the claim continued to progress within the constraints of the situation while maintaining professionalism and alignment.

Documentation as a Foundation

Documentation is central to litigation-aware claims handling. The claim file serves as the written record of events, decisions, and communication. Clear, structured documentation supports continuity and maintains alignment among stakeholders, ensuring the claim narrative remains understandable as conditions evolve.

Recording inspection observations establishes context. Notes should document site conditions, damage, timing, and limitations. Photographs, measurements, and supporting details clarify findings and provide a baseline for comparison as conditions and evaluations change.

Communication must be documented consistently. Recording conversations with all participants maintains alignment and preserves continuity. Notes should include information requests, scheduling, explanations, and responses. These records track claim progression, clarify expectations, and support coordination, particularly in multi-party environments.

Documentation should extend beyond individual notes. Maintaining structured files, timelines, and categorized information ensures clarity throughout the claim. Grouping inspection records, communication logs, and technical evaluations allows efficient access to relevant details. Organized documentation reduces confusion and supports disciplined claim management. A clear system enables the claim to be understood without reliance on memory or interpretation.

Documentation is foundational to professional claim handling. Clear records demonstrate how the claim was evaluated, how communication occurred, and how decisions were made. This structure supports transparency, continuity, and defensibility from initial report through final resolution. Documentation does not simply record the claim—it defines how the claim is understood over time.

REAL WORLD
Early Attorney Involvement in a Property Claim

An adjuster handled a residential claim with early legal involvement. Communication became more formal, and documentation was subject to increased scrutiny.

The adjuster ensured that all prior communication, inspection findings, and next steps were clearly documented and organized. Responses remained consistent, grounded in verified observations, and delivered with careful attention to tone and accuracy.

Through disciplined documentation and structured communication, the adjuster established a clear and defensible claim file. This approach managed increased scrutiny and allowed the claim to progress in a controlled and consistent manner.

Communication That Reduces Escalation

Many claim disputes arise from misunderstandings rather than significant differences in evaluation. Unclear timelines, incomplete explanations, or inconsistent updates can create frustration among stakeholders. Clear, disciplined communication reduces escalation and keeps the claim focused on resolution. In many cases, escalation is driven more by how information is communicated than by the decision itself.

Consistent updates help stakeholders understand the progress of claims. Explaining findings, outlining next steps, and clarifying timelines promote transparency. When participants understand what has occurred and what to expect, confusion decreases, and alignment is maintained.

Tone also influences escalation. Professional, neutral communication keeps discussions constructive, even during disagreement. A measured approach supports cooperation and maintains focus on claim requirements. Clear, respectful explanations help prevent conversations from becoming adversarial.

Documenting communication reinforces consistency. Recording key discussions, updates, and decisions ensures alignment as the claim evolves. These records track expectations and support continuity, particularly in multi-party claims. Direction is maintained through structured communication and reliable documentation.

Clear communication does not eliminate complexity—it ensures complexity is managed without escalation.

REAL WORLD
Attorney Involvement in an Auto Liability Claim

An adjuster managed an auto liability claim in which the claimant retained legal representation early in the process. Communication shifted to formal correspondence, and documentation requests increased as the claim progressed.

The adjuster maintained structured documentation of all communications, recorded the event timeline, and ensured updates were clear and consistent. Responses remained focused on the evaluation process and documented findings, avoiding informal or speculative discussion.

Through disciplined communication and consistent documentation, the adjuster established a clear and defensible claim file. This approach reduced confusion, aligned expectations, and allowed the claim to progress professionally despite increased scrutiny.

The Role of Professional Consistency

Consistency is essential in litigation-aware claims handling. Structured inspections, disciplined documentation, and reliable communication keep claims organized and understandable. Consistent handling reflects thoughtful, professional evaluation and supports clarity throughout the claim process.

Inconsistent handling creates uncertainty. Mixed messages, incomplete documentation, or shifting timelines can delay progression and confuse stakeholders. Reliable practices help prevent these issues and support clear, steady claim development.

Disciplined workflows reinforce professional consistency. Standardized documentation, consistent inspection records, and routine updates maintain alignment and reduce variation. This approach supports efficient review by supervisors or specialists and ensures that different reviewers can reach the same understanding of the claim.

Professional consistency reflects disciplined claims handling. Clear documentation, reliable communication, and organized workflows maintain clarity from inspection through resolution. These practices strengthen claim quality and support defensible decisions in complex environments. Consistency ensures that claims can be understood, reviewed, and defended without confusion.

Early Alignment Prevents Later Disputes

Many claim disputes begin with early misunderstandings. Unclear expectations or inconsistent communication at the outset can lead to confusion and larger disagreements later. Establishing alignment early reduces the risk of escalation.

Explaining the claim process at the start helps stakeholders understand what to expect. Outlining inspection timing, documentation requirements, and next steps supports coordination. Early communication clarifies roles and responsibilities, enabling more effective collaboration.

Regular updates preserve that alignment as the claim develops. Even when progress depends on new information, consistent communication maintains stability. Status updates, confirmed next steps, and documented developments reinforce coordination and keep the claim organized.

Early alignment sets the tone for the entire claim. Disciplined communication, clear expectations, and predictable updates help prevent disputes and support efficient handling from inspection through resolution. Establishing alignment early reduces the need for later correction and reinforces overall claim stability.

Handling Disagreements Professionally

Disagreements are a normal part of claims handling. Differences in scope, timing, documentation, or evaluation may arise as findings are reviewed. Professional communication is essential, as the way disagreements are managed determines whether the claim remains constructive or becomes adversarial.

Adjusters should focus on explanation rather than opposition. Clearly describing observations, inspection findings, and reasoning supports productive dialogue. Centering discussions on documented information keeps conversations professional and focused on the claim.

A calm, neutral tone reinforces effective handling. Consistent communication reduces tension and supports cooperation, even when viewpoints differ. Structured explanations clarify evaluations and help prevent escalation. Tone often determines whether disagreements remain constructive.

Documentation supports the professional management of disagreements. Recording discussions, questions, and next steps maintains clarity and alignment. These records preserve continuity, particularly when claims extend over time or involve multiple parties.

Professional handling of disagreements preserves the direction of the claim. Clear explanations, neutral communication, and consistent documentation reduce escalations and support resolution times. How disagreements are managed determines whether the claim remains organized or becomes adversarial.

Multi-Party Participation in Litigation-Aware Claims

Claims with litigation potential often involve additional participants, including public adjusters, consultants, contractors, engineers, attorneys, and carrier representatives. As more parties become involved, communication becomes more complex. Without structure, updates may fragment, and misunderstandings can develop. Disciplined communication sustains alignment in multi-party environments.

Adjusters should document requests and responses throughout the claim. Recording when information is requested, what is provided, and how updates are communicated helps track claim development and supports continuity. Clear records ensure all participants are working from consistent information.

Consistent communication keeps discussions focused on the claim. Clarifying next steps, confirming findings, and documenting updates maintain direction and reduce confusion. Structured communication makes multi-party participation manageable and reduces the risk of escalation.

Coordinating multiple participants requires organization. Tracking communication, documenting updates, and maintaining consistent workflows preserve clarity throughout the claim. Structured handling enables the adjuster to guide the process as stakeholder involvement increases. As participation expands, structure becomes essential to maintaining alignment.

Maintaining Objectivity

Objectivity is essential when litigation is possible. Adjusters should document observations carefully and avoid assumptions. Focusing on observed facts, supported by documentation and clear communication, maintains clarity and supports professional claim handling.

Recording facts rather than conclusions preserves neutrality. Documentation should reflect observed conditions, participant information, and communicated updates. Clear, factual notes demonstrate consistency, support transparency, and strengthen the claim file if questions arise.

Objectivity also supports the professional management of disagreements. Grounding discussions in documented observations keeps conversations constructive and focused on the claim. When stakeholders rely on the same information, next steps can be evaluated without becoming adversarial. Fact-based communication reduces escalation and maintains alignment.

Maintaining objectivity strengthens overall claim handling. Clear, factual documentation reduces confusion and keeps the claim grounded in what can be substantiated. This approach reinforces professionalism and supports defensible outcomes throughout the claim process.

Structured Decision-Making in Litigation-Aware Claims

Litigation awareness reinforces the need for disciplined decision-making. A structured evaluation process ensures decisions are consistent, well-supported, and aligned with the claim as it develops. This approach supports professional judgment and reduces uncertainty in complex environments.

Documenting reasoning strengthens transparency. Recording inspection findings, relevant information, and next steps explains how conclusions were reached and helps stakeholders understand the evaluation process. Clear reasoning supports defensibility and improves continuity across the claim lifecycle.

A disciplined approach to decision-making helps manage complexity. Breaking evaluation into stages—inspection, documentation, communication, and follow-up—improves organization and focus. This method allows adjusters to prioritize tasks, maintain alignment, and ensure critical details are not overlooked, even under pressure.

Organization supports reliable claim handling. Clear documentation, structured evaluation, and documented reasoning ensure decisions remain understandable and consistent. This disciplined approach strengthens claim quality and supports professional handling in litigation-aware environments. A defined process preserves alignment as claims become more complex.

The Modern Claims Environment

The rise in litigation reflects broader changes in the modern claims environment. Increased claim complexity, expanded stakeholder involvement, and greater policy awareness all contribute. Policyholders are more informed, contractors are more engaged, and claims often require extended evaluation. Adjusters must adapt by maintaining alignment, reliability, and disciplined handling throughout the process.

Clear documentation, consistent communication, and sound professional judgment support effective handling in litigation-aware environments. Recording findings, documenting interactions, and explaining next steps promote transparency. Organized information and clearly defined expectations reduce misunderstandings and maintain alignment as claims develop.

The adjuster's role continues to expand in this environment. Beyond evaluating damage, adjusters guide claims forward through structured handling. Organizing information, documenting decisions, and maintaining reliable communication support continuity across the claim lifecycle.

Litigation awareness is now part of modern adjusting. It does not change the purpose of the role but reflects the expectations of today's claims environment. Adjusters who maintain organization and alignment help ensure claims remain understandable, consistent, and professionally managed. Modern claims require disciplined management, not reactive response.

Leading Claims in a Litigation-Aware World

Adjusters operate in an environment where litigation is more common, and claim decisions are subject to closer review. This requires disciplined documentation, effective communication, and structured decision-making. A defined approach supports alignment and reinforces professional evaluation.

Leadership is demonstrated through claim management. Organized documentation, consistent updates, and clear explanations guide stakeholders through the process. Coordinated communication and documented decisions make claims more predictable and understandable, reducing uncertainty.

Leading claims in a litigation-aware environment does not change the purpose of adjusting—it strengthens the process. Clear documentation supports reasoning, reliable communication maintains alignment, and professional judgment informs decisions, keeping claims focused on evaluation and resolution.

As litigation becomes more prevalent, disciplined claims handling becomes increasingly important. Adjusters who maintain alignment, document thoroughly, and communicate professionally move claims forward effectively. Leadership in this environment is demonstrated through reliability, organization, and disciplined execution from initial handling through final resolution.

Practical Claim Leadership Actions

The Rise of Litigation in Claims Handling

Litigation exposure has increased across many claim environments. Adjusters must approach communication, documentation, and decision-making with defensibility in mind. Clear structure, consistent messaging, and careful documentation help reduce dispute risk and support professional credibility.

DOCUMENT WITH DEFENSIBILITY IN MIND

Claim files should clearly explain observations, reasoning, and next steps. Documentation becomes the foundation for understanding how decisions were made.

KEY ACTIONS:

Record observations objectively
Explain reasoning behind decisions
Document stakeholder communication
Identify pending follow-up actions

GO-TO LINES:

"Documentation reflects conditions observed at the time of inspection."
"This conclusion is based on documented findings."
"The evaluation process is ongoing as additional information is reviewed."

"All updates will be documented as they develop."

COMMUNICATE CAREFULLY AND PROFESSIONALLY

Communication tone and clarity can influence whether claims escalate. Structured messaging supports professionalism and alignment.

KEY ACTIONS:

Use neutral, factual language
Avoid assumptions or speculative statements
Confirm understanding during key conversations
Document important discussions promptly

GO-TO LINES:

"I want to ensure communication remains clear and consistent."
"This is based on current information available."
"We are continuing to evaluate as more information becomes available."
"I will confirm next steps as the process develops."

MAINTAIN CONSISTENCY ACROSS THE CLAIM

Inconsistent messaging can increase dispute risk. Alignment between documentation and communication strengthens defensibility.

KEY ACTIONS:

Align written and verbal communication
Maintain consistent updates
Clarify changes in direction
Reconfirm expectations when timelines shift

GO-TO LINES:

"I want to ensure all information remains aligned."
"Updates will reflect the current status of the claim."
"Any changes will be communicated clearly as they occur."
"Expectations will be confirmed as the claim progresses."

CLARIFY THE CLAIM PROCESS EARLY

Clear expectations help prevent misunderstandings that may later lead to disputes.

KEY ACTIONS:

Explain the evaluation process
Identify pending inspections or reports
Clarify documentation requirements
Provide next-step direction

GO-TO LINES:

"Here is how the evaluation process will proceed."
"These are the next steps in the claim."
"We are currently awaiting additional information to continue."
"I will provide updates as each stage is completed."

AVOID PREMATURE CONCLUSIONS

Litigation risk increases when decisions are communicated without sufficient support.

KEY ACTIONS:

Identify unknown factors
Document ongoing evaluation

Avoid early commitments
Reconfirm next steps as information develops

GO-TO LINES:

"This remains under review at this stage."
"Additional evaluation is required before conclusions are made."
"There are still factors being considered."
"Next steps will follow completion of the review."

These practices help adjusters maintain clarity, professionalism, and defensibility as litigation exposure increases. By combining structured documentation, disciplined communication, and consistent messaging, adjusters reduce dispute risk and guide claims effectively—even when outcomes remain under review and scrutiny is elevated.

CLAIM LEADERSHIP SUMMARY

Key Takeaway

Litigation has become an increasingly common outcome in modern claims handling. Documentation, communication, and decision-making are often reviewed beyond the claim itself. Adjusters must approach each file with clarity, consistency, and professional discipline, recognizing that their work may be examined in detail. In litigation-aware environments, the claim file must stand on its own as a complete, accurate, and understandable record.

In Practice

Maintain thorough documentation, explain decisions clearly, and communicate professionally throughout the claim. Record observations, reasoning, and next steps consistently. A structured file supports defensible handling, reduces escalation, and ensures the claim remains clear and aligned if reviewed later.

Questions for Reflection

1. Would my claim notes clearly explain my decisions if reviewed later?
2. Do I document both observations and reasoning consistently?
3. Am I maintaining a professional tone in all written communication?

Claim Leadership Principle

Consistent documentation and disciplined communication support defensible claim handling. Clarity is sustained when records, communication, and decisions remain aligned throughout the claim lifecycle.

CHAPTER 12

Documentation That Protects the Claim

Event Spotlight — Post-Storm Scope Disputes

Following widespread hail and severe convective storm events, including high-impact hail and wind losses across Texas, Colorado, and the Midwest, disputes frequently arose over roof damage, interior damage, and repair methods. In these high-frequency loss environments, policyholders, contractors, and carriers often differed in their interpretation of damage severity, causation, and required repairs. Many of these disagreements emerged early in the claim process, before formal dispute or litigation.

The financial impact of convective storm losses has been significant. In multiple years, insured losses from U.S. severe convective storms—including hail—have exceeded tens of billions of dollars annually, making them among the most frequent and costly drivers of property claims. Within these events, a large volume of claims required supplementation, reinspection, or escalation due to scope and documentation discrepancies.

Claims supported by detailed inspection notes, comprehensive photographs, and clearly documented observations consistently moved more efficiently toward resolution. In contrast, files lacking clarity often required additional review, extended timelines, and increased coordination among stakeholders. In high-volume environments, even small gaps in documentation were magnified across large claim inventories.

In many cases, these scope disputes marked the early stage of a larger escalation path. When documentation was incomplete or inconsistent, disagreements over damage and repair methodology became harder to resolve, increasing the likelihood of prolonged review or formal dispute.

Documentation forms the foundation for claim decisions. Clear notes, consistent observations, and organized photographic records provide structure to the file. The adjuster's documentation becomes the primary reference for all stakeholders. When documentation is complete and organized, the claim can be understood without relying on interpretation or repeated explanation.

CHAPTER FOCUS

Documentation protects both the claim and the adjuster. Clear records support decisions, reduce disputes, and improve consistency. Well-organized documentation ensures the claim remains clear, reliable, and defensible from initial inspection through resolution.

Documentation That Protects the Claim

Documentation is a critical responsibility in modern claims handling. While inspections, communication, and evaluation move the claim forward, documentation creates the record that holds the claim together. It captures observations, decisions, and communications so the file can be understood, reviewed, and relied upon over time.

Claims do not remain static. As new information emerges, follow-up inspections occur, and stakeholder communication expands, the claim continues to evolve. Without structured documentation, continuity is lost. Adjusters rely on written records to track developments, maintain alignment, and ensure consistent decision-making throughout the life of the claim.

Documentation also promotes transparency. When notes clearly reflect what was observed and how conclusions were reached, the claim becomes understandable to supervisors, reviewers, and stakeholders. In complex environments, this clarity builds confidence in both the process and the outcome.

Viewing documentation as protection reflects professionalism, not defensiveness. Disciplined records guide the claim, reduce the need for clarification, and preserve continuity throughout. Documentation does not simply support the claim—it defines how the claim is understood.

Documenting the Initial Inspection

The initial inspection lays the foundation for the claim. Recording site conditions, observed damage, and relevant environmental factors establishes a clear starting point and provides context for all subsequent decisions. When this stage is thoroughly documented, adjusters can track how the claim develops and maintain consistency as conditions change.

Photographs strengthen written documentation by providing a visual record of site conditions and damage at the time of inspection. Wide-angle images establish overall context, while detailed photographs capture specific conditions. When paired with written observations, these records enable both adjusters and stakeholders to reference the claim accurately as repairs progress or additional inspections occur.

Inspection timing should also be clearly recorded, including the date, access conditions, and any limitations encountered. In many claims, particularly those involving catastrophe events or restricted access, these details are essential for explaining what was observed and what required follow-up. Clear documentation of these conditions reinforces the integrity of the evaluation.

Industry experience consistently shows that claims with well-documented initial inspections progress more efficiently, whereas those lacking clear baseline records often require reinspection, clarification, or escalation. The difference is not the damage itself—it is how the damage was documented.

Initial inspection documentation establishes the claim baseline. Clear notes, organized photographs, and recorded timing provide structure for the entire claim. With that structure in place, adjusters are better positioned to track developments, communicate effectively, and maintain consistency from the initial inspection through resolution.

Recording Observations Clearly

Effective documentation records observations, not assumptions. Notes must clearly describe what was seen, measured, and identified during the inspection. The accuracy of the claim depends on the clarity of these observations. In high-pressure environments, there is no substitute for disciplined, observation-based documentation.

The responsibility for that clarity rests with the adjuster.

Documentation is not a secondary task. It is a core function of the role. The adjuster's record becomes the foundation for how the claim is understood, reviewed, and evaluated by all stakeholders. In many cases, it is the only consistent reference point throughout the claim.

Vague language introduces risk. General statements, incomplete descriptions, or missing details require interpretation, and interpretation leads to inconsistency. Specific descriptions of affected areas, visible conditions, and the extent of damage ensure that the claim can be understood without reliance on follow-up explanation. Precision in documentation supports alignment, reduces rework, and strengthens overall claim handling.

Documenting surrounding conditions—such as weather, access limitations, debris, or safety restrictions—provides essential context. These details explain how observations were made and clarify any limitations in the inspection. In catastrophe environments, where conditions change rapidly, this context becomes critical to maintaining continuity and credibility.

For catastrophe adjusters in particular, documentation is where leadership is demonstrated. Files move quickly, conditions evolve, and multiple stakeholders rely on the adjuster's record to make decisions.

Strong documentation reflects discipline, professionalism, and control. Over time, it becomes a defining factor in both performance and longevity in the field.

Clear, observation-based documentation is not optional. It is the standard. It ensures the claim remains understandable, supports consistent evaluation, and protects both the claim and the adjuster throughout the process.

Reviewing Prior Claims and Loss History

Prior loss history provides important context for claim evaluation. Tools such as industry claim history reports, often referred to as ISO reports, offer insight into prior claims, reported losses, and historical activity for a property or policyholder. Reviewing this information helps establish a broader understanding of the risk and supports consistent evaluation.

The responsibility for interpreting and documenting this information also rests with the adjuster. Prior loss history must be carefully reviewed and appropriately applied to the current claim. Clear documentation should distinguish between prior damage and current loss conditions, ensuring that findings are accurate and defensible.

Failure to clearly distinguish prior conditions from current damage creates confusion and increases the likelihood of dispute. When prior loss information is documented and clearly explained, it strengthens the claim file and supports professional handling.

Disciplined review and documentation of prior loss history enhances clarity, reduces misunderstandings, and contributes to a well-supported and defensible claim.

Documenting Communication

Communication drives the claim, and documentation ensures that communication remains aligned, consistent, and reliable over time. Every interaction, whether with a policyholder, contractor, or stakeholder, must be recorded to preserve clarity and direction.

The responsibility for that record rests with the adjuster.

Documentation should record who was contacted, what was discussed, and the actions or next steps established. These details are not administrative, they are structural. They ensure that expectations, timelines, and responsibilities remain clear as the claim progresses.

In complex or high-volume claims, multiple conversations occur among different parties at different times. Without consistent documentation, communication fragments quickly. Stakeholders receive conflicting interpretations, prior discussions are lost, and the claim begins to drift. Recording interactions helps the adjuster maintain continuity, reference prior discussions, and keep all parties aligned.

Documenting communication also reinforces transparency. Notes should capture the explanations provided, questions raised, and updates delivered. This creates a clear record of how the claim developed and ensures that all participants can follow the file's progression without relying on memory or interpretation.

For adjusters working in catastrophe or multi-party environments, documenting communication is a leadership function. It establishes control in situations where multiple voices and evolving conditions can easily create confusion. Strong documentation keeps the claim structured, aligned, and moving forward.

Communication documentation is not optional. It is a professional standard that ensures continuity, reduces misunderstandings, and supports consistent claim handling from initial contact through resolution.

Explaining Decision Reasoning

Documentation must also clearly show how decisions are made. Recording the reasoning behind conclusions ensures that the claim remains transparent, structured, and defensible over time.

The responsibility to explain decisions rests with the adjuster.

It is not enough to document what was decided. The file must show how and why the decision was made. This includes the observations considered, the information reviewed, and the factors that influenced the outcome. When this reasoning is clearly documented, any reviewer can understand the claim without additional explanation.

Without documented reasoning, decisions appear incomplete. Stakeholders may question conclusions, request clarification, or revisit previously addressed issues. This introduces delays, increases the likelihood of disputes, and weakens the overall structure of the claim.

Clear decision reasoning reinforces consistency. It links observations to conclusions and ensures that each step in the evaluation process is supported and traceable. As claims evolve and new participants join, this documentation preserves continuity and maintains alignment.

In high-pressure environments, the ability to document decisions is a defining professional skill. It reflects discipline, supports credibility, and ensures that the claim remains grounded in the evaluation process rather than in interpretation.

Documenting decision reasoning is not an extra step. It is an essential part of guiding the claim, ensuring conclusions are supported, and maintaining a clear, defensible file from beginning to end.

Supplements

In property claims—particularly for large or complex losses—supplements are a routine part of the claim lifecycle. As additional damage is identified, repair methods are refined, or new information emerges, the scope evolves. These changes often require revised estimates, additional review, and coordination among multiple stakeholders.

Supplements are not separate from the claim. They are a continuation of the evaluation.

As a result, the responsibility for maintaining alignment remains with the adjuster. The file must clearly document what has changed, why, and how those changes affect the scope and overall claim position. Without that clarity, supplements introduce inconsistency, increase the likelihood of dispute, and slow the claim.

This is also where technical capability becomes a professional advantage.

Adjusters who understand scope, interpret estimates, and navigate estimating platforms to review or amend line items add greater value to the process. They are better positioned to evaluate differences, communicate adjustments clearly, and maintain alignment between original and supplemental findings.

In many organizations, these skills create opportunities beyond field inspection, including roles focused on supplement review, estimate reconciliation, and file-level quality control. While technical proficiency is not the sole focus of the role, the ability to work effectively within the estimate strengthens the adjuster's ability to guide the claim and support consistent outcomes.

Structured supplement handling reinforces professionalism. Documentation should clearly identify what changed, the basis for those changes, and how they were evaluated. Communication should remain consistent to ensure that all stakeholders understand the updated scope and next steps.

Supplements do not create complexity. They reveal it.

Adjusters who can manage that complexity with clarity, discipline, and technical awareness maintain control of the claim and position themselves for long-term growth in the industry.

REAL WORLD
Incomplete Notes Leading to Rework

An adjuster returned to a claim several weeks after the initial inspection and found that prior documentation lacked sufficient detail. Inspection findings were not clearly recorded, references to prior loss history were incomplete, and next steps were inconsistently documented. As a result, additional time was required to reconstruct the evaluation, review the claim history, and clarify earlier decisions.

Supplemental activity increased the complexity. Revised estimates and newly identified damage required alignment with the original scope, but without clear documentation of prior observations and conclusions, it became difficult to distinguish new findings from previously evaluated conditions. What should have been a continuation of the claim became a reconstruction of the claim.

The gap was not in the claim itself. It was in the documentation.

Recognizing this, the adjuster adopted a more structured approach. Observations were recorded clearly, prior loss references were documented consistently, and each update included defined timelines and next steps. Documentation became deliberate rather than reactive.

As a result, rework decreased, continuity improved, and the claim advanced with greater clarity and efficiency. The file no longer required interpretation—it provided direction.

This example reinforces a core principle: documentation is not a record of the claim after the fact. It is the structure that enables the claim to move forward without interruption.

Tracking Claim Development

Claims rarely remain static. As follow-up inspections occur, new documentation is received, and communication expands, the claim continues to evolve. Tracking that evolution through documentation is essential to maintaining continuity, alignment, and control.

The responsibility for tracking claim progression rests with the adjuster.

Each update should clearly reflect what has changed, what has been confirmed, and what remains pending. Notes must capture new observations, revised timelines, and any shift in the claim's direction. Without this structure, the claim becomes fragmented, and sustaining progress becomes difficult.

Follow-up inspections must be documented with the same level of discipline as the initial inspection. Timing, observed changes, and updated findings should be clearly recorded. These details help the adjuster and stakeholders understand how conditions developed over time and ensure that decisions remain connected to the evolving facts of the claim.

When claim development is tracked consistently, the file tells a clear story. Each update builds on the last, and the claim progresses without the need for reconstruction or interpretation. Without that continuity, even routine changes can cause confusion and delay.

Tracking claim development is not administrative. It is a leadership function. It ensures the claim remains structured, aligned, and able to move forward as conditions evolve.

Documentation During High-Volume Events

Catastrophe events and high-volume claim environments place additional demands on adjusters. Managing multiple files simultaneously requires more than effort—it requires structure. In these conditions, documentation becomes the primary means of maintaining organization and control.

The responsibility for maintaining that structure remains with the adjuster.

Without clear documentation, claims blur together. Pending actions are missed, timelines become unclear, and continuity is lost during file transitions. Structured notes ensure that each claim remains distinct, organized, and actionable, even at high volume.

Clear documentation helps the adjuster move between files without losing direction. When returning to a claim, notes should provide immediate context—what has been observed, what has been communicated, and what must happen next. This eliminates the need to re-evaluate the file and allows work to continue efficiently.

Consistency is critical in high-volume environments. Using a structured format to document observations, communication, and follow-up actions reduces variation and ensures that each claim is handled with the same level of clarity and discipline. This consistency supports both individual performance and overall operational alignment.

For catastrophe adjusters, documentation is the foundation of control. Conditions change quickly, assignments shift, and claim volume increases. In these environments, well-structured documentation enables the adjuster to manage workload, preserve continuity, and uphold professional standards across every file.

High-volume events do not reduce the need for documentation; they increase it.

Disciplined documentation ensures that even under pressure, claims remain clear, organized, and on track toward resolution.

Using Documentation as a Stability Anchor

Documentation serves as a stability anchor in complex claims. When conditions change or new information emerges, clear notes provide direction. Adjusters rely on documented information rather than re-evaluating prior discussions, thereby maintaining continuity and reducing confusion as the claim evolves.

The responsibility for maintaining that stability rests with the adjuster.

In high-volume or high-pressure environments, it is common to feel pulled to "complete the work now and document later." Over time, this creates gaps. Details are lost, timelines blur, and the claim becomes harder to follow. What was clear in the moment becomes difficult to reconstruct later.

Documentation must occur as part of the work—not after it.

Recording next steps helps maintain momentum. Documenting pending inspections, requested information, and follow-up actions keeps tasks visible, supports prioritization, and reduces the risk of missed steps. When documentation is current, the file provides direction. When it is delayed, the file creates uncertainty.

In long-duration claims involving multiple inspections, participants, and updates, documentation preserves continuity. Clear records help both the adjuster and stakeholders understand the claim's progression without relying on memory or repeated explanations.

For catastrophe adjusters, documentation is the primary means of maintaining control. Workloads increase, conditions shift, and files move quickly. In these environments, disciplined documentation enables the adjuster to manage volume without losing clarity.

Documentation is not something to return to later. It is what keeps the claim stable while everything else changes.

Avoiding Gaps in Documentation

Incomplete documentation introduces uncertainty into the claim file. Missing notes, unclear descriptions, or undocumented conversations require clarification, delay progress, and increase the likelihood of rework. Consistent documentation prevents these breakdowns.

Gaps often arise when documentation is delayed. Recording observations immediately after inspections and communicating promptly after conversations ensures accuracy and preserves continuity. Timeliness is not optional—it is required to maintain a reliable record.

Consistent documentation practices reduce gaps. A structured approach to inspection notes, communication logs, and follow-up actions ensures that key information is captured as the claim develops. This structure helps the file remain complete, organized, and actionable at every stage.

Avoiding gaps strengthens both the claim and the adjuster's performance. Clear, timely, and consistent documentation maintains organization, supports efficient handling, and reduces the need for reconstruction or correction.

In high-pressure environments, the difference between control and confusion often comes down to documentation.

Documentation in Multi-Party Claims

Claims involving multiple stakeholders require disciplined documentation to maintain alignment. In these environments, information arrives from diverse sources at different times and often with varying perspectives. Without structure, communication fragments, and the claim becomes difficult to manage.

The responsibility for maintaining alignment rests with the adjuster.

Documentation should clearly identify who provided information, when it was received, and what actions or follow-up are required. Recording requests, updates, and responses creates a reliable timeline and ensures expectations remain consistent across all participants.

As discussions evolve, documentation becomes the central point of reference. Adjusters must be able to return to prior notes to confirm what was communicated, what was agreed upon, and what remains outstanding. This continuity prevents conflicting interpretations and reduces the need for repeated clarification.

In multi-party claims, documentation is how control is maintained. It allows the adjuster to coordinate among stakeholders, track information flow, and ensure the claim continues to move forward in a structured, organized manner.

Well-documented files reduce confusion, support alignment, and enable efficient coordination from initial inspection through resolution.

Writing With Professional Precision

Documentation must be clear, well-structured, and professional. Notes should capture observations, communication, and the reasoning behind decisions without unnecessary complexity. The goal is not volume—it is clarity.

The responsibility for that clarity rests with the adjuster.

Concise documentation ensures that the claim can be understood quickly and accurately by any reviewer. Each entry should contribute to the overall understanding of the file, eliminating the need for interpretation or follow-up explanations.

Organizing documentation chronologically strengthens continuity. Recording inspections, communications, and updates in sequence allows the claim to be followed from beginning to end, ensuring that each development builds on the previous one.

Professional precision is reinforced through consistent language. Disciplined descriptions, clear terminology, and structured entries maintain accuracy and ensure others understand the claim without ambiguity.

In complex or high-pressure environments, precision becomes a defining professional standard. Clear, consistent documentation ensures that information remains accessible, the claim remains organized, and decisions remain understandable throughout the claim lifecycle.

Documentation as Professional Leadership

Documentation is a direct reflection of leadership in claims handling. It provides direction, supports decision-making, and maintains organization as the claim progresses from inspection through resolution. In complex environments, the quality of the documentation often determines how effectively the claim advances.

The responsibility for that leadership rests with the adjuster.

Well-structured documentation ensures that each step of the claim is clear, connected, and actionable. Notes that capture observations, updates, and next steps enable the file to guide itself, reducing the need for clarification and preventing delays. When documentation is disciplined, the claim remains aligned even as conditions evolve.

Documentation also strengthens communication. Clear records of discussions, findings, and expectations ensure that all stakeholders share a common understanding. This reduces redundant conversations, minimizes misinterpretation, and reinforces consistency across the claim.

Leadership in claims is demonstrated not only by decisions but also by how those decisions are documented. Organized, well-developed records reflect professionalism, establish reliability, and allow the claim to progress without interruption.

Documentation is not administrative. It is the system that moves the claim forward.

Protecting the Claim Through Alignment

Documentation protects the claim by preserving alignment from the initial inspection through final resolution. Recording observations, communications, and the reasoning behind decisions ensures that the file reflects not only what was done but also how and why it was done.

When documentation is clear and organized, the claim can be understood without relying on memory or interpretation. This clarity promotes consistency, reduces misunderstandings, and strengthens confidence in the evaluation process.

Claims often involve multiple inspections, evolving conditions, and participation by several stakeholders. Without structured documentation, this complexity leads to fragmentation. With it, the claim remains connected. Each update builds on the last, and the claim's progression remains clear and traceable.

Alignment is maintained through disciplined documentation. Organized notes, documented decisions, and consistent communication ensure that each stage of the claim supports the next. This continuity enables the claim to move forward with clarity, even in complex or high-pressure environments.

In modern claims handling, documentation is not a support function. It is a protective function. It preserves structure, reinforces professionalism, and ensures the claim remains clear, consistent, and defensible from start to finish.

Practical Claim Leadership Actions

Documentation That Protects the Claim

Documentation is central to claim clarity, alignment, and defensibility. Clear, structured documentation supports continuity, reduces confusion, and strengthens decision-making. Adjusters who treat documentation as a leadership tool can effectively guide the claim.

DOCUMENT OBSERVATIONS CLEARLY

Accurate observations form the foundation of defensible documentation.

KEY ACTIONS:

Record site conditions objectively
Document damage observations clearly

Identify relevant details
Avoid assumptions in documentation

GO-TO LINES:

"Documentation reflects observed conditions at the time of inspection."
"These observations are based on what was visible during evaluation."
"Conditions have been recorded as documented at the time of inspection."
"Additional observations will be documented as they develop."

EXPLAIN DECISION REASONING

Documentation should reflect how conclusions were reached. This supports clarity and continuity.

KEY ACTIONS:

Connect findings to decisions
Document coverage considerations
Explain scope conclusions
Identify pending evaluation items

GO-TO LINES:

"This conclusion is based on documented findings."
"The evaluation reflects the information available at this time."
"Additional review may be required as more information becomes available."
"Next steps will follow completion of the evaluation."

TRACK COMMUNICATION CONSISTENTLY

Documenting communication helps maintain alignment across stakeholders.

KEY ACTIONS:

Record key conversations
Document timelines discussed
Identify next steps communicated
Confirm updates provided

GO-TO LINES:

"This communication reflects the current status of the claim."
"Updates have been provided based on available information."
"Next steps have been outlined and documented."
"Additional updates will follow as information develops."

MAINTAIN ORGANIZED FILE STRUCTURE

Structured documentation helps prevent confusion and supports continuity.

KEY ACTIONS:

Use consistent note format
Track claim status clearly
Identify follow-up actions
Maintain chronological documentation

GO-TO LINES:

"The file has been updated to reflect current claim status."
"Documentation has been organized to maintain continuity."
"All updates are recorded in chronological order."
"Follow-up actions have been documented for tracking."

REVIEW PRIOR LOSS HISTORY AND CLAIM DATA

Prior loss history can influence claim evaluation and the clarity of documentation. Industry claim history tools, often referred to as ISO reports, provide insight into prior claims, reported losses, and historical activity associated with a property or policyholder. Reviewing this information helps establish context for current findings and supports consistent evaluation.

KEY ACTIONS:

Review prior claim history when available
Identify previously reported damage or losses
Distinguish between prior and current conditions
Document how prior loss information relates to the current claim

GO-TO LINES:

"Prior claim history has been reviewed as part of the evaluation."

"Observed conditions have been compared with prior documented losses."

"This assessment reflects current findings in relation to prior claim activity."

"Documentation distinguishes between previously reported and current conditions."

UPDATE DOCUMENTATION AS THE CLAIM EVOLVES

Claims develop over time. Documentation should reflect evolving information.

KEY ACTIONS:

Add supplemental observations
Update decisions when needed
Document timeline changes
Reconfirm next steps

GO-TO LINES:

"Documentation has been updated to reflect new information."
"This update reflects changes in claim evaluation."
"Timeline adjustments have been recorded."
"Next steps have been reconfirmed based on current findings."

DOCUMENT IN REAL TIME

Documentation must occur as part of the work, not after it.

KEY ACTIONS:

Record notes immediately following inspection
Document communication promptly after conversations
Capture next steps before moving to the next file
Avoid relying on memory to reconstruct the claim

GO-TO LINES:

"Documentation reflects observations recorded at the time of inspection."

"This update reflects information documented during the most recent review."

"All notes have been recorded to reflect current claim activity."

"Next steps have been documented as part of ongoing claim handling."

ALIGN SUPPLEMENTS WITH THE ORIGINAL SCOPE

Supplements must remain connected to the original evaluation to maintain consistency and defensibility.

KEY ACTIONS:

Compare supplemental findings to the original scope

Document what has changed and why
Identify new vs. previously evaluated conditions
Maintain alignment between estimates and documentation

GO-TO LINES:

"This supplement reflects updated findings based on additional inspection."

"Changes have been documented in relation to the original scope."

"New information has been evaluated and incorporated into the claim file."

"Documentation maintains alignment between original and revised findings."

MAINTAIN CONTROL IN MULTI-PARTY COMMUNICATION

KEY ACTIONS:

Track who provided information and when
Document differing viewpoints clearly
Confirm aligned next steps across stakeholders
Prevent conflicting interpretations through documentation

GO-TO LINES:

"Information has been documented as provided by involved parties."
"All updates have been aligned across stakeholders."
"Next steps have been confirmed and documented."
"Documentation reflects current multi-party communication."

These practices help ensure documentation supports clarity, defensibility, and professional claim leadership. By maintaining structured documentation, consistent communication, and clear decision reasoning, adjusters create claim files that remain understandable, aligned, and defensible as conditions evolve.

CLAIM LEADERSHIP SUMMARY

Key Takeaway

Documentation provides the structure that holds the claim together. It supports consistent decision-making, maintains alignment, and ensures the claim remains understandable throughout the process. Clear notes, organized photographs, and disciplined observations reduce disputes and guide resolution. The adjuster's file becomes the primary reference for all stakeholders. When documentation is complete and well-structured, the claim does not require explanation—it provides direction.

In Practice

Document observations clearly and in real time. Align photographs with written notes, so both reflect the same conditions. Record the reasoning behind decisions and next steps consistently so the file remains actionable. Structured documentation reduces reinspection, limits confusion, and allows the claim to progress without interruption, even as conditions evolve.

Questions for Reflection

1. Do my notes clearly describe what was observed without interpretation?
2. Are my photographs aligned with my documentation and easy to follow?
3. Am I documenting decisions and next steps as part of the work, not after the work is done?
4. Would my file remain clear and complete if reviewed weeks later?

Claim Leadership Principle

Documentation is a leadership function. Clarity is maintained when documentation, communication, and decision-making remain consistently aligned. In high-pressure environments, the quality of the documentation determines the stability of the claim.

CHAPTER 13

Communication That Prevents Escalation

Event Spotlight — Claim Escalation Following Repair Delays

Following widespread storm damage during and after the COVID-19 pandemic, repair timelines were significantly extended because of contractor shortages, labor constraints, and material supply disruptions. Events such as Winter Storm Uri and Hurricane Ida further increased claim volume during a period when repair capacity was already constrained. As a result, policyholders faced prolonged delays, leading to frustration and uncertainty throughout the claim process.

Billions in insured losses were associated with these events, but operational delays and communication gaps added another layer of complexity. Policyholders sought updates, clarity, and reassurance while timelines remained uncertain or continued to shift. In many cases, escalation was not driven by the scope of damage but by a lack of consistent communication about what was happening and what to expect next.

In this environment, communication became a determining factor in claim outcomes. Claims supported by clear expectations, regular updates, and consistent messaging were more likely to remain stable, even amid persistent delays. In contrast, files lacking proactive communication often escalated into complaints, disputes, or formal review.

Communication became a central function of claims leadership. The adjuster's role extended beyond documenting damage to guiding the policyholder through uncertainty. Clear explanations, timely updates, and a professional tone helped maintain alignment and reduce the risk of escalation.

The adjuster's words influenced the direction of the claim. How information was communicated often shaped the experience of the delay.

CHAPTER FOCUS

Strong communication prevents escalation. Adjusters who set clear expectations and provide consistent updates improve claim outcomes. Structured communication keeps alignment, even when timelines are uncertain.

Communication That Prevents Escalation

Effective communication is essential to stable claims handling. Clear expectations, consistent updates, and structured explanations help keep claims moving forward in alignment. When communication is unclear or delayed, uncertainty increases, and the likelihood of escalation increases. Adjusters who communicate clearly and consistently help stabilize the process.

Claims often arise in high-stress conditions. Policyholders may be managing property damage, displacement, or business interruption, while contractors and other stakeholders coordinate repairs and timelines. In these environments, communication is not a support function; it is a control function.

The responsibility for maintaining that control rests with the adjuster. Disciplined communication prevents escalation. It prioritizes clarity, consistency, and professionalism over volume. Structured updates, clearly defined next steps, and documented conversations reduce uncertainty and keep the claim moving forward. Escalation is often not caused by the decision itself but by how it is communicated.

Preventing escalation does not require lengthy conversations. It requires consistent, clear communication to keep stakeholders informed, aligned, and aware of what comes next.

Setting Expectations Early

Escalations often stem from unclear expectations. When timelines, documentation requirements, or next steps are not defined early, stakeholders fill the gaps with assumptions. These assumptions often lead to repeated questions, frustration, and escalation.

Setting expectations early provides structure.

Adjusters should clearly explain the claim process at the outset, including inspection schedules, documentation requirements, and how updates will be communicated. When stakeholders understand the process, communication becomes more focused and productive.

Expectation-setting also includes acknowledging uncertainty. Potential delays—such as access limitations, high claim volume, contractor availability, or weather conditions—should be identified early. Proactively communicating these factors prepares stakeholders for changes and reduces the likelihood of reactive escalation when timelines shift.

Early communication sets the tone for the claim. When expectations are clear, stakeholders remain aligned even as conditions change. When expectations are unclear, even routine developments can create tension. Establishing expectations early is not optional. It is a leadership action that stabilizes the claim from the outset and reduces the risk of escalation throughout the process.

Consistent Updates Build Confidence

Consistent communication maintains alignment throughout the claim. Regular updates—whether or not there is a significant change, reduce uncertainty and reinforce professionalism. In high-pressure environments, silence is often interpreted as inaction. Consistent updates prevent that gap.

The responsibility for maintaining that consistency rests with the adjuster.

Effective updates should clearly reflect the claim's status, including inspection progress, documentation review, pending information, and defined next steps. When stakeholders understand where the claim stands and what is expected next, unnecessary follow-up and duplicate inquiries are reduced.

Consistency matters more than frequency. Communication should follow a predictable structure, such as after inspections, at key milestones, or upon receiving new information. This predictability allows stakeholders to anticipate updates rather than seek them.

Confidence is built on reliability. When communication is consistent, the process feels controlled—even when timelines are uncertain. When communication is inconsistent, even minor delays can cause concern.

Consistent updates do not accelerate the claim; they stabilize it.

Explaining Decisions Clearly

Decisions without context create confusion. Explaining how and why a decision was made strengthens understanding, supports transparency, and reduces the likelihood of escalation. The responsibility for clearly explaining decisions rests with the adjuster.

Effective communication links observations to conclusions. Adjusters should describe what was observed, identify the information reviewed, and outline the next steps. This ensures that decisions are understood as part of a structured evaluation rather than isolated outcomes.

A professional tone is essential. Clear, neutral, and respectful communication reinforces cooperation and keeps discussions focused on resolution, even when perspectives differ. Tone often determines whether a conversation remains constructive or turns adversarial.

When decision-making reasoning is communicated clearly, stakeholders are less likely to challenge the outcome and more likely to remain aligned with the process. Explaining decisions does not eliminate disagreement. It prevents confusion.

Appraisal Communication

During the appraisal process, communication becomes even more critical. Policyholders and stakeholders may not fully understand the roles involved, the purpose of the process, or how decisions will be made. Without a clear explanation, uncertainty increases, and the risk of escalation remains high.

The responsibility for maintaining clarity lies with the adjuster.

Communication during the appraisal should clearly explain the process, define roles, outline expected timelines, and identify next steps. When stakeholders understand how the process works, discussions remain focused and constructive, even in a formal dispute setting.

Consistency is essential. Messaging should align with prior communication and documentation to ensure that the transition into appraisal does not create confusion or contradict earlier discussions. Structured, professional communication maintains stability, even as the claim moves into a more formal stage of evaluation.

Appraisal does not remove the need for communication. It increases the need for communication.

Supplement requests

Supplement requests are a routine part of property claims, often involving contractor estimates, newly identified damage, or changes to repair methodology. While common, they introduce additional complexity and heighten the need for disciplined communication.

Maintaining alignment remains the adjuster's responsibility.

Each supplement must be evaluated within the context of the original scope and existing documentation. Clear communication should explain how new information is reviewed, what factors influence approval or revision, and how any changes affect the overall claim.

Unstructured handling of supplements creates confusion. Repeated conversations, inconsistent messaging, and unclear decisions lead to misaligned expectations and increase the likelihood of escalation. When supplements are not clearly documented and communicated, the claim begins to fragment.

Structured review, consistent documentation, and clear messaging maintain alignment. Each update should link back to the original evaluation to ensure continuity and reinforce defensibility. Supplements do not cause escalation. Inconsistent communication about them does.

Managing Difficult Conversations

Claims handling often involves difficult conversations about scope, timing, documentation, or expectations. These moments test the adjuster's ability to maintain control. How the conversation is managed determines whether the claim remains constructive or escalates.

The responsibility for maintaining that control rests with the adjuster.

Effective communication in these situations is grounded in explanation, not opposition. Clearly describing observations, clarifying findings, and outlining next steps keeps the discussion structured and focused on the claim. Grounding communication in documented information reduces emotion and reinforces professionalism.

Listening is equally important. Allowing stakeholders to express concerns helps identify misunderstandings and gaps in expectations. Acknowledging those concerns and responding with clear, structured explanations supports alignment and reduces tension.

Documentation completes the process. Recording the discussion, the concerns raised, and the next steps ensures continuity and prevents later conflicting interpretations. Difficult conversations do not cause escalation. Poorly managed conversations do.

Communication During Delays

Delays are a normal part of claims handling. Access limitations, weather conditions, inspection scheduling, high claim volume, and expert involvement can all extend timelines. When delays are not communicated, stakeholders assume inaction, increasing the likelihood of escalation.

The responsibility for maintaining clarity during delays rests with the adjuster.

Clear communication should explain the reason for the delay, identify what is currently in progress, and outline what happens next. Even when timelines are uncertain, structured updates maintain direction and reduce speculation.

Regular communication is more important than perfect answers. Confirming status and reinforcing next steps are often sufficient to maintain alignment. Predictable updates help stakeholders understand that the claim is progressing, even when progress is not immediately visible.

Communication during delays is a leadership responsibility. Transparent, consistent updates maintain stability, reinforce professionalism, and ensure the claim continues to move forward without unnecessary escalation.

Delays do not cause escalation. Lack of communication during delays does.

Tone and Professionalism

Tone determines how communication is received. Clear, respectful communication keeps discussions constructive, encourages cooperation, and maintains focus on the claim—even when conditions are challenging.

The responsibility for maintaining that tone lies with the adjuster.

In high-pressure environments, communication can easily become reactive. Questions may be repeated, timelines may be uncertain, and expectations may differ. A reactive response introduces tension and reduces control. A disciplined tone—focused on observations, updates, and next steps—keeps communication structured and productive.

A calm, neutral tone reinforces reliability. It signals that the claim is being handled consistently and professionally, even when outcomes are not immediate. Stakeholders respond to that consistency. When communication remains steady, conversations are more likely to stay constructive.

Professional tone is not situational. It is a standard.

In complex or multi-party claims, tone serves as a stabilizing force. It supports alignment, reduces the risk of escalation, and keeps communication focused on resolution rather than reaction.

Tone is not separate from communication. It defines communication.

REAL WORLD
Preventing Escalation Through Early Alignment

An adjuster managed a claim in which the policyholder expected immediate approval of repairs. Because expectations were not clearly established at the outset, follow-up calls increased and frustration grew.

The adjuster addressed the issue through structured communication. The evaluation process was clearly explained, pending items were identified, and next steps were outlined. Communication remained focused on process and timing rather than on immediate outcomes.

As expectations aligned, the frequency of follow-up calls decreased. The policyholder understood what to expect and when. The claim progressed without escalation.

The shift was not in the decision but in the communication. Structured, professional communication established alignment early, reduced unnecessary workload, and enabled the claim to move forward with stability.

Documenting Communication

Documentation reinforces communication by preserving consistency over time. Recording conversations ensures that updates, explanations, and next steps remain clear and aligned as the claim progresses.

The responsibility for maintaining that consistency rests with the adjuster.

Each entry should clearly document who was contacted, what was discussed, and what actions or follow-up were established. These details create a reliable record that supports continuity and allows the claim to be understood without relying on memory or interpretation.

Documenting communication also tracks claim development. Clear notes allow adjusters to reference prior discussions, prevent confusion, and maintain alignment across all participants. This becomes especially important in multi-party claims, where information is received from different sources and at different times. Without structured documentation, communication fragments and conflicting interpretations increase.

Well-documented communication strengthens the claim file. Organized records provide continuity, support transparency, and ensure that the claim remains structured from initial contact through resolution.

Communication documentation is not administrative. It is how alignment is maintained.

Communication in High-Volume Events

Catastrophe and high-volume claims environments significantly increase communication demands. Adjusters often receive simultaneous requests from multiple stakeholders, each seeking updates, clarification, or direction. Without structure, communication quickly becomes fragmented.

The responsibility for maintaining control under these conditions rests with the adjuster.

Consistent communication practices are essential. Clear, structured updates that identify claim status, pending items, and next steps reduce duplicate inquiries and help manage the workload efficiently. When messaging is consistent, stakeholders remain aligned even as volume increases.

Structure is more important than frequency. Grouping communication into defined intervals—such as after inspections, documentation reviews, or key checkpoints—helps adjusters stay responsive without disrupting workflow. This approach balances accessibility with productivity.

Managing communication volume is a leadership function. Without structure, communication becomes reactive and inefficient. With structure, it becomes controlled and purposeful.

High-volume environments do not change the need for communication. They increase the need for disciplined communication. Clear, consistent updates maintain stability, reduce escalation, and ensure that claims continue to progress, even under pressure.

Communication in Multi-Party Claims

Claims involving multiple stakeholders require disciplined communication to maintain alignment. In these environments, information is shared among participants at different times and often with differing perspectives. Without structure, messaging becomes inconsistent, and the claim begins to fragment.

The responsibility for maintaining alignment rests with the adjuster.

Structured communication ensures that all participants share a common understanding. Each interaction should be clearly documented, including who requested information, what was communicated, and what follow-up is expected. These records create a reliable timeline and allow the claim to progress without confusion or conflicting interpretations.

A professional tone is essential. Neutral, respectful communication supports constructive dialogue, even when perspectives differ. In multiparty claims, tone helps maintain cooperation and keeps discussions focused on resolution rather than disagreement.

Managing communication among multiple stakeholders requires organization. Structured messaging, documented updates, and consistent practices preserve clarity and enable the adjuster to guide the claim forward with control.

In multi-party environments, communication is how coordination is achieved.

Leadership Through Communication

Communication is a direct expression of leadership in claims handling. Adjusters who communicate clearly, explain decisions, and document conversations provide direction and stability for complex claims.

The responsibility for that leadership rests with the adjuster.

Effective communication reduces confusion and improves efficiency. When stakeholders understand the claim status, the rationale for decisions, and the next steps, they are more likely to stay aligned. This reduces repeated inquiries and prevents unnecessary escalation.

Communication also manages complexity. As the number of participants grows and conditions evolve, structured messaging becomes essential. Clear, consistent communication ensures that the claim remains coordinated and progresses without interruption.

Leadership in claims is demonstrated not only by decisions but also by how those decisions are communicated.

Disciplined communication guides the claim, maintains alignment, and ensures clarity from initial contact through to final resolution.

Preventing Escalation Through Clarity

Escalation often begins with uncertainty. When timelines are unclear, decisions are not explained, or updates are inconsistent, stakeholders assume the claim has stalled. That assumption breeds frustration and increases the likelihood of escalation.

The responsibility for preventing that uncertainty rests with the adjuster.

Clarity maintains control. Structured communication ensures stakeholders understand the claim's status and what to expect next.

Confirming inspection progress, identifying pending information, and outlining next steps keep the claim moving forward in alignment.

Even brief updates reduce uncertainty. When communication is consistent, stakeholders do not need to seek information—they receive it. This reduces redundant inquiries and helps maintain focus on resolution rather than clarification.

Explaining decisions is equally important. When stakeholders understand the observations, the information reviewed, and the reasoning behind the conclusions, misunderstandings are less likely. Clear explanations keep discussions grounded in the evaluation process and support professional dialogue.

Preventing escalation is not about increasing effort. It is about maintaining consistency. Adjusters who communicate clearly, document updates, and provide direction stabilize the claim and preserve momentum, even in complex or high-pressure situations.

Clarity does not eliminate challenges. It prevents confusion.

Practical Claim Leadership Actions

Communication That Prevents Escalation

Communication determines how claims develop. Clear, consistent messaging helps reduce misunderstandings, manage expectations, and prevent unnecessary escalation. Adjusters who communicate with structure and professionalism help stabilize the claim, even when conditions are complex. In high-pressure claims, communication often determines whether a situation stabilizes or escalates. Communication does not reduce complexity—it ensures that complexity is managed without escalation.

SET THE TONE EARLY

The first conversations in a claim influence expectations and perception. Clear, calm communication helps establish professionalism and direction.

KEY ACTIONS:

Explain the claim process clearly
Set expectations for communication timing
Identify next steps early
Confirm understanding with stakeholders

GO-TO LINES:

"Here is how the claim process will proceed."
"These are the next steps we will be taking."
"I will provide updates as the claim progresses."
"Please let me know if anything needs clarification."

USE STRUCTURED UPDATES

Consistent communication helps prevent frustration and repeated inquiries. Structured updates reinforce clarity.

KEY ACTIONS:

Provide status updates regularly
Confirm completed actions
Identify pending review items
Communicate next steps clearly

GO-TO LINES:

"Here is the current status of your claim."
"These steps have been completed."

"We are currently reviewing the next phase."
"I will update you as soon as there is progress."

WAYS TO ADDRESS SUPPLEMENTS

Supplements test consistency. Leadership ensures alignment.

KEY ACTIONS:

Review supplemental information against original documentation
Identify new vs previously evaluated conditions
Document reasoning for approval, revision, or denial
Communicate decisions clearly and consistently
Reconfirm scope, timelines, and next steps

GO-TO LINES:

"This supplement is being reviewed against the original scope and documentation."

"Additional items are being evaluated based on new information provided."

"The decision reflects documented findings and current evaluation."

"Updates will be provided once review is complete."

ADDRESS QUESTIONS PROACTIVELY

Unanswered questions can lead to confusion and escalation. Proactive communication helps maintain alignment.

KEY ACTIONS:

Anticipate common questions
Clarify timelines realistically
Explain evaluation steps
Reconfirm expectations when conditions change

GO-TO LINES:

"Let me walk through what to expect next."
"Here is what is currently under review."
"Timelines may adjust based on new information."
"I will confirm updates as they are available."

MAINTAIN PROFESSIONAL TONE UNDER PRESSURE

Emotionally charged conversations require calm, structured responses. Professional tone helps stabilize the interaction.

KEY ACTIONS:

Use neutral, respectful language
Avoid defensive responses
Focus on facts and process
Confirm next steps before closing the conversation

GO-TO LINES:

"I want to ensure we keep communication clear and focused."
"Let's walk through the process step by step."
"This is based on the information available at this time."
"I will confirm next steps before we close this conversation."

DOCUMENT COMMUNICATION CLEARLY

Clear documentation helps maintain consistency and supports defensibility.

KEY ACTIONS:

Record key conversations
Document expectations discussed
Identify follow-up actions

Track communication timeline

GO-TO LINES:

"This communication has been documented in the claim file."
"The discussion reflects the current status of the claim."
"Next steps have been recorded for follow-up."
"Updates will be documented as the claim progresses."

COMMUNICATE DURING DELAYS

Delays create uncertainty. Communication maintains control.

KEY ACTIONS:

Explain the reason for delays clearly
Identify what is currently in progress
Provide realistic expectations
Reconfirm next steps during inactivity

GO-TO LINES:

"There is a delay due to [reason], and here is what is currently in progress."
"We are waiting on additional information to move forward."
"I will provide an update once this step is complete."
"The claim is still active, and I will continue to keep you updated."

EXPLAIN DECISIONS CLEARLY

Decisions without explanation create confusion. Explanation creates alignment.

KEY ACTIONS:

Connect observations to conclusions
Reference documentation used

Clarify what influenced the decision
Outline next steps following the decision

GO-TO LINES:

"This decision is based on documented findings and evaluation."
"Here is how we arrived at this conclusion."
"This reflects the information available at this time."
"Next steps will follow this stage of the process."

MANAGE COMMUNICATION VOLUME

High communication volume requires structure to maintain control.

KEY ACTIONS:

Group updates into defined intervals
Prioritize critical communications
Avoid reactive, fragmented responses
Maintain consistent messaging across stakeholders

GO-TO LINES:

"Updates will be provided at key stages of the claim."
"I will consolidate updates to keep communication clear."
"Here is the current status and next steps moving forward."
"All updates will reflect the most current information available."

These practices help adjusters reduce escalation, maintain professionalism, and preserve claim clarity. By combining structured communication, consistent updates, and a disciplined professional tone, adjusters guide conversations with control—even when timelines are uncertain, emotions are elevated, and conditions continue to evolve.

The responsibility for maintaining that control rests with the adjuster. Communication does not eliminate complexity. It determines whether complexity creates confusion or control.

CLAIM LEADERSHIP SUMMARY

Key Takeaway

Communication determines whether a claim remains stable or escalates. As timelines shift or information evolves, stakeholders rely on clear updates, realistic expectations, and consistent direction. Adjusters who communicate with structure and clarity reduce uncertainty and maintain alignment throughout the claim process. Consistent communication keeps the claim under control—even as conditions change.

In Practice

Provide structured updates at regular intervals. Explain delays early, clarify next steps, and reinforce expectations throughout the claim. Communicate even when there is no significant change to maintain alignment. A professional tone and transparent messaging reduce frustration, limit repeated inquiries, and keep the claim progressing steadily.

Questions for Reflection

1. Do I provide updates even when there is no visible progress?
2. How clearly do I explain delays and evolving timelines?
3. Am I reinforcing expectations in every interaction?
4. Would my communication prevent confusion if the claim became more complex?

Claim Leadership Principle

Communication is a leadership function. Consistency, clarity, and professionalism determine whether a claim remains aligned or escalates. In high-pressure environments, communication does not eliminate complexity; it controls how that complexity is experienced.

CHAPTER 14

Bad Faith Allegations and Adjuster Exposure

Event Spotlight — Claim Handling Disputes Leading to Bad Faith Allegations

Following major property losses, disputes occasionally escalated into allegations of delayed handling, insufficient investigation, or inconsistent communication. These allegations most often focused on claim timelines, documentation quality, and the clarity of decisions. In these situations, adjusters and carriers were required to demonstrate that the claim was handled in a structured, timely, and reasonable manner, given the information available.

Financial exposure from bad-faith litigation can significantly exceed the value of the original claim. In many cases, the focus of review shifts from the loss itself to how the claim was handled. Legal review often examines claim notes, communication history, and the reasoning behind decisions in detail. Documentation is evaluated not only for accuracy but also for timing, consistency, and completeness across the entire claim lifecycle.

The claim file becomes the primary evidence.

Adjusters play a central role in establishing that record. Each entry contributes to the documented timeline of the claim, showing what was known, what actions were taken, and how decisions were made. Gaps in documentation, delayed updates, or inconsistent communication can create uncertainty, even when the underlying evaluation is sound.

Bad-faith allegations often stem not from a single decision but from how the claim is perceived over time.

Consistent communication, timely action, and thorough investigation reduce that risk. When expectations are clear, updates are documented, and decisions are explained, the claim remains structured and understandable. Professional consistency demonstrates that the claim was handled in good faith.

The adjuster's professionalism is evident in the file. When documentation is clear, communication is consistent, and actions are timely, the claim demonstrates reasonableness from the initial report through resolution.

CHAPTER FOCUS

Bad-faith exposure rises when claim handling lacks clarity, consistency, or timeliness. Adjusters must approach each claim with structure, disciplined documentation, and professional communication. A well-maintained file demonstrates that decisions were reasonable, timely, and based on the information available at each stage of the claim.

Documentation does not prevent scrutiny. It ensures the claim can withstand scrutiny.

Bad Faith Allegations and Adjuster Exposure

Bad-faith allegations are among the most serious risks in modern claims handling. While most claims are handled professionally and without dispute, the risk of allegations has increased alongside heightened litigation awareness, policyholder advocacy, and more complex claim environments. Adjusters must operate with the understanding that communication, documentation, and decision-making may be scrutinized in detail long after the claim is completed.

The responsibility for managing that exposure rests with the adjuster.

Bad-faith concerns typically arise when a stakeholder believes a claim was not handled fairly, promptly, or consistently. These perceptions often stem from delays, communication gaps, unclear explanations, or inconsistent handling. Whether allegations are substantiated or not, they frequently stem from misunderstanding, incomplete documentation, or a lack of structured communication.

Exposure is not created solely by the decision. It arises when the decision cannot be clearly explained, supported, or followed in the claim file.

Clear documentation, consistent communication, and structured workflows reduce that risk. These practices promote transparency, ensure continuity, and ensure the claim remains understandable at any point in its lifecycle. When the file reflects what was known, what actions were taken, and how decisions were reached, the claim demonstrates reasonableness over time.

In litigation-aware environments, perception is shaped by consistency. Gaps in notes, delayed updates, or shifting explanations create uncertainty, even when the underlying evaluation is sound. Consistent handling ensures that each stage of the claim aligns with the next.

Managing bad-faith exposure is not a reactive process. It is built into daily claim handling through discipline, clarity, and professional consistency. Adjusters who document thoroughly, communicate clearly, and act within a structured process reduce uncertainty and strengthen the defensibility of the claim.

Exposure does not come from decisions. It comes from how clearly and consistently those decisions are documented and communicated.

Understanding How Allegations Develop

Bad-faith allegations rarely stem from a single moment. They develop over time through a series of small breakdowns, delays without explanation, inconsistent communication, or unclear decisions. What begins as uncertainty can gradually become concern, and over time, that concern can become an allegation.

The responsibility for halting that progression rests with the adjuster.

Many allegations stem from communication gaps. When updates are inconsistent or absent, stakeholders are left to interpret the status of the claim. Questions go unanswered, expectations become unclear, and frustration builds. Under these conditions, perception shifts from uncertainty to doubt.

Documentation gaps contribute in the same way. When notes do not clearly reflect observations, decisions, or timelines, the claim can appear inconsistent or incomplete. Even when the underlying evaluation is sound, the file may not demonstrate it, creating additional questions and increasing scrutiny.

Allegations often stem from accumulated uncertainty, not isolated error.

Understanding how they develop enables adjusters to respond proactively. Clear communication, timely updates, and structured documentation reduce uncertainty at each stage of the claim. When the file consistently reflects what is happening and why, the likelihood of escalation is significantly reduced.

Appraisal and Umpire

In certain claims, particularly those involving disputes over scope or valuation, the appraisal process may be invoked as a structured method of resolution. This process typically involves an appraiser for each party and, when necessary, an independent umpire to resolve differences when the parties cannot agree.

When an appraisal is requested, the claim enters a formal dispute environment.

The responsibility for maintaining structure and clarity rests with the adjuster.

Documentation, communication, and scope definition become even more critical at this stage. The claim file must clearly support the position presented, as appraisal outcomes often depend on the strength, consistency, and completeness of the documented findings. Each observation, estimate, and communication may be reviewed in detail.

The role of the umpire is to evaluate differing positions and reach a determination when agreement is not possible. In doing so, the clarity and organization of the documentation directly influence how each position is understood.

Appraisal does not replace disciplined claim handling. It tests the claim handling.

Adjusters who maintain consistent documentation, clear communication, and structured scope development are better positioned to support the claim through appraisal and to maintain alignment throughout the process.

Timeliness and Claim Progression

Timeliness is a critical factor in bad-faith exposure. Delays may arise from access limitations, additional evaluations, expert coordination, or high claim volume. While these delays are often unavoidable, a lack of communication during those periods creates risk. When progress is not visible, stakeholders may assume the claim has stalled, leading to frustration and increased scrutiny.

The responsibility for maintaining that clarity rests with the adjuster.

Providing updates during delays shows the claim remains active. Explaining the reasons for timing changes, identifying pending items, and outlining next steps reinforces transparency. Even when new information is still being gathered, consistent communication confirms the claim is progressing.

Documentation reinforces timeliness. Recording inspections, communications, requests for information, and follow-up actions creates a clear timeline of activity. These records demonstrate how the claim has progressed and ensure that progress remains visible, even over extended timeframes.

Timeliness does not require rushing decisions. It requires consistent communication and documentation that clearly reflects the ongoing claim activity.

Consistency in Decision-Making

Inconsistent decisions create uncertainty and increase exposure. When conclusions appear to shift without explanation, stakeholders may question the evaluation's structure and reliability.

The responsibility for maintaining consistency lies with the adjuster.

Structured evaluation supports consistent decisions. Documenting observations, identifying the information reviewed, and recording the reasoning behind decisions ensure that conclusions are clear and traceable. When decisions are grounded in documented findings, the claim becomes understandable.

When new information changes the claim, documentation must reflect that change. Recording updated observations, revised timelines, and evolving findings explains how decisions developed over time. This continuity demonstrates that adjustments are based on new information, not on inconsistency.

Consistency is not about maintaining the same outcome. It is about maintaining a clear, well-supported process.

Communication That Reduces Risk

Communication plays a central role in reducing exposure to bad-faith conduct. When stakeholders understand how the claim is being handled, uncertainty decreases and discussions remain more constructive.

The responsibility for maintaining that clarity rests with the adjuster.

Clear explanations of inspection findings, timelines, and next steps demonstrate that the claim is progressing in a structured manner. This transparency supports professional handling and reduces misunderstandings.

Regular updates maintain alignment throughout the claim. Even when there are no significant changes, communication confirms that the claim remains active. Identifying pending items, confirming follow-up actions, and outlining next steps reinforces continuity and prevents assumptions.

Tone also shapes how communication is received. Professional, neutral communication supports cooperation, especially when timelines shift or questions arise. A steady tone keeps discussions focused on the claim and reduces the risk of escalation. Documentation completes the process. Recording discussions, updates, and next steps ensures consistency across interactions and maintains alignment over time.

Clear communication does not eliminate exposure. It reduces the conditions that cause it.

REAL WORLD
Managing Perception in a Coverage Dispute

An adjuster managed a property claim in which coverage was disputed after a large loss. As additional information was requested during the evaluation, the policyholder expressed concern about delays and questioned whether the claim was being handled fairly.

The risk was not only in the decision. It was in the perception of how the claim was handled.

The adjuster maintained consistent, structured communication throughout the process. Each interaction was clearly documented, including requests for information, explanations of the evaluation process, and updates on claim status. Communication remained grounded in policy language and supported by documented observations, with careful attention to tone and clarity.

As concerns about timing persisted, the adjuster addressed them directly. The steps required to complete the evaluation were explained, and the rationale for each stage of the process was documented. Follow-up actions and next steps were consistently recorded, ensuring the claim remained aligned and understandable.

The outcome of the claim was important, and the consistency of the process was critical.

By maintaining disciplined documentation and clear, professional communication, the adjuster reduced misunderstandings and strengthened the file's defensibility. This example demonstrates that in coverage disputes, perception is shaped not only by the outcome but also by how clearly and consistently the claim is handled over time.

Documentation as Protection

Documentation is one of the strongest protections against bad-faith allegations. The claim file must clearly document how the claim was evaluated, how communication occurred, and how decisions were made.

The responsibility for building that record rests with the adjuster.

Clear documentation establishes the claim narrative. Recording observations, updates, and follow-up actions provides structure and continuity, enabling the claim to be understood at any point in the process. Without that structure, even well-handled claims can appear inconsistent.

Timing is a critical component of documentation. Recording when inspections occurred, when communication took place, and when information was received establishes a clear progression of events. A well-documented timeline demonstrates that the claim progressed in a consistent and reasonable manner.

Documenting the reasoning behind decisions strengthens that protection. Recording observations, identifying the information considered, and outlining next steps ensure that conclusions are clear and supported. This level of detail allows the file to demonstrate how and why decisions were reached.

Strong documentation protects both the claim and the adjuster. Organized, consistent records preserve continuity, maintain alignment, and demonstrate disciplined handling from the initial inspection through final resolution.

Documentation does not prevent allegations. It ensures the claim can withstand them.

Managing Expectations

Unclear expectations can heighten the risk of bad-faith concerns. When stakeholders expect immediate resolution or specific outcomes, frustration may arise as timelines shift or additional information is required. Setting expectations early helps align stakeholders and reduces this risk.

Stakeholders enter the claims process with varying levels of experience. Some may have prior loss experience and a strong understanding of the process, while others may be navigating a claim for the first time. In either case, expectations may not align with how the claim must be evaluated.

The responsibility for establishing that alignment rests with the adjuster.

Explaining timelines, documentation requirements, and next steps provides structure. Identifying potential delays—such as access limitations, expert involvement, or high claim volume—prepares stakeholders for changing conditions. Proactive communication reduces uncertainty and helps sustain constructive dialogue.

Some stakeholders may require more detailed communication or challenge aspects of the process more directly. In these situations, consistency is critical. Clear explanations, structured updates, and a professional tone help maintain control and prevent conversations from becoming reactive.

Providing consistent updates reinforces expectations over time. Confirming progress, clarifying pending items, and outlining next steps ensure that stakeholders remain informed and aligned as the claim develops.

Managing expectations does not eliminate challenges. It reduces the conditions that lead to escalation.

Handling Disagreements Professionally

Disagreements are a normal part of claims handling. Differences in scope, timing, documentation, or evaluation may arise as stakeholders review findings. These situations do not necessarily signal conflict, but they do require disciplined communication.

The responsibility for maintaining control during these discussions rests with the adjuster.

Effective handling of disagreements focuses on explanation, not opposition. Clearly describing observations, clarifying findings, and outlining next steps keeps the discussion grounded in the claim. When communication is anchored in documented information, conversations are more likely to remain structured and productive.

Some disagreements may become more persistent or more direct. In these situations, tone and consistency are critical. Professional, neutral communication helps maintain cooperation and keeps the discussion focused on resolution rather than on reaction.

Documentation reinforces this process. Recording what was discussed, the concerns raised, and the identified next steps helps preserve continuity and prevent conflicting interpretations. These records ensure the claim remains aligned as it progresses.

Disagreements do not cause escalation. Unstructured responses to them do. Clear explanations, consistent communication, and documented follow-up maintain control and keep the claim moving forward.

Avoiding Assumptions

Assumptions introduce risk into claims handling. When conclusions are formed without clear support, documentation becomes vulnerable, and the evaluation becomes harder to defend.

The responsibility for maintaining objectivity rests with the adjuster.

Effective documentation is grounded in observation. Notes should reflect what was seen, measured, or communicated, rather than inferred. Recording observed conditions, receiving information, and documenting updates ensures accuracy and preserves transparency throughout the claim.

Fact-based documentation strengthens continuity. When the file clearly reflects observed conditions and communicated information, stakeholders can understand the evaluation without interpretation. This reduces confusion and supports consistent claim progression.

Avoiding assumptions also strengthens communication. Conversations remain focused on documented conditions rather than speculation, helping maintain professionalism and reducing the likelihood of misunderstanding.

Objectivity is not a preference. It is a requirement for defensible claims handling. Clear, fact-based documentation reduces uncertainty and limits exposure created by unsupported or unclear conclusions.

Multi-Party Claims and Exposure

Claims involving multiple stakeholders increase complexity and, with it, exposure. Contractors, public adjusters, engineers, representatives, and other participants provide information and request updates throughout the claim. As participation expands, the risk of misalignment increases.

The responsibility for maintaining alignment rests with the adjuster.

Structured communication is essential in these environments. Without coordination, messaging can become inconsistent, and the claim can fragment. Clear, consistent updates ensure that all participants share the same understanding.

Documentation is critical. Recording requests, responses, and updates creates a reliable record of how information was shared and how the claim progressed. These records preserve continuity and prevent conflicting interpretations, especially when discussions span time or involve multiple parties.

A professional tone supports coordination. Neutral, respectful communication helps sustain constructive dialogue, even when perspectives differ. This keeps discussions focused on resolution rather than on disagreement.

Managing multi-party claims requires structure. Consistent documentation, aligned communication, and disciplined handling reduce exposure and ensure the claim remains clear, coordinated, and defensible throughout its lifecycle. In multi-party environments, alignment is not assumed. It is achieved through communication.

Maintaining Professional Boundaries

Maintaining professional boundaries is essential to consistent claims handling. Adjusters explain the process, document observations, and outline next steps, but should not make commitments beyond what the evaluation supports. When communication goes beyond the facts, expectations can become misaligned, increasing risk.

The responsibility for maintaining those boundaries rests with the adjuster.

Clear, measured communication keeps expectations aligned with the claim process. Avoiding informal assurances, especially regarding outcomes, timelines, or decisions, prevents confusion and protects the integrity of the evaluation. Statements made before the evaluation is complete can create expectations that the claim file may not support.

Communication should remain structured, neutral, and documented. When explanations are grounded in observed conditions and include defined next steps, stakeholders understand how the claim is progressing without relying on assumptions or interpretation.

Professional boundaries maintain control. By reinforcing a neutral, process-driven role, adjusters keep discussions focused on documented findings and structured handling. This reduces the likelihood of disputes and supports consistent, professional communication.

Boundaries do not limit communication. They ensure it remains accurate.

Leadership Through Alignment

Reducing bad-faith exposure depends on consistent alignment throughout the claim. That alignment is established and maintained by leadership.

The responsibility for that leadership rests with the adjuster.

Adjusters guide the claim with reliability, professional communication, and sound judgment. Structured documentation and coordinated communication provide stability, especially in complex or evolving claims. When each stage of the claim supports the next, the file remains clear and defensible.

Well-documented records show the progression of the claim. Recording inspections, communications, and the reasoning behind decisions creates a coherent narrative that stakeholders can follow. This continuity reduces uncertainty and reinforces transparency.

Consistent communication sustains alignment. Providing updates, explaining decisions, and outlining next steps ensures that all participants remain informed and focused on the process. When communication is clear, discussions remain constructive, and the claim continues to move forward.

Leadership in claims is demonstrated through alignment. Organization, reliability, and disciplined communication reduce confusion and support defensible outcomes from the initial report through resolution.

Alignment is not assumed. It is sustained through consistent leadership.

Protecting the Adjuster Through Professional Practice

Adjuster exposure is reduced through disciplined, consistent claims handling. Clear documentation, structured communication, and organized workflows ensure the claim remains understandable from start to finish. When the file reflects thoughtful evaluation and steady progression, it supports both the claim and the adjuster.

The responsibility for building that record rests with the adjuster.

Professional practice is grounded in transparency. Recording observations, documenting communication, and explaining the reasoning behind decisions demonstrate how the claim was handled. These records show what information was considered and how conclusions were reached, reducing uncertainty and limiting misunderstandings.

Consistency strengthens that foundation. Standardized documentation, regular updates, and neutral communication ensure continuity throughout the claim lifecycle. This structure enables the claim to progress in a predictable, organized manner.

Professional claims handling does not change the adjuster's role. It strengthens it. Adjusters who document clearly, communicate consistently, and maintain organized workflows manage claims with control and clarity.

In modern claims environments, awareness of bad-faith considerations is part of professional practice. Through consistency, documentation, and clear communication, adjusters reduce exposure and promote disciplined claim handling. In complex claims, expertise alone does not create clarity. Coordination does.

The adjuster's role is not to replace expert input. It is to ensure that information connects in a way that advances the claim.

Practical Claim Leadership Actions

Bad Faith Allegations and Adjuster Exposure

Bad-faith allegations often stem from perceived delays, unclear communication, or inconsistent documentation. Exposure is not created by a single decision it develops when the claim file fails to clearly demonstrate how and why decisions were made over time.

The responsibility for managing that exposure rests with the adjuster.

Adjusters reduce risk by maintaining structure, documenting decisions carefully, and communicating clearly throughout the claim. In high-risk or disputed claims, consistent documentation and communication demonstrate that handling was reasonable, timely, and disciplined.

MAINTAIN CLEAR DOCUMENTATION

Defensible documentation explains how the claim was evaluated and how decisions were made.

KEY ACTIONS:

Document observations objectively
Explain decision reasoning clearly
Record stakeholder communication
Identify pending actions and timelines

GO-TO LINES:

"Documentation reflects observed conditions and the evaluation conducted."

"This conclusion is based on documented findings."

"The file reflects the information available at the time of review."

"Updates will be documented as additional information is received."

COMMUNICATE TIMELINES REALISTICALLY

Unclear or unrealistic timelines increase frustration and raise exposure risk.

KEY ACTIONS:

Explain evaluation steps clearly
Identify potential delays early
Avoid premature commitments
Update timelines as conditions change

GO-TO LINES:

"This review may take additional time as we complete the evaluation."
"Timelines will be updated as information develops."
"We are working through the process step by step."
"I will provide updates as each stage progresses."

MAINTAIN CONSISTENT COMMUNICATION

Consistency prevents misunderstandings and stabilizes the claim.

KEY ACTIONS:

Provide structured updates
Confirm next steps
Clarify changes in direction
Reconfirm expectations throughout the claim

GO-TO LINES:

"I want to ensure all communication remains consistent."
"Here is the current status of the claim."

"Next steps are confirmed as follows."
"Updates will reflect the current stage of the process."

AVOID PREMATURE CONCLUSIONS

Decisions must be communicated carefully while the evaluation is ongoing.

KEY ACTIONS:

Identify pending information
Document ongoing review activity
Avoid early commitments
Communicate the process clearly

GO-TO LINES:

"This remains under review at this stage."
"Additional evaluation is required before conclusions are made."
"There are still factors being considered."
"Next steps will follow completion of the review."

MAINTAIN PROFESSIONAL DISCIPLINE

Professional consistency reinforces credibility and reduces risk.

KEY ACTIONS:

Use neutral, factual language
Document communication promptly
Track follow-up actions
Maintain organized file notes

GO-TO LINES:

"Communication reflects the current information available."
"All updates are documented in the claim file."

"Follow-up actions have been recorded for continuity."
"The claim is being handled in a structured and consistent manner."

These practices reduce exposure by creating clarity, consistency, and continuity throughout the claim. When documentation is structured, communication is consistent, and decisions are clearly explained, the claim file demonstrates reasonableness over time.

Exposure is not prevented by avoiding scrutiny. It is reduced by ensuring the claim can withstand scrutiny.

CLAIM LEADERSHIP SUMMARY

Key Takeaway

Bad-faith exposure arises when communication, timelines, or documentation lack clarity. Adjusters establish the official record of claim handling through notes, decisions, and interactions. Consistent, structured handling ensures the file clearly shows how and why decisions were made over time. When communication and documentation remain aligned, the claim becomes understandable, defensible, and less vulnerable to dispute.

In Practice

Respond promptly, document decisions clearly, and maintain consistent communication throughout the claim. Explain the reasoning behind decisions, record timelines, and eliminate gaps in documentation. Each entry should reflect what was known, what actions were taken, and what steps were followed. A disciplined approach demonstrates reasonable, timely, and professional handling while maintaining alignment as the claim progresses.

Questions for Reflection

1. Do my notes clearly document timelines, actions, and decision points?
2. Am I clearly explaining my reasoning in both documentation and communication?
3. Would the file be understandable if reviewed without my involvement?
4. Are there any gaps that could create uncertainty or misinterpretation?

Claim Leadership Principle

Exposure is reduced when the claim file demonstrates clarity, consistency, and continuity. Communication, documentation, and decision-making must align at every stage of the claim. In high-risk environments, documentation does not prevent scrutiny; it ensures the claim can withstand it.

CHAPTER 15

Working with Attorneys, Engineers, and Experts

Event Spotlight — Structural Loss Requiring Engineering Evaluation

After a significant structural loss, engineers were engaged to evaluate the cause and extent of the damage and to provide repair recommendations. Attorneys reviewed liability exposure and policy interpretation as the claim continued to develop. The adjuster coordinated communication among all parties as findings evolved.

Structural losses introduce greater complexity and financial exposure. Following major catastrophes such as Hurricane Katrina and Hurricane Sandy, engineering evaluations played a critical role in determining causation, structural integrity, and the scope of repairs. Disputes in these contexts often centered on differing interpretations of damage, repair methods, and coverage application.

Expert opinions are rarely static. They evolve over time and may shift as new information is identified, reviewed, and applied. In today's claims environment, multiple expert perspectives often emerge simultaneously and are reviewed by carriers, policyholders, and legal representatives. These findings are frequently evaluated alongside claim documentation to assess consistency, methodology, and alignment.

The responsibility for maintaining that alignment rests with the adjuster.

Multi-expert claims require structured communication and disciplined documentation. Engineers, attorneys, and other experts provide specialized analysis, but the claim must serve as a single, coherent evaluation. Without coordination, information fragments make the claim difficult to interpret.

The adjuster's role shifts to integration and leadership. Each expert perspective must be documented, understood, and linked to the overall claim. How that information is organized and communicated determines whether the claim remains clear or becomes disjointed.

In complex claims, expertise alone does not create clarity. Alignment does.

CHAPTER FOCUS

Working with attorneys, engineers, and other experts requires disciplined communication, organization, and leadership. Adjusters must coordinate multiple perspectives while maintaining consistency throughout the claim. Effective integration ensures that expert input contributes to a clear, structured, and defensible claim narrative.

Working with Attorneys, Engineers, and Experts

Modern claims handling often involves collaboration with attorneys, engineers, and other technical experts. As claims grow more complex and litigation awareness rises, adjusters work in multidisciplinary environments where technical findings, legal interpretation, and claim evaluation develop simultaneously.

The responsibility for maintaining clarity and alignment rests with the adjuster.

Attorneys may evaluate liability and interpret policy. Engineers assess causation, structural integrity, and repair methodology. Other experts provide specialized analysis. Each perspective adds value but also introduces complexity. The claim must still serve as a single, coherent evaluation.

Working with experts adds complexity to claim handling. Reports may be pending, technical conclusions may require interpretation, and timelines often depend on external availability. These moving parts must be managed without disrupting communication or delaying claim progression.

The adjuster's role is not to replace expert input. It is to integrate it.

Adjusters coordinate information, maintain structured communication, and ensure that all findings are documented and linked to the overall claim. Without this coordination, information fragments, making the claim difficult to follow.

The involvement of attorneys and experts does not shift responsibility. Adjusters continue to guide the claim by maintaining communication, documenting developments, and ensuring consistent and appropriate information sharing.

Structured collaboration prevents confusion. Organized documentation and clear communication keep all parties aligned and enable the claim to progress steadily. Coordination does not reduce complexity. It ensures that complexity is managed under control.

The Role of Technical Experts

Engineers and technical specialists are often engaged when claims involve structural concerns, complex causation questions, or large losses. Their evaluations provide additional analysis to support claim handling and clarify conditions that may not be immediately apparent during the initial inspection. These experts may inspect the property, review documentation, analyze damage patterns, and prepare written reports. Their findings become part of the overall claim evaluation.

The responsibility for integrating that information rests with the adjuster.

Adjusters coordinate expert involvement and document key timing throughout the process. Recording when experts are assigned, inspections occur, and reports are received establishes a clear timeline. This documentation shows how technical input was incorporated and ensures continuity as the claim develops. Structured notes also help track pending items and required follow-up.

Technical findings often require interpretation. Adjusters explain how expert reports affect the claim, whether additional evaluation is needed, and what the next steps will be. Clear, structured updates ensure stakeholders understand how technical input affects the claim process.

Working with technical experts requires organization and control. Tracking assignments, documenting communications, and recording receipt of reports ensure that technical evaluations are clearly integrated into the claim.

Technical input does not create clarity on its own. It must be connected to something.

Collaboration with Attorneys

Attorneys may become involved when claims include disputes, liability issues, or litigation. Their role may include reviewing documentation, advising on communication, and addressing legal issues. As legal involvement increases, communication becomes more formal and more closely reviewed.

The responsibility for maintaining structure and clarity remains with the adjuster.

All interactions with legal representatives should be documented. Recording requests for information, materials provided, and the timing of communications ensures the claim remains organized and aligned. These records demonstrate how legal involvement influenced claim development and preserve continuity throughout the process.

Adjusters must approach these interactions with professionalism and precision. Communication should remain structured, consistent, and grounded in documented information. Clear records of discussions, updates, and follow-up actions ensure the claim file reflects a complete and reliable history.

Collaborating with attorneys does not change the claims process. It increases the need for disciplined communication and documentation.

Working Across Experience Levels in the Industry

Claims environments often bring together professionals with varying levels of experience. Adjusters may work alongside seasoned experts who rely on field judgment developed over time and newer professionals who depend more heavily on structured workflows and evolving practices.

These differences can affect communication style, pace, and expectations. The responsibility for maintaining alignment rests with the adjuster.

Effective coordination requires clarity, professionalism, and respect. Differences in experience should not lead to inconsistent handling. Structured communication, consistent documentation, and a defined approach ensure that all participants remain aligned, regardless of perspective.

Professional alignment does not require changing approaches. It requires maintaining clarity so that all participants understand the claim's direction.

Consistency bridges experience gaps. Without it, variation increases, making the claim harder to manage.

REAL WORLD
Navigating Differences in Experience and Approach

An adjuster managed a large commercial loss, coordinating with an experienced engineer and a senior claims supervisor. The engineer relied on extensive field experience and preferred verbal summaries, whereas the supervisor required detailed written documentation and structured updates.

The challenge was not the quality of the information. It was how the information was communicated. Differences in communication style created early friction. Information was shared, but not always in a format that supported alignment across all parties.

The adjuster ensured consistency. All findings were clearly documented, key points were summarized in writing after discussions, and next steps were confirmed in a structured format. Verbal conversations were consistently followed by written summaries to ensure clarity and continuity.

This approach created a shared understanding.

The engineer's input was accurately captured, and the supervisor's documentation expectations were met. Each perspective was preserved, but the claim was managed through a single, consistent process.

By maintaining disciplined documentation and structured communication, the adjuster reduced miscommunication and aligned all participants. The claim progressed with clarity and remained defensible despite differences in experience and work style.

Alignment did not require changing perspectives. It required establishing a consistent way to connect them.

Coordinating Multi-Disciplinary Teams

Claims involving technical experts often require coordination among multiple participants. Engineers, contractors, consultants, and attorneys contribute information at different stages, with overlapping timelines and differing priorities. Without structure, communication fragments, and the claim becomes difficult to manage.

The responsibility for maintaining that alignment rests with the adjuster.

Effective coordination requires clear documentation and consistent communication. Recording who provided information, what was requested, and when updates were received creates a reliable record of the claim's progress. These notes ensure that all participants work from consistent information and that follow-up actions remain visible.

Inspection coordination is equally important. Experts may need access at different stages, and their findings often inform subsequent evaluations. Documenting inspection timing, site access, and follow-up actions ensures the claim progresses in a logical sequence.

Coordination is not passive; it is structured.

Clear documentation, organized scheduling, and consistent communication enable the adjuster to guide multidisciplinary teams while maintaining control of the claim. When coordination is structured, expert input aligns rather than fragments.

Multi-disciplinary claims do not become complex because of the number of participants. They become complex when those participants are misaligned.

REAL WORLD
Coordinating Expert Input in a Structural Claim

A commercial property claim involved structural damage that required input from a structural engineer and a contractor. The engineer recommended further testing due to potential integrity concerns, while the contractor proposed immediate repairs based on visible damage.

The challenge was not the difference in opinion. It was how those opinions were integrated.

The adjuster clearly documented both perspectives and coordinated a structured discussion to clarify each recommendation and identify the additional information required. Each viewpoint was recorded and linked to the overall evaluation process.

The policyholder was informed that the claim remained under review pending final engineering confirmation. The differing opinions were explained as part of a thorough evaluation, not a conflict.

This communication maintained confidence in the process.

By maintaining clear documentation, structured communication, and defined next steps, the adjuster aligned the expert inputs. The final scope reflected both structural requirements and practical repair considerations, allowing the claim to move forward with clarity and consistency.

Alignment did not require agreement. It required structure.

Managing Timelines with Expert Involvement

Expert involvement often extends claim timelines. Inspections must be scheduled, reports prepared, and findings reviewed before decisions can be finalized. When multiple experts are involved, these steps may occur sequentially or overlap, increasing complexity and lengthening the evaluation process.

The responsibility for maintaining clarity throughout this process rests with the adjuster.

Clear communication is essential for managing expectations. Providing updates on expert scheduling, anticipated report timing, and next steps helps stakeholders understand the claim's progress. Even when timelines depend on external availability, structured communication reinforces that the claim remains active and moving forward.

Visibility reduces uncertainty.

Documenting the timeline of activities further strengthens this process. Recording when inspections occur, when reports are received, and when findings are reviewed establishes a clear progression of events. These records demonstrate how expert input influenced the evaluation and provide continuity throughout the claim lifecycle.

Managing timelines in multi-expert environments requires discipline. Consistent communication, documented milestones, and structured updates enable the adjuster to guide the claim while keeping all participants aligned.

Timelines do not create risk. Lack of visibility does.

Interpreting Technical Information

Technical reports often contain specialized terminology, detailed observations, and complex analysis. Adjusters serve as the bridge between expert findings and claim progression. This requires translating what the findings mean for the claim process without going beyond what is documented.

The responsibility for maintaining that clarity rests with the adjuster.

Adjusters should focus on explaining how technical findings affect next steps rather than attempting to reinterpret expert conclusions.

Communicating whether additional inspections are required, documentation is pending, or review is ongoing keeps stakeholders informed while maintaining accuracy.

Process clarity prevents misinterpretation.

Documentation reinforces this role. Recording when reports are received, when updates are provided, and which follow-up actions are identified creates a clear record of how technical information is incorporated into the claim. These notes ensure continuity and help the claim remain understandable as it develops.

Handling technical information requires organization and discipline. Structured communication, documented updates, and clearly defined next steps ensure that expert findings are integrated without causing confusion.

Technical information does not create clarity on its own. It must be communicated precisely.

Maintaining Professional Neutrality

Working with attorneys and technical experts requires maintaining professional neutrality. Adjusters coordinate communication, document findings, and guide the claim without exceeding the documented record.

The responsibility for maintaining neutrality rests with the adjuster.

Communication should remain factual, structured, and process-focused. Explaining timing, next steps, and documentation requirements ensures that stakeholders understand how the claim is progressing without introducing assumptions or bias. Avoiding conclusions beyond documented findings preserves consistency and reduces the risk of misunderstanding.

Neutrality also supports coordination. In multi-party environments, clear, objective communication ensures that information is shared consistently among all participants. This prevents conflicting interpretations and helps maintain alignment.

Neutrality maintains control.

When communication remains objective, and documentation remains consistent, the claim progresses with clarity and stability—even with multiple expert perspectives.

Documentation of Expert Activity

Documentation becomes critical when experts participate in a claim. Recording assignment dates, inspection times, and report receipt establishes a clear timeline of activity and demonstrates how expert input influenced claim development.

The responsibility for maintaining that record rests with the adjuster.

Structured documentation supports continuity. Notes should document when experts are assigned, when inspections occur, and when reports are received. This creates a clear progression of the claim and ensures that expert involvement is clearly integrated into the evaluation.

Communication regarding expert findings must also be documented. Recording when updates are provided, what information is shared, and what follow-up actions are required helps maintain consistency among all participants. These records ensure that information remains aligned and accessible throughout the claim lifecycle.

Documenting expert activity provides structure to complex claims. Clear timelines, recorded communications, and organized follow-up actions help keep the claim coordinated, even when multiple experts are involved.

Without documentation, expert involvement adds complexity. With structure, it brings clarity.

Communication with Stakeholders

Stakeholders often have questions when technical experts become involved in a claim. Scheduling inspections, awaiting reports, and reviewing findings can extend timelines. Without communication, these steps may be perceived as delays.

The responsibility for maintaining clarity lies with the adjuster.

Providing structured updates on expert involvement maintains alignment and reduces uncertainty. Communicating when experts are assigned, when inspections are scheduled, and what next steps are expected helps stakeholders understand the claim's progress.

Communication should remain clear, professional, and process-focused. Explaining the sequence of events—rather than speculating about outcomes—ensures expectations remain realistic and aligned with the evaluation.

Consistency reinforces confidence. Even when there are no significant updates, confirming the status and next steps shows that the claim remains active.

Documentation supports this process. Recording when updates are provided, what information is shared, and what follow-up actions are identified ensures continuity across all interactions.

Clear communication with stakeholders does not shorten timelines. It ensures those timelines are understood.

Managing Multiple Reports

Some claims involve multiple expert reports. Engineers, consultants, and other specialists may each provide findings that inform the overall evaluation. These reports are often received at different stages and may address distinct aspects of the loss.

The responsibility for maintaining organization among these inputs rests with the adjuster.

Structured tracking is essential. Recording when each report is received, who reviewed the findings, and the next steps identified creates a clear, reliable record. This ensures that all technical input is accounted for and integrated into the claim.

Sequencing matters. One report may prompt additional evaluation, clarification, or a follow-up inspection. Documenting how reports relate to one another preserves continuity and ensures the claim's progression remains clear.

Without structure, multiple reports create confusion. With organization, they add depth.

Managing multiple reports requires discipline. Clear records, documented communication, and structured tracking help the adjuster maintain consistency and guide the claim toward a coordinated outcome.

Coordinating Follow-Up Inspections

Expert involvement often triggers follow-up inspections. Additional evaluations may be required based on new findings, clarification requests, or evolving conditions. These inspections must be carefully coordinated to ensure the claim continues to progress.

The responsibility for that coordination rests with the adjuster.

Documenting follow-up inspections is critical. Recording inspection timing, participants, and observations establishes a clear sequence of evaluation. These records demonstrate how findings evolved and support continuity throughout the claim.

Communication about follow-up activity must also be documented. Recording the dates of inspections, stakeholder notifications, and updates ensures that all participants remain aligned. These notes help maintain a consistent understanding of the claim's direction.

Follow-up coordination is not administrative; it is structural.

Organized scheduling, consistent documentation, and clear communication ensure that evolving evaluations remain aligned and that the claim progresses in a coordinated and defensible manner.

Leadership Through Coordination

Working with attorneys, engineers, and technical experts requires leadership from the adjuster. Multiple participants contribute information at different stages, often with varying timelines and perspectives. Without coordination, that input can become fragmented.

The responsibility for maintaining alignment rests with the adjuster.

Adjusters lead by coordinating communication, tracking timelines, and documenting developments. Structured coordination ensures that information from experts, attorneys, and other stakeholders remains consistent and aligned. Recording assignments, inspections, and report receipts creates a clear timeline that supports continuity throughout the claim.

Coordination creates clarity.

The adjuster's leadership is evident in how collaboration is managed. Providing structured updates, documenting interactions, and maintaining organized workflows ensure that technical input is integrated effectively. These practices allow the claim to progress steadily, even as complexity increases.

Multi-disciplinary claims do not require more information. They require better organization.

Guiding Complex Claims Through Expert Collaboration

The involvement of attorneys, engineers, and technical experts reflects the complexity of modern claims handling. These participants provide analysis, documentation, and guidance that support evaluation. Despite this collaboration, the adjuster retains responsibility for coordination and alignment.

A defined approach is essential.

Adjusters manage complex claims by tracking expert involvement, managing timelines, and documenting communications. Recording assignments, inspections, and report receipts preserves continuity and ensures that each stage of the claim is clearly connected. Regular updates help stakeholders understand how expert input influences the evaluation.

Expert input must be integrated, not accumulated.

Clear communication, neutral coordination, and organized documentation ensure that technical findings are linked to the overall claim. Without structure, multiple inputs create confusion. With discipline, they strengthen the evaluation.

Adjusters who maintain alignment and organization guide complex claims with control. Through coordination, communication, and documentation, expert collaboration is structured and supports clear, defensible claim handling.

Practical Claim Leadership Actions

Working with Attorneys, Engineers, and Experts

Complex claims often require coordination among attorneys, engineers, consultants, and other experts. These stakeholders provide specialized input that shapes scope, causation, and decision-making. Adjusters must maintain structure, clarify roles, and ensure communication remains aligned.

The responsibility for maintaining that alignment rests with the adjuster.

Effective coordination prevents confusion and supports defensible claim handling. In multi-expert claims, clarity depends on how well roles, communication, and information are structured and integrated.

ESTABLISH ROLES EARLY

Clear role definitions prevent overlap and miscommunication.

KEY ACTIONS:

Identify involved experts and stakeholders
Clarify each party's role in the claim
Confirm communication channels
Establish update expectations

GO-TO LINES:

"These are the roles of each party involved in the claim."
"We are coordinating responsibilities across all participants."
"Communication will follow a structured process."
"I will provide updates as information is confirmed."

COORDINATE COMMUNICATION CAREFULLY

Multiple stakeholders increase the risk of conflicting information.

KEY ACTIONS:

Align communication across parties
Confirm information before sharing externally
Document coordination discussions
Provide consistent updates

GO-TO LINES:

"I want to ensure all communication remains aligned across parties."
"We are confirming information before it is shared."
"Updates will reflect verified information only."
"Coordination is ongoing across all stakeholders."

TRACK EXPERT INPUT CLEARLY

Expert findings influence the direction of the claim and must be documented precisely.

KEY ACTIONS:

Document expert observations
Record report timelines
Identify pending evaluations
Update the claim file as findings develop

GO-TO LINES:

"Expert findings are being documented as they are received."
"We are currently awaiting additional expert input."
"Reports will be incorporated into the claim as they are finalized."
"The file reflects the current status of expert evaluation."

MAINTAIN CLAIM DIRECTION

Experts provide input. The adjuster guides the claim.

KEY ACTIONS:

Identify next steps following expert input
Clarify how findings affect the claim
Communicate direction to stakeholders
Maintain consistent follow-up

GO-TO LINES:

"Based on current findings, these are the next steps."
"This is how the expert input affects the claim direction."
"We are maintaining a structured approach as information develops."
"Follow-up actions have been identified and will be tracked."

MANAGE EXPECTATIONS AROUND EXPERT REVIEW

Expert involvement may extend timelines.

KEY ACTIONS:

Explain the need for expert involvement
Clarify expected review timelines
Reconfirm next steps after evaluation
Update stakeholders when timelines change

GO-TO LINES:

"Expert review is required to complete the evaluation."
"Timelines may extend based on the review process."
"Next steps will follow completion of expert analysis."
"Updates will be provided as timelines are confirmed."

HANDLE CONFLICTING EXPERT OPINIONS

Differences in expert conclusions are common and must be carefully managed.

KEY ACTIONS:

Document each expert's findings clearly
Identify where opinions differ
Avoid taking positions beyond documented findings
Coordinate additional review when needed

GO-TO LINES:

"There are differing expert perspectives under review."
"Each opinion is being documented and evaluated."
"Additional clarification may be required to align findings."
"Next steps will follow completion of the review process."

DOCUMENT DECISION ALIGNMENT

Defensibility depends on how expert input is linked to decisions.

KEY ACTIONS:

Connect expert findings to claim decisions
Document how conclusions were reached
Record changes based on new information
Ensure the file reflects a clear evaluation path

GO-TO LINES:

"This decision reflects the combined evaluation of expert findings."
"The conclusion is based on documented information and analysis."
"Updates reflect new information received during evaluation."
"The file outlines how the final position was reached."

These practices ensure that expert collaboration strengthens the claim rather than complicates it. Structured coordination, consistent communication, and disciplined documentation enable multiple perspectives to function as a single, coherent evaluation.

Expert input does not create clarity on its own. It must be aligned.

When alignment is maintained, the claim remains organized, understandable, and defensible—even as complexity grows.

CLAIM LEADERSHIP SUMMARY

Key Takeaway

Complex claims require collaboration among attorneys, engineers, and technical experts. Each brings specialized insight, but clarity depends on how well those inputs are coordinated. The adjuster establishes the structure that integrates these perspectives into a single, coherent claim. When expert input is aligned through clear communication and disciplined documentation, the claim remains understandable, organized, and defensible.

In Practice

Clarify roles early and define how information will be communicated and documented. Record expert findings, track timelines, and link evolving conclusions to the overall evaluation. Provide consistent updates to all stakeholders to ensure alignment. Organized coordination ensures that each contribution supports the claim rather than complicates it.

Questions for Reflection

1. Do I clearly understand and document each expert's role in the claim?
2. Am I linking expert findings to the overall claim narrative?
3. Is my communication consistent across all stakeholders?
4. Would the claim remain clear if multiple expert opinions were reviewed together?

Claim Leadership Principle

Coordination is a leadership function. Clarity is maintained when expert input is integrated through structured communication and disciplined documentation. In complex claims, information alone does not create understanding; alignment does.

PRELUDE

Influence Without Control

Adjusters often lead without formal authority. Multiple stakeholders may be involved in a claim, including policyholders, contractors, attorneys, engineers, and carrier representatives. In this environment, leadership is not defined by position. It is demonstrated through communication, organization, and consistency.

The responsibility for maintaining direction rests with the adjuster.

Leading the claim requires establishing direction and sustaining alignment. Adjusters clarify next steps, manage expectations, and coordinate communication across all participants. This influence allows the claim to progress, even when the adjuster does not control every decision.

Leadership is demonstrated through structure.

Working without authority also requires adaptability. Conversations may shift, priorities may change, and new information may emerge. Adjusters must respond with professionalism and composure, guiding discussions while reinforcing process expectations. This consistency maintains continuity across the claim lifecycle.

Influence is not about control. It is about clarity.

Adjusters who communicate clearly, maintain structure, and reinforce alignment lead effectively in complex environments. When direction is consistent, the claim progresses with greater stability and fewer disruptions.

PART IV

Leadership Inside the Claim

Leadership in claims handling does not begin with authority. It develops through the daily interactions, decisions, and communication that shape a claim's direction. Adjusters work in collaborative environments that include policyholders, contractors, engineers, attorneys, carriers, and other stakeholders. In these situations, the adjuster does not control every participant, yet the claim still requires direction. The responsibility for providing that direction rests with the adjuster.

Leadership emerges from clarity, consistency, and professional presence. Adjusters lead by maintaining structure, guiding communication, and keeping the process moving forward. Complex claims require adjusters to organize information, guide conversations, and maintain alignment as conditions evolve. Disagreements may arise over scope, valuation, timelines, or coverage interpretation. Policyholders may be navigating disruption while seeking certainty, contractors may focus on repair timelines, and technical specialists may evaluate damage from different perspectives. Without structure, these competing viewpoints create confusion.

Clarity stabilizes the claim.

The adjuster's ability to communicate calmly, document findings, and define next steps keeps the claim on track and moving forward. Leadership within the claim also requires disciplined decision-making under pressure. Adjusters work in time-sensitive environments where inspections must be scheduled, information gathered, and decisions communicated efficiently. Access limitations, claim volume, and evolving details require careful evaluation.

Responsiveness must be balanced with accuracy.

Documenting findings, recording limitations, and communicating expectations ensure that decisions remain clear and defensible. Consistent decision-making reduces uncertainty and improves the overall quality of the claim. In many situations, adjusters lead without formal authority. They may not control contractors, engineers, or policyholders' decisions, yet progress depends on coordination among these participants.

Influence replaces control.

Adjusters shape outcomes by coordinating communication, clarifying responsibilities, and aligning expectations. Structured updates, documented next steps, and consistent follow-up sustain momentum. In this environment, leadership is operational. It is demonstrated through organization, communication, and steady direction rather than hierarchy.

Conflict management is another critical component of leadership in claims. Differences in scope, valuation, or repair approach can create tension. Policyholders may become frustrated when timelines extend or information changes. Contractors may advocate for specific repair methods. These dynamics are expected.

Structure prevents escalation.

Adjusters must acknowledge concerns while maintaining professional neutrality. Clear documentation and consistent communication keep discussions grounded in observed conditions and in claim requirements. This approach reduces escalation and supports resolution.

Sustaining performance during extended claims also requires leadership. Catastrophe deployments, large losses, and litigation-prone claims may persist for extended periods. Adjusters must remain organized, track developments, and continue providing updates.

Consistency sustains momentum.

Structured workflows, documented follow-up, and clear communication ensure continuity as conditions change. Leadership in this phase focuses on maintaining clarity over time.

Leadership within the claim is defined by presence and discipline. Adjusters who communicate clearly, document consistently, and guide stakeholders stabilize complex environments. Their influence stems from organization, professionalism, and steady direction.

This section explores how adjusters lead within the claim. The chapters that follow examine leading without authority, managing stakeholder conflict, making decisions under pressure, sustaining performance during extended deployments, and navigating the evolving role of the adjuster.

Leadership within the claim is not separate from claims handling. It is embedded in communication, documentation, and decision-making. Clarity, consistency, and structure define it.

CHAPTER 16

Leading the Claim Without Authority

Event Spotlight — Multi-Carrier Commercial Loss

A large commercial property loss required coordination among multiple carriers, contractors, engineers, and building stakeholders. Each party contributed to the claim, but no single individual controlled all decisions. The adjuster worked in an environment where direction had to be set without formal authority.

The claim involved overlapping inspections, evolving repair estimates, and differing timelines among stakeholders. Contractors sought approval to proceed, engineers required additional evaluation, and carriers required documentation to support decisions. These parallel processes created pressure points where expectations could diverge.

In large-scale losses, similar coordination challenges have been observed in events such as the Surfside condominium collapse, where multiple parties contributed to the investigation, evaluation, and resolution without centralized control. In these environments, alignment—not authority—determines how effectively outcomes are achieved.

In this claim, the risk was not a lack of activity but a lack of alignment. Without coordination, communication could become inconsistent, timelines could conflict, and decisions could stall.

The adjuster's role was to maintain structure by clarifying next steps, documenting progress, and ensuring information flowed consistently across all parties.

Progress depended on how well the process was managed. The adjuster influenced outcomes by coordinating communication, reinforcing timelines, and maintaining continuity in the claim file. Even without authority over each participant, consistent direction allowed the claim to move forward in a structured manner.

Operating without formal authority requires disciplined coordination. Influence is built on reliability, clarity, and consistency. Without structure, multi-party claims fragment. With structure, they align.

CHAPTER FOCUS

Adjusters frequently lead claims without formal authority. In complex, multi-party environments, leadership is shown through structured communication, organized documentation, and consistent direction. Coordination—not control—advances the claim.

Leading the Claim Without Authority

Adjusters are responsible for guiding claims without formal authority over the participants involved. Contractors, policyholders, consultants, engineers, and internal stakeholders all contribute to the process, yet the adjuster does not control their actions. The claim still requires direction.

The responsibility for providing that direction rests with the adjuster.

Leading without authority requires clarity rather than control. Adjusters guide the claim by setting timelines, communicating expectations, documenting developments, and coordinating information. These actions create structure. With structure in place, stakeholders understand how the claim is progressing and what steps are required.

Clarity creates movement.

This form of leadership is practical and process-driven. Adjusters do not rely on positional authority. Instead, they provide structure. The claim progresses because communication is clear, documentation is consistent, and next steps are defined. This approach maintains alignment among participants, even when priorities differ.

Leading without authority is not a secondary skill. It is a defining requirement of modern claims handling. In complex, multi-party environments, progress depends on how effectively direction is established and maintained.

Influence is built through consistency.

The Adjuster as the Central Point of Coordination

Claims often involve multiple participants who contribute information at different stages. Policyholders, contractors, consultants, internal teams, and technical experts each provide input that shapes the claim. Without coordination, communication fragments and timelines become unclear. The adjuster provides the structure that connects these inputs.

Coordinating the claim includes tracking inspections, documenting communications, and clarifying next steps. Recording updates, identifying follow-up actions, and maintaining structured timelines ensure that information remains consistent across all participants. These activities create a clear path forward.

Organization replaces confusion.

The adjuster's coordination does not depend on authority over others. It depends on consistency. When documentation is disciplined and communication is structured, the claim progresses steadily. Stakeholders respond to clarity, not control.

Serving as the central point of coordination is a core function of leading without authority. Through organization, documentation, and consistent communication, the adjuster integrates multiple perspectives into a single, aligned process.

Coordination creates control.

Establishing Structure Early

Leadership in claims handling begins with structure. When adjusters define the process early, stakeholders gain a clear understanding of expectations and direction from the outset.

The responsibility for establishing that structure rests with the adjuster.

Outlining how inspections will be conducted, what documentation is required, and how communication will be managed creates a defined process. Establishing timelines, identifying information needs, and clarifying next steps ensure that participants understand their roles and responsibilities.

Early clarity prevents later confusion.

When expectations are communicated early, stakeholders are better prepared to provide information, coordinate access, and respond to requests. Communication becomes more focused, follow-up actions are more consistent, and the claim progresses with fewer disruptions.

Structure creates efficiency.

Leading without authority begins with organizing the claim. A defined process enables the adjuster to guide activity, maintain alignment, and ensure consistent handling from the start.

Communication as Leadership

Communication is a primary means of leading without authority. Adjusters guide the claim by providing updates, clarifying expectations, and outlining next steps throughout the process. The responsibility for maintaining that communication rests with the adjuster.

Consistent updates help stakeholders understand the progress of the claim. Even when activity is limited, communication shows that the claim remains active and moving forward. Clear explanations of inspections, documentation, and timelines reduce misunderstandings and prevent unnecessary escalation.

Consistency builds alignment.

A professional tone reinforces control. Clear, respectful, and neutral communication sustains constructive interactions, even in challenging conditions. Stakeholders are more likely to respond productively when communication remains structured and process-focused.

Communication provides direction.

When updates are clear and expectations are understood, stakeholders remain aligned. Leadership is demonstrated through clarity, consistency, and the ability to guide the claim without relying on authority.

Managing Multiple Stakeholders

Claims often involve participants with different perspectives and priorities. Contractors may focus on the scope of repairs, policyholders on timelines, and consultants on technical analysis. These competing viewpoints can create complexity if communication is not coordinated.

The responsibility for maintaining alignment rests with the adjuster.

Structured communication brings consistency. Documenting requests, responses, and follow-up actions creates a clear record of how information is shared and applied. These notes help prevent conflicting messages and ensure that all participants share the same understanding.

Clarity reduces friction.

Defining next steps for all participants further supports coordination. Identifying required documentation, inspection schedules, and communication intervals ensures expectations remain clear. When direction is defined, collaboration becomes more efficient, and the claim progresses with fewer disruptions.

Managing multiple stakeholders requires discipline. Organization and consistent communication help the adjuster align perspectives and guide the claim through complexity.

Alignment does not happen automatically. It is created.

Maintaining Momentum

Claims slow when direction is unclear. Delays in communication, missing documentation, or scheduling challenges can stall progress. Maintaining momentum requires consistent direction and clear next steps.

The responsibility for sustaining that momentum rests with the adjuster.

Identifying and documenting follow-up actions keeps the claim moving forward. Recording what is needed, who is responsible, and when updates are expected ensures tasks remain visible and actionable. This structure prevents delays from turning into stagnation.

Momentum is created through clarity.

Regular updates reinforce progress. Even incremental steps—such as scheduling inspections or reviewing documentation—demonstrate that the claim remains active. Stakeholders are more likely to stay engaged when they understand what happens next.

Consistency sustains movement.

Maintaining momentum demonstrates leadership in claims handling. Clear direction, documented follow-up, and structured communication move the claim forward, even when conditions are complex or timelines shift.

Using Financial Decisions to Maintain Claim Direction

Financial decisions shape the course of a claim. Setting reserves, issuing payments, and providing advances are not administrative tasks. They influence expectations, signal progress, and stabilize the claim.

The responsibility for using these decisions to maintain direction rests with the adjuster.

Reserves reflect the current understanding of exposure. They should be updated as information develops to ensure internal alignment and consistent evaluation of the claim. As new findings emerge, reserve adjustments document the claim's evolution.

Accuracy preserves credibility.

Payments and advances directly influence claim momentum. Timely payments reduce uncertainty, support recovery, and signal that the claim is progressing. In complex losses, advances may provide necessary support during evaluation, allowing operations or repairs to proceed.

Movement reduces friction.

These decisions must remain structured and clearly documented. Payments should align with verified findings, reserves should reflect current exposure, and communication should explain what is being issued and why. Consistent, transparent financial decisions reinforce alignment across all stakeholders.

Financial decisions are not separate from claim leadership. They are integral to it.

In environments where adjusters lead without authority, financial decisions are a key mechanism for maintaining direction. Structured documentation, clear communication, and timely updates ensure that these decisions support progress rather than create confusion.

REAL WORLD
Coordinating a Multi-Stakeholder Commercial Claim

An adjuster managed a commercial property claim involving business interruption, structural damage, and multiple vendors. The business owner required clarity on reopening timelines, contractors submitted repair scopes, and financial documentation was needed to assess loss exposure. Each stakeholder had different priorities.

The challenge was not the level of activity. It was aligning competing expectations.

The adjuster established structure early by clarifying roles, defining next steps, and maintaining a consistent communication schedule. Financial decisions were integrated into that structure. Partial payments and updates were aligned with documented findings and clearly communicated to all parties, creating visible progress.

Updates were consistently documented and shared, ensuring stakeholders understood how decisions connected to the overall claim. Contractors proceeded within the defined scope, the policyholder understood the status of recovery, and internal teams maintained alignment on exposure.

By coordinating communication, documenting decisions, and using financial actions to reinforce direction, the adjuster aligned competing priorities. The claim progressed with clarity, reduced delays, and remained organized despite its complexity.

Financial decisions did not just support the claim. They guided it.

Professional Neutrality in Leadership

Leading without authority requires professional neutrality. Adjusters coordinate participants, document information, and guide the claim without favoring any perspective. The responsibility for maintaining that neutrality rests with the adjuster.

Neutrality ensures that the claim proceeds on documented information rather than assumptions. When communication remains objective, stakeholders receive consistent information, and discussions remain focused on the process rather than on competing viewpoints.

Objectivity preserves control.

Communication should remain structured and process-focused. Explaining what has occurred, what information is required, and what steps will follow helps maintain alignment. Avoiding conclusions beyond documented findings reduces misunderstanding and supports consistency across interactions.

Neutral leadership also strengthens coordination. In multi-party environments, consistent, objective communication ensures that information is shared evenly and accurately. This prevents fragmentation and helps maintain a unified direction.

Neutrality is not passive. It is disciplined.

Adjusters who maintain objectivity, structure, and consistency guide complex claims and reinforce professionalism and stability.

Setting Clear Next Steps

Uncertainty arises when next steps are unclear. Stakeholders may not know what is required, when updates will be provided, or how the claim will progress.

The responsibility for providing that direction rests with the adjuster. Defining next steps creates structure. Identifying required documentation, scheduling inspections, and outlining follow-up actions ensures that participants understand expectations and can respond accordingly.

Direction creates movement.

When expectations are clear, coordination becomes more efficient, and the claim progresses with fewer delays. Stakeholders are more likely to act when next steps are defined and consistently communicated. Documenting next steps reinforces continuity. Recording pending actions, responsibilities, and expected updates ensures progress is visible and trackable. These records maintain alignment across interactions.

Clear next steps are not administrative. They are directional.

Handling Disagreements

Disagreements are a normal part of claims handling. Differences in scope, timing, documentation, or interpretation may arise among participants. The adjuster is responsible for managing these situations.

Control is maintained through explanation, not opposition. Describing observations, citing documented information, and outlining next steps keep discussions grounded in the claim. This approach reduces escalation and supports productive dialogue.

Clarity stabilizes conflict.

Documenting disagreements strengthens consistency. Recording discussions, concerns raised, and follow-up actions ensures that issues are tracked and addressed systematically. These records provide continuity and demonstrate how the claim progressed through its complexity.

Professional handling of disagreements demonstrates leadership. Objective communication, disciplined documentation, and clear next steps enable the claim to move forward, even when perspectives differ.

Alignment is maintained by structure.

REAL WORLD
Leading Without Authority in a Multi-Party Claim

An adjuster managed a claim involving independent contractors, third-party vendors, and internal teams, none of whom reported directly to the adjuster. With multiple parties working in parallel, communication risked becoming fragmented and timelines unclear.

The challenge was not activity. It was alignment.

Without formal authority, the adjuster set direction through structure. Next steps were defined, responsibilities were confirmed with each participant, and expectations were reinforced through consistent updates. Key milestones were communicated in advance, and follow-up actions kept progress visible.

This created continuity across all parties.

By maintaining disciplined communication and organization, the adjuster aligned stakeholders and reduced confusion. The claim progressed steadily, demonstrating that leadership is reinforced by reliability, coordination, and consistent execution—even without direct authority.

Direction replaced control.

Using Documentation to Guide the Claim

Documentation is a primary leadership tool in claims handling. Clear records provide continuity and direction, particularly in multi-party environments where information evolves across multiple interactions.

The responsibility for maintaining that record rests with the adjuster.

Recording communications, observations, and next steps ensures that stakeholders understand what has occurred and what will follow. These notes prevent confusion and provide a consistent reference for coordination.

Documentation creates continuity.

Structured records also help manage complexity. Claims involving multiple inspections, participants, and evolving conditions require organized documentation. Clear timelines and recorded updates ensure that the claim's progression remains visible and understandable.

Documentation is not passive. It directs the claim.

Building Confidence Through Consistency

Consistency builds confidence in the claims process. When communication, documentation, and scheduling follow a structured approach, stakeholders understand what to expect and how the claim is progressing.

Consistency builds trust.

Inconsistent handling creates uncertainty. When communication varies, timelines shift without explanation, or documentation is incomplete, stakeholders may question the claim's direction. Structured workflows prevent these disruptions.

Clear communication intervals, documented updates, and organized follow-up actions maintain alignment. Stakeholders are more likely to stay engaged when progress is predictable and visible.

Reliability reinforces leadership. In multi-party environments, progress depends on consistency rather than control. When communication and documentation remain consistent, confidence in the process increases.

Leading Complex Claims

Complex claims require coordination among multiple participants, evolving timelines, and ongoing communication. These conditions define leadership within the claim. The responsibility for maintaining that direction rests with the adjuster.

Structured documentation and consistent communication support this leadership role. Recording inspections, tracking expert involvement, and identifying follow-up actions ensure continuity as the claim develops. Clear updates help stakeholders understand how each step fits into the overall process.

Organization creates alignment.

The adjuster's leadership is evident in how effectively the claim is structured. When communication is consistent and documentation is clear, collaboration becomes more efficient, and the claim remains stable.

Complex claims do not require more control. They require more structure. Through coordination, communication, and disciplined documentation, adjusters guide complex claims with clarity and consistency—even in settings where authority is limited.

The Adjuster as Claim Leader

The modern adjuster leads through alignment, communication, and organization. Formal authority is not required to lead a claim. Direction is set by structure, and progress is sustained by consistency.

The responsibility for that leadership rests with the adjuster.

Coordinating stakeholders, documenting developments, and defining next steps create alignment among all participants. These actions ensure that information remains reliable, follow-up activities are tracked, and the claim progresses in a structured manner.

Organization creates direction.

Leading without authority reflects the evolving role of the adjuster. Claims now involve multiple participants, technical input, and shifting conditions. Adjusters manage this complexity by maintaining consistent communication and disciplined documentation.

Consistency creates control.

In modern claims environments, leadership is defined by how well claims are organized and communicated. Adjusters who establish a clear process guide claims from evaluation through resolution, providing clarity and stability.

Leadership is not a position within the claim. It depends on how the claim is managed.

Practical Claim Leadership Actions

Leading the Claim Without Authority

Adjusters often guide claims in environments where authority is shared among multiple stakeholders. Contractors, policyholders, attorneys, and internal teams all influence the process. In this context, leadership is demonstrated through clarity, organization, and consistent communication rather than formal control.

The responsibility for maintaining direction rests with the adjuster. In shared-authority environments, influence is established through consistency, not position.

CREATE STRUCTURE WITHOUT CONTROL

Leadership begins with organizing the claim and defining direction.

KEY ACTIONS:

Establish the claim process early
Clarify next steps consistently
Identify stakeholder roles
Maintain a defined communication timeline

GO-TO LINES:

"Here is how the claim process will proceed."
"These are the next steps we will be following."
"Roles have been identified across all stakeholders."
"Updates will follow a structured timeline."

GUIDE COMMUNICATION ACROSS STAKEHOLDERS

Multiple voices create risk. Structured communication preserves clarity.

KEY ACTIONS:

Align messaging across all parties
Confirm expectations clearly
Document communication consistently
Provide regular, structured updates

GO-TO LINES:

"I want to ensure all communication remains aligned."
"Expectations have been confirmed across all parties."
"Updates will reflect the current status of the claim."
"We are maintaining consistent communication across stakeholders."

MAINTAIN DIRECTION AS THE CLAIM EVOLVES

Shared authority can cause claims to drift. Direction must be consistently reinforced.

KEY ACTIONS:

Identify next steps after each interaction
Reconfirm timeline expectations
Clarify pending actions
Maintain organized claim notes

GO-TO LINES:

"Based on current information, these are the next steps."
"Timelines are being confirmed as the claim progresses."
"Pending actions have been identified and are being tracked."
"The claim is continuing to move forward as planned."

USE FINANCIAL DECISIONS TO MAINTAIN DIRECTION

Financial decisions influence momentum and reinforce structure.

KEY ACTIONS:

Set reserves based on current documented exposure
Update reserves as information develops
Issue payments aligned with verified findings
Consider advances when appropriate to support recovery
Document reasoning behind financial decisions
Communicate clearly regarding payments and next steps

GO-TO LINES:

"Reserves will be updated as additional information becomes available."

"This payment reflects the portion of the claim that has been evaluated."

"Additional amounts may be considered as the review continues."

"An advance may be issued based on current findings."

"This payment is based on documented conditions at this stage."

"I will provide updates as additional evaluation is completed."

HANDLE MISALIGNMENT EARLY

Differences in expectations, scope, or timelines must be addressed before escalation.

KEY ACTIONS:

Identify conflicting information early
Clarify differences through documentation
Reconfirm expectations across stakeholders
Maintain neutral, process-focused communication

GO-TO LINES:

"There are differences in understanding that we are working to align."
"We are reviewing the information to ensure consistency."
"Expectations will be clarified based on documented findings."
"Next steps will follow once alignment is confirmed."

INFLUENCE THROUGH CONSISTENCY

Consistency builds credibility and strengthens leadership.

KEY ACTIONS:

Provide structured updates
Maintain documentation clarity
Set realistic expectations
Close conversations with direction

GO-TO LINES:

"I will continue to provide structured updates."
"Documentation reflects the current status of the claim."
"Expectations are being set based on current conditions."
"We will proceed with the next steps as outlined."

These practices enable adjusters to lead effectively in shared-authority environments. Structure, communication, and documentation provide direction when control is limited.

Influence is not asserted. It is demonstrated.

When communication is consistent, documentation is clear, and next steps are defined, stakeholders align with the process. The claim progresses not because authority is imposed, but because direction is maintained.

CLAIM LEADERSHIP SUMMARY

Key Takeaway

Adjusters often lead claims without formal authority over all stakeholders. Contractors, engineers, carriers, and policyholders may each influence decisions, creating a shared environment. Direction still must be set. Leadership in this setting is defined by clarity, communication, and consistency rather than by position. When structure is maintained, the claim remains aligned even when control is distributed.

In Practice

Establish structure early, define next steps consistently, and maintain clear communication with all stakeholders. Document updates, track responsibilities, and reinforce timelines to ensure alignment. When communication is structured and documentation is consistent, the claim progresses with direction—even when decisions are shared.

Questions for Reflection

1. How do I maintain direction when authority is shared among stakeholders?
2. Do I consistently define and communicate next steps?
3. Am I using documentation and communication to keep the claim aligned?

Claim Leadership Principle

Leadership without authority is demonstrated by consistency. Direction is maintained when communication, documentation, and next steps remain clear, structured, and aligned across all stakeholders.

CHAPTER 17

Managing Conflict with Policyholders

Event Spotlight — Total Loss Valuation Dispute

After a significant property loss, disagreements arose over valuation, scope, and replacement expectations. Policyholders compared contractor estimates, questioned timelines, and expressed frustration with perceived limitations. The claim required clear communication to move toward resolution.

During large-scale events such as Hurricane Katrina, similar disputes arose as policyholders and carriers differed on valuation, causation, and coverage interpretation. These conditions highlighted how quickly disagreements can escalate when expectations are misaligned and communication is unclear.

Financial exposure varied, but emotional intensity remained high. Policyholders were managing disruption while trying to understand their coverage and valuation. In modern claims environments, perceptions of fairness often shape how policyholders respond to claim decisions. Adjusters must maintain professionalism while navigating disagreement.

The risk is not disagreement but escalation. Conflict is a common part of claims handling. The adjuster's tone, clarity, and consistency determine whether disagreement stabilizes or intensifies. Structured communication helps maintain direction in difficult conversations.

How conflict is managed determines whether the claim advances or becomes adversarial.

CHAPTER FOCUS

Managing conflict requires calm, structured communication and clear explanations. Adjusters must maintain professionalism while guiding toward resolution. Consistent communication reduces escalation and helps maintain alignment throughout the claim.

Maintaining Professional Boundaries in Policyholder Relationships

Policyholder relationships can become more personal during major losses or extended claims. Adjusters often work with individuals and families facing disruption, displacement, and financial uncertainty. Ongoing communication and repeated interactions can create a sense of familiarity.

Empathy is necessary. Boundaries are essential. The responsibility for maintaining them rests with the adjuster. The adjuster's role is to provide clarity, structure, and direction—not to become personally involved in the outcome. When relationships become overly personal, objectivity can weaken, communication can shift, and decisions may become less consistent.

Professional communication must remain structured, respectful, and focused on the claim. Clear explanations, defined next steps, and documented updates maintain alignment without creating dependency or confusion. Empathy supports the interaction, and structure maintains the claim.

Maintaining this balance protects both the policyholder and the adjuster. Decisions remain grounded in evaluation and policy, and communication remains professional and consistent throughout the process.

Managing Conflict with Policyholders

Conflict is a natural part of claims handling. Policyholders may be dealing with damage, disruption, and uncertainty while seeking clarity about outcomes. Differences in scope, timing, or documentation can create tension when expectations are misaligned.

The responsibility for managing that conflict rests with the adjuster.

Most conflict stems from uncertainty. When timelines, evaluation methods, or next steps are unclear, frustration rises. Questions are repeated, expectations shift, and conversations may become more difficult.

Uncertainty fuels escalation.

Managing conflict requires clarity. Adjusters who explain the process, document observations, and consistently communicate next steps help stabilize discussions. Clear, structured communication keeps conversations focused on the claim rather than on personal positions.

Clarity reduces tension.

Tone reinforces control. Neutral, respectful communication supports productive dialogue, even when concerns are raised. Avoiding reactive responses and staying focused on documented information helps guide conversations toward resolution.

Conflict is not avoided. It is managed.

When communication is consistent and expectations are clear, conflict becomes structured rather than disruptive. Adjusters maintain direction by reinforcing the process, documenting discussions, and identifying next steps.

Conflict does not undermine the claim. Unclear communication does.

Understanding the Source of Conflict

Policyholder conflict most often stems from misaligned expectations. A policyholder may expect immediate resolution, a broader scope, or faster timelines than the claim process allows. When these expectations do not align with the requirements of inspections, documentation review, or expert involvement, tension can arise.

The responsibility for recognizing that gap rests with the adjuster.

When expectations are not clarified, assumptions take their place. Policyholders may interpret delays as inaction and limitations as inconsistency. These perceptions increase frustration and can lead to escalation.

Uncertainty creates conflict.

Communication gaps further contribute to the problem. Delayed updates or unclear explanations leave stakeholders without direction. When information is not provided, stakeholders often assume the claim is not progressing. Consistent communication reduces these misunderstandings and reinforces that the claim remains active.

Clarity restores alignment.

Documentation questions also play a role. Policyholders may seek explanations of observations, decisions, or next steps. These conversations require structured responses grounded in documented findings. Clear reasoning keeps discussions focused on the claim and supports consistency.

Understanding the source of conflict enables the adjuster to respond with structure rather than reacting. Clear explanations, documented updates, and consistent communication reduce misunderstandings and advance the claim.

Maintaining Professional Tone

Tone determines how communication is received. In conflict situations, a professional and consistent tone helps sustain constructive conversations, even when frustration is expressed. The responsibility for maintaining that tone rests with the adjuster.

A calm, structured tone keeps discussions focused on the claim rather than on emotion. When communication remains neutral and process-focused, conversations are more likely to be productive. Tone stabilizes interaction.

Avoiding reactive responses prevents escalation. Measured, factual communication keeps the discussion focused on observations, documentation, and next steps. This structure reduces misunderstandings and supports alignment.

A professional tone also reinforces confidence. Stakeholders are more likely to engage constructively when communication is respectful, consistent, and clear. Well-delivered explanations enhance transparency and help maintain direction.

Professionalism is not situational. It is consistent.

Maintaining a disciplined tone supports effective conflict management. Structured communication, calm delivery, and consistent updates guide the claim through difficult conversations, preserving alignment and progress.

Listening to Clarify Concerns

Listening is a critical component of conflict management in claims handling. Policyholders may raise concerns about scope, timing, documentation, or communication. Allowing them to explain their perspective helps identify the source of the misunderstanding and provides context for the discussion.

The responsibility for clarifying those concerns rests with the adjuster.

Listening does not require agreement. It requires understanding. When concerns are acknowledged, and responses are grounded in documented information and include defined next steps, conversations remain focused on the claim.

Understanding creates direction.

Clarifying questions strengthen alignment. Requesting specific details about concerns ensures precise communication and reduces assumptions. This keeps discussions focused on documented conditions and claim progression.

Listening reduces tension and supports productive dialogue. When policyholders feel heard, communication becomes more focused, and the claim remains organized.

Listening is not passive. It is structured.

REAL WORLD
Maintaining Professional Boundaries During an Extended Claim

An adjuster managed a residential fire claim involving structural damage and temporary displacement. Over several weeks, communication intensified as inspections, documentation, and next steps were coordinated.

As the claim progressed, communication began to shift. The policyholder reached out more frequently between scheduled updates, sharing personal frustrations and seeking reassurance beyond claim-related matters. The communication structure began to erode.

The risk was not the volume of communication but the loss of boundaries.

The adjuster maintained professionalism by acknowledging the situation and redirecting communication to the claim process. Updates were provided at defined intervals, discussions remained focused on claim status and next steps, and all communication was consistently documented. Structure was restored.

By maintaining clear boundaries and disciplined communication, the adjuster reduced unnecessary follow-ups and preserved alignment. The claim continued to progress in a structured, professional manner despite the emotional context.

Boundaries protect direction.

Explaining the Claims Process

Many conflicts arise when the claims process is unclear. Policyholders may not understand inspection timelines, documentation requirements, the role of experts, or the sequence of next steps. Without this context, delays or additional evaluation may seem inconsistent or unexpected.

The responsibility for providing that clarity rests with the adjuster.

Structured explanations reduce uncertainty. Outlining what has occurred, what is under review, and what will follow helps stakeholders understand how the claim is progressing.

Clarity prevents escalation.

Explaining the process also manages expectations. When policyholders understand that inspections, documentation review, and expert involvement take time, they are less likely to interpret delays as inactivity. Clear communication reinforces that the claim is moving forward.

Consistent explanations ensure stability.

Explaining the claims process is a core part of conflict management. Structured communication, clear expectations, and defined next steps help guide the claim and maintain alignment throughout the process.

Managing Scope Disagreements

Scope disagreements are common in claims handling. Policyholders may hold different views on damage, repair methods, or the extent of coverage. Without structured communication, these differences can create tension and slow claim progression. The adjuster is responsible for managing these disagreements.

Maintaining focus on documented observations keeps discussions grounded. Explaining inspection findings, identifying the reviewed documentation, and outlining next steps improve understanding and reduce ambiguity. Documentation anchors the discussion and keeps conversations centered on the claim rather than on opinion.

Neutral, process-focused communication preserves professionalism. Avoiding argumentative responses and maintaining a measured tone keeps discussions constructive and reduces the risk of escalation. Precision in communication helps prevent misunderstandings from escalating.

Documenting scope discussions supports continuity. Recording conversations, identifying concerns, and follow-up actions ensure consistency and provide a clear record of how disagreements were addressed. These records demonstrate how the claim progressed through differing perspectives while maintaining alignment.

Managing scope disagreements requires precision, professionalism, and disciplined documentation. When communication remains clear and grounded in documented findings, disagreements become manageable rather than disruptive.

Maintaining Ethical Boundaries in Contractor Interactions

Adjusters must maintain clear ethical boundaries when interacting with policyholders and contractors. Recommending specific contractors or vendors can create conflicts of interest and increase exposure within the claim. The responsibility for maintaining that neutrality rests with the adjuster.

Providing direction without endorsement preserves the integrity of the claim. Adjusters should guide policyholders to general processes, carrier guidelines, or qualification standards without recommending specific service providers. This approach ensures that decisions remain independent and defensible.

Maintaining this boundary protects credibility. When contractor selection is separate from claim evaluation, scope review, and payment decisions, those decisions are less likely to be questioned. Professional boundaries reinforce objectivity and support consistent claim handling.

REAL WORLD
Avoiding Contractor Recommendation Conflicts

During a wind-loss claim, a policyholder asked the adjuster to recommend a contractor to begin repairs quickly. The policyholder expressed urgency and concern about selecting a reliable provider. The risk was not the request itself but the potential loss of neutrality.

The adjuster clarified that recommending specific contractors was outside the scope of the role and could create a conflict of interest in the claim process. Instead, the adjuster explained the repair process, cited carrier guidance, and encouraged the policyholder to select an independently licensed and qualified contractor.

This approach maintained neutrality while still providing direction. The claim was supported by clear documentation, and all scope and estimate evaluations remained independent of contractor selection. By maintaining professional boundaries, the adjuster protected the integrity of the claim and reduced the risk of perceived bias.

Communication During Frustration

Policyholders may become frustrated at various points in the claims process. Delays, uncertainty, scope questions, or complex evaluations can heighten emotions. Communication during these moments is critical. The adjuster is responsible for stabilizing the conversation. A calm, structured response helps maintain focus on claim progression rather than emotion.

Acknowledging concerns demonstrates professionalism. Recognizing that the policyholder is experiencing uncertainty or frustration shows attentiveness without agreeing with conclusions. Clear updates on claim status and next steps help restore alignment and reduce uncertainty. When information is provided consistently, conversations remain constructive.

Calm communication prevents escalation. Structured messaging that focuses on documented observations, timelines, and follow-up actions keeps the discussion grounded in the claim. This approach moves conversations forward and prevents them from becoming reactive.

Communication during frustration demonstrates leadership in action. Clear, consistent responses guide the claim and maintain alignment, even when discussions are difficult.

Setting Clear Boundaries

Effective conflict management requires clear communication boundaries and a defined scope. Adjusters provide explanations, document findings, and communicate next steps, but should avoid making commitments outside the scope of the evaluation. The responsibility for maintaining those boundaries rests with the adjuster.

Avoiding informal assurances helps prevent confusion. Statements implying guaranteed outcomes or timelines can create expectations that do not align with the claim development process. Communication should remain structured, factual, and documented to ensure clarity and consistency.

Professional boundaries keep discussions focused. When communication centers on observations, documentation, and next steps, conversations remain productive and aligned with the claim. This reduces escalation and supports organized handling.

Clear boundaries support effective conflict management. Structured, professional communication maintains alignment and ensures the claim continues to progress with clarity and control.

REAL WORLD
Resolving a Scope Disagreement

An adjuster handled a claim in which the policyholder disagreed with the proposed scope of repairs, creating tension as expectations diverged. The conversation risked escalating without clear guidance.

The adjuster maintained a calm, professional tone and focused on explaining how the scope was developed. This included outlining the evaluation process, citing supporting documentation, and identifying next steps. All discussions were documented to ensure consistency and transparency.

The shift was not in the outcome. It was in the clarity of the explanation.

By reinforcing structured communication and maintaining a steady approach, the adjuster reduced conflict and kept the conversation productive. The claim progressed toward resolution, with a shared understanding of the scope and the process used to reach it.

Clarity restored alignment.

Documenting Conflict Conversations

Documentation is essential for managing conflict. Recording conversations ensures consistency and continuity across multiple interactions. The adjuster is responsible for maintaining that record. Notes should reflect the concerns raised, the information provided, and the next steps identified. This creates a clear reference point and helps ensure that communication remains aligned over time.

Documentation preserves continuity.

When frustration leads to repeated questions or follow-up conversations, clear records help track developments and reinforce prior discussions. These notes ensure consistent communication and make the progression of the claim visible.

Documenting conflict also reinforces professionalism. Recording how concerns were addressed and the actions taken demonstrates structured handling and supports defensibility. Documentation provides direction. Clear, consistent records reduce confusion and guide the claim through challenging discussions while maintaining alignment.

Managing Multi-Party Conflict

Some claims involve multiple participants in the discussion. Contractors, representatives, consultants, and policyholders may each provide input on scope, timing, or documentation. As the number of perspectives grows, communication becomes more complex.

The responsibility for maintaining alignment across these discussions rests with the adjuster.

Disciplined communication provides structure. Clarifying what information has been shared, identifying pending documentation, and outlining next steps keep participants focused on the claim rather than on competing viewpoints. Recording requests and responses ensures that information remains consistent across all parties.

Structure reduces complexity.

A professional tone is critical in multi-party discussions. Neutral, factual communication helps sustain constructive dialogue and prevents conversations from becoming adversarial. When communication remains process-focused, coordination improves.

Managing multi-party conflict requires organization and consistency. Structured communication, documented interactions, and clearly defined next steps help maintain clarity and enable the claim to progress, even in complex environments.

Alignment is maintained through coordination.

Maintaining Objectivity

Objectivity is essential during conflict. Adjusters should focus on documented observations, inspection findings, and claim process steps to keep communication grounded in available information. The responsibility for maintaining objectivity rests with the adjuster.

Avoiding assumptions supports clarity. Communication should reflect what has been observed, what documentation has been reviewed, and what next steps are planned. Keeping conversations factual reduces the likelihood of misunderstanding and helps prevent escalation.

Objectivity also promotes consistency across discussions. When communication remains focused on documented conditions and claim progression, stakeholders better understand the process. This helps maintain alignment and supports resolution.

Maintaining objectivity strengthens conflict management. Neutral, factual communication guides discussions and supports structured claim handling.

De-Escalating Through Structure

Structure is one of the most effective ways to reduce conflict. Clear timelines, documented decisions, and consistent communication provide direction. When stakeholders understand what has happened and what will follow, uncertainty decreases and discussions become more stable.

The responsibility for providing that structure rests with the adjuster.

Providing next steps helps move conversations forward. Identifying required documentation, scheduling inspections, or outlining follow-up actions shifts the focus from disagreement to progress. This approach promotes alignment and reduces tension.

Disciplined communication further supports de-escalation. Keeping discussions focused on claim progression, documented findings, and timelines maintains professionalism and prevents conversations from becoming reactive.

Structure is a key tool for managing conflict. Organized communication, documented updates, and clearly defined next steps guide the claim and support constructive resolution.

Leading Through Difficult Conversations

Managing conflict requires leadership. Adjusters guide difficult conversations by maintaining professionalism, documenting communications, and clarifying next steps. These practices keep discussions focused on the claim rather than on emotion and help sustain forward progress.

Difficult conversations are a normal part of claims handling. Disagreements about scope, timing, documentation, or expectations may arise as the claim progresses. Clear explanations and calm communication help manage these interactions and keep discussions constructive.

Documentation plays a critical role in these situations. Recording concerns raised, information provided, and follow-up actions helps maintain continuity and ensures that future discussions remain consistent. Structured documentation enhances clarity and direction.

The adjuster's leadership is evident in how conflict is handled. A professional tone, objective communication, and clearly defined next steps guide discussions and support resolution. In modern claims environments, conflict is not a disruption to the process; it is part of it. The standard is not to avoid conflict but to manage it with clarity, consistency, and control.

Practical Claim Leadership Actions

Managing Conflict with Policyholders

Conflict may arise when expectations differ, timelines extend, or coverage questions develop. Clear communication, professional tone, and consistent documentation help reduce tension and maintain direction. In conflict situations, how communication is delivered often determines whether the claim stabilizes or escalates. The responsibility for managing that communication rests with the adjuster.

ADDRESS CONCERNS EARLY

Unresolved concerns can escalate quickly. Early communication helps stabilize the claim and reduce uncertainty.

KEY ACTIONS:

Listen to policyholder concerns
Clarify the claim process
Confirm next steps
Reaffirm communication timeline

GO-TO LINES:

"I want to make sure I understand your concerns."
"Let me walk through how the process works."
"Here are the next steps we will be taking."
"I will continue to provide updates as the claim progresses."

MAINTAIN PROFESSIONAL TONE

Emotionally charged conversations require calm, structured responses. Tone often determines whether conflict stabilizes or escalates.

KEY ACTIONS:

Use neutral, respectful language
Focus on facts and process
Avoid defensive responses
Confirm understanding

GO-TO LINES:

"I want to ensure we keep communication clear and respectful."
"This is based on the information available at this time."
"Let's focus on the process and next steps."
"Please let me know if anything needs clarification."

CLARIFY EXPECTATIONS

Misaligned expectations often drive conflict. Clear communication helps reduce misunderstanding and maintain alignment.

KEY ACTIONS:

Explain evaluation steps
Set realistic timelines
Clarify pending reviews
Reconfirm expectations

GO-TO LINES:

"Here is how the evaluation process will proceed."
"Timelines may adjust based on new information."

"This is currently under review."
"I will confirm updates as the process continues."

USE DOCUMENTATION TO SUPPORT CLARITY

Documenting communication helps maintain consistency and defensibility, especially in conflict.

KEY ACTIONS:

Record key conversations
Document expectations discussed
Identify follow-up actions
Track communication timeline

GO-TO LINES:

"This conversation has been documented in the claim file."
"Expectations discussed are reflected in the documentation."
"Next steps have been recorded for follow-up."
"Updates will be documented as the claim progresses."

These practices help adjusters reduce escalations, maintain professionalism, and improve claim clarity. By combining structured communication, consistent updates, and a disciplined professional tone, adjusters guide conversations effectively—even when expectations differ, emotions run high, and conditions continue to evolve. Conflict is not eliminated from the process. It is managed through clarity, consistency, and control.

CLAIM LEADERSHIP SUMMARY

Key Takeaway

Conflict is common in claims handling, especially when valuation, timelines, or coverage expectations differ. Policyholders may be navigating disruption while trying to understand complex information. The adjuster is responsible for keeping these conversations stable. Calm, consistent communication and clear explanations help maintain alignment and keep the claim moving forward. When communication remains structured and professional, conflict is less likely to escalate into a dispute.

In Practice

Listen carefully, acknowledge concerns, and provide clear, structured explanations. Avoid emotional reactions and stay focused on documented information, timelines, and next steps. Consistent communication and a professional tone help reduce escalation, reinforce alignment, and support resolution as the claim progresses.

Questions for Reflection

1. How do I maintain clarity when policyholders disagree with claim decisions?
2. Do I acknowledge their concerns while remaining professionally objective?
3. Am I using consistent, structured communication during difficult conversations?

Claim Leadership Principle

Calm, structured communication helps de-escalate conflict and supports resolution. Clarity is maintained when communication remains consistent, objective, and focused on the claims process.

CHAPTER 18

Decision-Making Under Pressure

Event Spotlight — Catastrophe Deployment with Limited Information

During a large-scale catastrophe deployment, adjusters were assigned multiple claims before all information was available. Access challenges, incomplete reports, and evolving conditions required timely decisions. Prioritization became essential to effectively manage the workload.

During major events such as Hurricane Ian, adjusters worked in high-volume environments where inspections were delayed, access was limited, and initial decisions were made before full documentation was available. These conditions reflect the reality of modern catastrophe response.

Losses from catastrophe events often run into billions, yet individual claim decisions still require careful judgment. Adjusters must determine scope, set expectations, and document findings under time pressure. In high-volume environments, decisions are often made with incomplete information as conditions continue to evolve. Each decision shapes the direction of the claim.

Pressure does not eliminate precision; it demands it. Adjusters must balance speed and accuracy. A defined decision-making approach supports reliability during high-demand deployments. Disciplined decisions ensure that speed does not compromise accuracy or alignment.

CHAPTER FOCUS

Decision-making under pressure requires discipline and structure. Adjusters must carefully evaluate information while maintaining efficiency. Consistent decision-making helps preserve claim quality even in high-demand environments.

Decision-Making Under Pressure

Adjusters routinely make decisions in environments defined by time constraints, incomplete information, and competing priorities. Claims may require immediate attention even as additional documentation is pending. Policyholders often seek answers before all facts are available, and external factors such as weather conditions, access limitations, and workload volume can further complicate the process. These conditions create pressure that directly affects decision-making.

Decision-making under pressure requires clarity and structure. Adjusters must balance speed with accuracy while communicating next steps and documenting the reasoning behind their actions. The ability to make thoughtful, well-supported decisions under these conditions is a defining aspect of modern claims handling. It reflects not only technical knowledge, but also professional discipline.

Pressure does not eliminate the need for consistency. Even in fast-moving environments, disciplined evaluation ensures that decisions remain clear and defensible. Documentation and communication provide stability, allowing decisions to be understood both in the moment and as the claim develops. These practices help guide the claim through uncertainty.

Effective decision-making under pressure is ultimately about maintaining direction. Adjusters who rely on structure and documentation ensure that claims progress with clarity, even as conditions evolve. Pressure does not change the standard—it reveals whether a structured approach is in place to support sound decisions.

The Nature of Time-Sensitive Decisions

Many claims require timely decisions. Emergency mitigation, inspection scheduling, and stakeholder communication often demand immediate attention. Adjusters must evaluate available information, determine appropriate next steps, and communicate direction without unnecessary delay. Timely action helps prevent further damage, supports the policyholder's needs, and keeps the claim moving forward.

Time-sensitive decisions are often made before all details are known. Adjusters may need to act on preliminary observations, initial documentation, or limited field information. In these situations, documenting the decision is especially important. Recording what information was available, what actions were taken, and what follow-up is expected preserves alignment and provides continuity as additional details emerge.

However, timeliness should not be allowed to replace accuracy. A defined evaluation approach helps balance urgency with careful review. Acting promptly while documenting the reasoning allows adjusters to maintain sound judgment under pressure. This approach ensures that early decisions remain understandable, even as new information emerges and the claim evolves.

Understanding the nature of time-sensitive decisions helps adjusters maintain reliability in high-pressure environments. Disciplined documentation, effective communication, and careful evaluation support alignment and ensure that claim activity remains structured, even when rapid response is required.

Working With Incomplete Information

Claims frequently develop in stages. Documentation may be pending, inspections may be scheduled, and expert evaluations may still be in progress. Adjusters are often required to make decisions while additional information is still being gathered. Working with incomplete information requires structure, clarity, and disciplined documentation.

The responsibility for maintaining clarity under these conditions rests with the adjuster.

Explaining that the evaluation is ongoing helps manage expectations. Communicating what is known, what remains pending, and the planned next steps supports transparency. When stakeholders understand that the claim is progressing—even without full information—uncertainty is reduced, and alignment is maintained.

Documenting preliminary decisions is essential. Recording the observations available at the time, the actions taken, and the expected follow-up creates a clear record of how the claim is developing. As additional information is received, these records demonstrate continuity and support consistent decision-making.

Working with incomplete information does not prevent progress. It requires structure. Adjusters who communicate clearly, document consistently, and define next steps ensure that the claim remains organized as conditions evolve.

Balancing Speed and Accuracy

Pressure introduces urgency into claims handling. Policyholders may request immediate responses, mitigation may require quick decisions, and inspections may need to be scheduled without delay. At the same time, decisions must remain accurate and supported by available information. Balancing speed and accuracy is essential for professional claims handling.

The responsibility for maintaining that balance rests with the adjuster.

Structured workflows support consistent decision-making under pressure. Documenting observations, identifying next steps, and communicating timelines allow adjusters to move forward without sacrificing clarity. When actions are recorded and communication remains consistent, progress can occur while evaluation continues.

Rushed decisions without documentation can create confusion later in the claim. Delayed decisions without communication can create frustration and uncertainty. Both introduce risk. Structured handling reduces this risk by ensuring that decisions are both timely and explainable.

Balancing speed and accuracy is not a trade-off. It is a disciplined approach. Clear documentation, structured communication, and thoughtful prioritization ensure that decisions made under pressure remain organized, defensible, and aligned with the progression of the claim.

Auto Claims

In auto claims, supplements commonly arise during the repair process when additional damage is discovered after teardown or further inspection. Initial estimates may not capture all underlying issues, especially in complex or impact-related losses. As repair facilities identify additional damage, revised estimates must be evaluated and aligned with prior documentation.

The responsibility for maintaining consistency during this process rests with the adjuster.

Adjusters must carefully review supplements to ensure that additional items are supported by documented findings and consistent with the loss. Clear communication with repair facilities and policyholders helps manage expectations and prevent delays. As information develops, decisions must remain aligned with prior documentation while adapting to new findings.

Supplement handling reflects decision-making under pressure. It requires balancing speed, accuracy, and consistency as conditions evolve.

Supplements test consistency. Leadership ensures alignment across every stage of the claim.

Prioritization During High Workload

High claim volume increases pressure on adjusters. Managing multiple files simultaneously requires disciplined prioritization to maintain clarity and organization. Without structure, important follow-up actions may be delayed, and communication may become inconsistent.

The responsibility for prioritization rests with the adjuster.

Identifying which claims require immediate attention guides decision-making. Safety concerns, access limitations, ongoing damage, and time-sensitive mitigation often determine urgency. Establishing consistent prioritization criteria ensures that decisions remain structured and defensible, even in high-volume environments.

Documenting priorities strengthens organization. Recording which claims require follow-up, which inspections are pending, and which updates are needed helps effectively track the workload. These records reduce the need for repeated evaluations and ensure tasks are addressed in a logical sequence.

Prioritization is not reactive. It is structured.

Clear prioritization, documented follow-up actions, and consistent communication enable adjusters to manage their workload effectively while maintaining claim quality.

Communication During Rapid Decisions

Communication becomes critical when decisions must be made quickly. Stakeholders benefit from understanding what actions are being taken and what will follow. Even brief updates help maintain alignment and reduce uncertainty in time-sensitive situations.

The responsibility for maintaining that communication rests with the adjuster.

Providing concise, structured updates helps manage expectations. Explaining that the evaluation is ongoing, that additional information may be pending, or that follow-up actions are scheduled supports transparency. This approach enables adjusters to act promptly while keeping stakeholders informed and aligned.

Disciplined communication reinforces professionalism under pressure.

Documenting communication further improves clarity. Recording updates, identifying next steps, and noting pending information ensure that claim development remains consistent and understandable. These records support continuity across conversations and decisions.

Communication supports decision-making under pressure. Clear updates, documented interactions, and consistent messaging guide the claim through fast-moving conditions while maintaining structure and alignment.

Avoiding Reactive Decisions

Pressure can lead to reactive responses. Adjusters may feel compelled to provide immediate answers without fully documenting observations or considering next steps. While responsiveness is important, reactive decisions can create confusion and inconsistency when they lack structure.

The responsibility for maintaining control under pressure rests with the adjuster.

Disciplined decision-making helps prevent reactive responses. Taking a moment to document observations, identify available information, and outline next steps promotes clarity. This brief pause helps keep decisions organized while still addressing urgency. Structure reduces the likelihood of error.

Professional judgment is strengthened by documentation and consistency. Decisions based on recorded information are easier to explain, track, and refine as the claim evolves. Organized handling ensures that communication remains aligned with documented findings.

Avoiding reactive decisions strengthens performance under pressure. Thoughtful evaluation and disciplined communication enable consistent, defensible claim handling.

REAL WORLD
Rapid Decision-Making in a Farm Claim

An adjuster handled an agricultural claim involving crop damage and equipment loss after a severe weather event. Conditions were time-sensitive, with the risk of additional loss if action was delayed. Access to complete information was limited, and field conditions continued to change as the situation evolved.

The adjuster documented site conditions immediately and prioritized actions to stabilize the loss. Initial actions were based on observable damage and available information, with clear communication outlining what was known, what remained under review, and what steps would follow. Early decisions were made to protect the claim while allowing further evaluation as conditions evolved.

As additional information became available, the adjuster updated the documentation, refined the scope, and confirmed next steps with all parties involved. Each decision was documented with supporting observations to maintain clarity and continuity.

By applying disciplined decision-making, the adjuster balanced urgency and accuracy. This approach allowed the claim to move forward efficiently, reduced the risk of additional loss, and maintained a clear, defensible record. Structured decisions ensured that speed supported the claim rather than compromising it.

Documenting Decision Reasoning

Documentation plays a critical role in high-pressure environments. Recording how decisions are made supports transparency and continuity, especially when timelines are compressed. Clear notes ensure that actions remain understandable both in the moment and as the claim progresses.

The responsibility for documenting that reasoning rests with the adjuster.

Notes should document observations, information considered, and identified next steps. Recording what was known at the time, along with planned follow-up actions, helps track claim progression and supports continuity as additional information becomes available.

Documenting reasoning also strengthens confidence. Adjusters can rely on recorded information when revisiting decisions or providing updates, thereby reducing uncertainty and supporting consistent communication.

Documentation reinforces disciplined decision-making. Clear records, structured notes, and well-defined reasoning help guide the claim through time-sensitive situations while maintaining alignment and control.

Managing Changing Conditions

Claims handled under pressure often involve evolving conditions. Additional damage may become visible, inspections may be rescheduled, and communication may broaden as new participants join. Adjusters must adapt to these changes while maintaining clarity and continuity. Structured handling ensures that updates remain organized throughout the claim.

The responsibility for maintaining continuity through change rests with the adjuster.

Recording changes is essential for tracking claim development. Documenting updated observations, revised timelines, and new follow-up actions provides a clear progression of events. These records ensure that changes are understood and that prior decisions remain linked to new information. This continuity supports alignment throughout the claim lifecycle.

Communicating changes maintains alignment among all stakeholders. Explaining why updates were made and what the next steps will be reduces uncertainty and keeps discussions focused on claim progression. Clear, structured communication reinforces professionalism and supports consistency.

Managing changing conditions requires flexibility supported by organization. Documentation, communication, and clearly defined follow-up actions help ensure that the claim remains aligned as conditions evolve.

Maintaining Professional Judgment

Pressure can undermine confidence in decision-making. Adjusters may revisit earlier conclusions or question whether additional evaluation is needed as new information emerges. Maintaining professional judgment requires disciplined evaluation, structured documentation, and a defined decision-making approach.

The responsibility for maintaining that judgment rests with the adjuster.

Documenting reasoning reinforces confidence. Recording observations, information considered, and next steps provides a clear reference for future review. These records ensure that decisions remain understandable, even as conditions change, and help maintain continuity throughout the claim.

Disciplined evaluation strengthens judgment. Systematically reviewing available information, identifying pending items, and documenting updates ensures decisions remain consistent. This approach prevents reactive decision-making and keeps the evaluation grounded in documented conditions.

Professional judgment is sustained by structure. Clear documentation, consistent communication, and disciplined evaluation enable adjusters to maintain confidence and reliability under pressure.

Decision-Making in Multi-Party Claims

Claims involving multiple stakeholders often heighten decision pressure. Contractors, policyholders, consultants, and internal teams may request guidance simultaneously. Without structure, communication can become fragmented, and decisions may lose alignment. Adjusters must coordinate these interactions to maintain organization and clarity.

The responsibility for maintaining alignment among participants rests with the adjuster.

Recording requests and responses supports consistency. Documenting who requested information, which decisions were required, and which next steps were identified helps track claim progression. These records reduce confusion and ensure consistent communication across all parties.

Prioritizing decisions by urgency improves clarity. Safety concerns, mitigation needs, and time-sensitive inspections often require immediate attention. Documenting priorities and follow-up actions ensures decisions remain organized and that critical tasks are addressed without delay.

Managing multi-party decisions requires discipline and structure. Clear communication, documented reasoning, and defined next steps enable adjusters to guide complex claims while maintaining alignment and direction.

Leading Through Pressure

Decision-making under pressure requires leadership. Adjusters guide claims by maintaining structure, documenting their reasoning, and communicating clear next steps. These practices keep discussions focused and ensure the claim continues to progress, even when conditions are uncertain. Leadership under pressure is defined by clarity, consistency, and control.

The responsibility for maintaining that clarity rests with the adjuster.

Clear documentation shows how decisions were made and how the claim has progressed. Recording observations, timeline changes, and follow-up actions creates transparency and supports continuity. These records ensure that decisions remain understandable as new information is introduced.

Consistent communication reinforces direction. Providing updates, explaining changes, and confirming next steps help ensure that stakeholders remain aligned throughout the claim. When communication remains structured, confusion is reduced, and coordination improves.

Pressure is a constant in modern claims handling. High volume, evolving conditions, and multi-party involvement require adjusters to make timely decisions while staying organized. Disciplined decision-making helps adjusters manage this environment without losing clarity or professionalism.

The adjuster's leadership is evident in how decisions are made under pressure. Structure, documentation, and communication work together to maintain direction and support claim progression.

Pressure does not determine the outcome. Leadership does.

Practical Claim Leadership Actions

Decision-Making Under Pressure

Adjusters frequently make decisions with evolving information, compressed timelines, and multiple stakeholders. In these conditions, a defined decision-making approach is essential to maintain alignment and reliability. Pressure does not remove the need for discipline; it increases the need for it. A structured process ensures that decisions remain sound, even when information is incomplete.

EVALUATE BEFORE DECIDING

Pressure can lead to rushed conclusions. A deliberate evaluation process strengthens understanding and supports sound judgment.

KEY ACTIONS:

Review available information
Identify unknown factors
Consider next steps carefully
Document decision reasoning

GO-TO LINES:

"This decision is based on the information currently available."
"There are still factors under review."
"We are evaluating the next steps carefully."
"All findings are being documented as part of the evaluation."

COMMUNICATE DECISIONS CLEARLY

Clear communication prevents misunderstanding and reduces escalation. Decisions must be explained in a way that maintains alignment across all stakeholders.

KEY ACTIONS:

Explain the basis for decisions
Clarify next steps
Confirm stakeholder understanding
Document communication

GO-TO LINES:

"Here is how this decision was determined."
"These are the next steps moving forward."
"Please let me know if any clarification is needed."
"This communication has been documented for consistency."

MAINTAIN FLEXIBILITY AS INFORMATION EVOLVES

Decisions made under pressure may require adjustment as new information becomes available. Flexibility ensures that the claim remains aligned as conditions change.

KEY ACTIONS:

Identify pending evaluations
Revisit decisions when necessary
Communicate updates promptly
Document changes clearly

GO-TO LINES:

"This decision may be updated as additional information becomes available."

"We are continuing to review as conditions evolve."

"Updates will be provided as soon as they are confirmed."

"Changes have been documented to reflect new findings."

USE STRUCTURE TO MANAGE PRESSURE

Organization reduces decision fatigue and supports consistency. Structured handling allows adjusters to manage high workloads without losing clarity.

KEY ACTIONS:

Track claim status clearly
Identify pending actions
Maintain organized documentation
Set realistic timelines

GO-TO LINES:

"The claim status is being tracked to maintain clarity."

"Pending actions have been identified and documented."

"Documentation reflects the current stage of the claim."

"Timelines are being managed based on current conditions."

These practices help adjusters make sound decisions while maintaining professionalism under pressure. By combining structured evaluation, clear communication, and disciplined documentation, adjusters ensure that decisions remain consistent, defensible, and aligned—even when timelines are compressed, and information continues to develop.

Decision-making under pressure is not defined solely by speed.

It is defined by structure.

CLAIM LEADERSHIP SUMMARY

Key Takeaway

Decision-making under pressure is a constant in catastrophe and high-volume claims environments. Limited information, compressed timelines, and workload demands require adjusters to balance speed with accuracy. In these conditions, disciplined thinking and a defined evaluation approach provide stability. When decisions follow a structured process, alignment is maintained—even when information is incomplete, and conditions continue to evolve.

In Practice

Prioritize available information, document observations clearly, and avoid rushed conclusions. Confirm key details when possible and communicate expectations with precision. A structured approach ensures that decisions remain consistent, understandable, and aligned—even when made quickly.

Questions for Reflection

1. How do I prioritize decisions when information is limited?
2. Do I document my reasoning when working under time pressure?
3. Am I maintaining consistency while balancing efficiency and accuracy?

Claim Leadership Principle

A disciplined decision-making approach preserves alignment under pressure. Clarity is sustained when evaluation, communication, and documentation remain consistent—even in high-demand environments.

CHAPTER 19

Sustaining the Adjuster: Resilience in High-Stakes Claims

Event Spotlight — Extended Catastrophe Deployment

During extended catastrophe deployments, adjusters often work long days across multiple claims. Travel demands, emotionally intense conversations, and sustained claim volume create continuous pressure on performance. Over time, fatigue can impair communication, documentation, and decision-making.

Large-scale catastrophes may persist for weeks or months. Adjusters manage repeated inspections, evolving claim discussions, and ongoing administrative requirements while remaining responsive across multiple files. In these environments, performance is not measured by initial response alone—it is measured by the ability to remain consistent over time. As workload and duration increase, maintaining that consistency becomes more challenging.

The responsibility for sustaining performance rests with the adjuster.

Resilience in this context is operational. It is demonstrated by the ability to manage energy, maintain focus, and preserve communication precision over extended periods. A steady, disciplined presence supports claim quality and reinforces professional leadership throughout the deployment.

Sustained performance under pressure depends on maintaining alignment over time. When communication remains consistent, documentation remains organized, and decisions remain disciplined, the claim continues to progress—even as fatigue sets in.

CHAPTER FOCUS

Resilience supports reliable claims handling. Adjusters who manage fatigue effectively maintain alignment, clear communication, and professional consistency. Sustained performance depends on maintaining focus, structure, and reliability under extended demand.

Sustaining the Adjuster: Resilience in High-Stakes Claims

Claims handling is demanding work. Adjusters routinely manage heavy workloads, complex losses, time-sensitive decisions, and emotionally charged conversations. Catastrophic events, litigation-aware claims, and multi-party environments further intensify these demands. Over time, sustained pressure can impair focus, decision-making, and overall performance. Maintaining resilience is therefore essential to long-term effectiveness.

Resilience in claims handling is not about eliminating pressure. The work itself is inherently urgent, uncertain, and high-stakes. Instead, resilience is demonstrated by maintaining clarity, professionalism, and consistency during demanding periods. Adjusters who rely on structure and organization are better positioned to sustain performance and guide claims effectively.

The responsibility for sustaining that performance rests with the adjuster.

The modern adjusting environment demands endurance. High-volume assignments, travel demands, and continuous communication create cognitive and emotional strain. Adjusters must balance responsiveness with sustained focus. Disciplined workflows, structured documentation, and consistent communication practices help reduce this strain and maintain control.

Sustaining the adjuster is not separate from claims handling—it is integral to it. Maintaining resilience supports clarity, decision-making, and consistent claim leadership. Resilience does not reduce pressure; it ensures that pressure does not undermine performance.

The Demands of High-Stakes Claims

High-stakes claims often involve significant losses, multiple stakeholders, and time-sensitive decisions. These conditions increase the adjuster's level of responsibility. Accurate documentation, clear communication, and structured evaluation must occur simultaneously, requiring sustained focus over extended periods.

Catastrophe events amplify these demands. Adjusters may manage numerous claims while coordinating travel, inspections, and communication across wide geographic areas. The pace of work often remains elevated for extended periods, with limited downtime between decisions. In these environments, organization is not optional; it is essential.

Emotional demands are also present in high-stakes claims. Policyholders may be experiencing disruption, displacement, or financial uncertainty. Conversations may involve frustration, urgency, or concern. Adjusters must maintain professionalism while guiding these discussions, which requires composure and disciplined communication.

Recognizing these demands supports resilience. When adjusters maintain structure, document consistently, and communicate clearly, they are better able to sustain performance under pressure. Organization, clarity, and consistency help the claim progress even in high-demand environments.

Cognitive Load and Decision Fatigue

Sustained decision-making increases cognitive load. Adjusters make ongoing judgments about prioritization, communication, inspections, and evaluation. Over time, this mental demand can lead to decision fatigue, especially in high-volume, time-sensitive environments. Recognizing this effect is essential to maintaining clarity during prolonged claim activity.

The responsibility for managing cognitive load rests with the adjuster.

Decision fatigue may present as difficulty prioritizing tasks, delayed responses, or reduced detail in documentation. Adjusters may revisit decisions repeatedly or experience uncertainty when identifying next steps. These responses are natural under sustained workloads, but without structure, they can undermine consistency and overall performance.

Disciplined workflows reduce cognitive strain. Consistent documentation routines, prioritized follow-up actions, and defined communication intervals reduce the need for repeated decisions. This structure allows adjusters to focus on evaluation rather than reorganization, preserving clarity across multiple claims.

Managing cognitive load is a key component of resilience. Structured workflows, consistent documentation, and disciplined communication help sustain performance during extended periods of continuous decision-making.

Maintaining Organization Under Pressure

Organization is a core component of resilience in high-stakes claims. When claim files are clearly structured, adjusters can transition between claims efficiently without losing context. Clear documentation provides a reference point, enabling adjusters to understand status, pending items, and next steps without re-evaluating the entire file. This reduces cognitive strain and supports continuity.

The responsibility for maintaining that organization rests with the adjuster.

Tracking next steps improves consistency. Recording pending inspections, documentation requests, and follow-up communications keeps actions visible and organized. When tasks are documented, adjusters can move between claims while maintaining clarity and direction.

This approach reduces the risk of missed actions and supports reliable handling.

Structured grouping further improves efficiency. Organizing claims by location, severity, or status—such as inspection routes, pending documentation, or priority level—streamlines workflow. This allows adjusters to focus more on evaluation and less on reorientation.

Maintaining organization supports sustained performance under pressure. Clear documentation, tracked follow-ups, and structured workflows strengthen resilience and ensure consistent claim handling, even in high-volume environments.

Communication Boundaries and Focus

Communication demands often rise during high-stakes claims. Policyholders, contractors, internal teams, and experts may request updates simultaneously. Without structure, constant communication can interrupt evaluation, fragment attention, and reduce efficiency. Establishing communication boundaries is essential to maintaining focus and sustaining performance.

The responsibility for maintaining those boundaries rests with the adjuster.

Establishing clear communication routines supports alignment while preserving work time. Providing updates at regular intervals—rather than responding reactively—helps manage expectations. Stakeholders remain informed, and adjusters maintain dedicated time for inspections, evaluation, and documentation. This balance promotes clarity and reduces disruption.

Documenting communication further improves efficiency. Recording updates, next steps, and timelines ensures information remains consistent across interactions. Clear notes allow adjusters to reference prior discussions and reduce duplicate inquiries. This continuity supports both organization and responsiveness.

Managing communication boundaries is a key component of resilience. Structured communication, documented updates, and scheduled responses help adjusters sustain focus and maintain performance during high-demand periods.

Professional Detachment and Objectivity

Adjusters must maintain professionalism in emotionally charged situations. Policyholders may express frustration, urgency, or concern, especially during high-stakes claims. Maintaining calm, objective communication helps stabilize interactions and keeps discussions focused on claim progression. Professional composure promotes clarity.

The responsibility for maintaining that objectivity rests with the adjuster.

Professional detachment does not mean a lack of empathy. It means staying focused on documented observations, timelines, and next steps while acknowledging stakeholder concerns. This approach helps adjusters remain supportive without losing objectivity. Clear, structured communication guides conversations constructively.

Objectivity also supports consistent decision-making. Documenting observations, identifying available information, and recording the reasoning behind decisions ensure that conclusions remain grounded in the claim. Clear documentation reduces uncertainty and reinforces professional judgment over time.

Professional detachment supports sustained performance. Calm communication, objective evaluation, and disciplined documentation help adjusters remain consistent and effective, even in demanding claims environments.

Managing Workload Over Time

High-stakes claims often span weeks or months. Sustaining performance during long-duration assignments requires disciplined workload management. Without structure, repeated evaluations, fragmented communication, and missed follow-ups can undermine consistency. Organized workflows support continuity as claims evolve and enable adjusters to maintain control over extended periods.

The responsibility for managing workload over time rests with the adjuster.

Recording progress preserves alignment. Documenting inspections, communications, and next steps keeps claim development clear and organized. These records enable adjusters to transition between files efficiently without re-evaluating previously reviewed information, reducing cognitive strain and supporting continuity.

Prioritization strengthens workload management. Identifying urgent tasks, pending follow-ups, and scheduled inspections guides daily decision-making. A defined prioritization approach keeps critical actions visible and ensures sustained progress across multiple claims.

Managing workload over time is a key component of resilience. Disciplined documentation, structured workflows, and intentional prioritization help adjusters maintain alignment and consistency during extended claim activity.

REAL WORLD
Maintaining Performance During Extended Catastrophe Deployment

An adjuster worked an extended catastrophe deployment marked by sustained high claim volume, long hours, and limited downtime. As the deployment continued, fatigue became a significant risk—not only to personal capacity but also to consistency in communication, documentation, and decision-making.

Recognizing this early, the adjuster established structured routines to sustain performance. Defined start and end times, protected rest periods, and a consistent daily schedule became part of the operational approach. Rather than working continuously without structure, the adjuster created a repeatable rhythm that supported energy, focus, and decision quality over multiple days.

Structured workflows reinforced this approach. Daily responsibilities were organized into clear priorities, with repeatable processes for inspections, documentation, and follow-ups. Communication was scheduled at defined intervals, reducing constant interruptions and allowing focused evaluation and task completion.

Disciplined documentation practices further supported performance. Notes, decisions, and next steps were consistently recorded, reducing rework and enabling efficient task transitions—even under sustained pressure.

By combining structured workflows with intentional routines, the adjuster sustained performance over time. This approach shows that in catastrophe environments, effective claims handling is not sustained by effort alone. It is sustained through organization, clarity, and the ability to manage energy while maintaining professional consistency.

Recognizing Signs of Strain

Adjusters may experience strain during high-volume assignments or extended catastrophe deployments. As workload increases, difficulty prioritizing tasks, delayed responses, or reduced focus may emerge. If not addressed, these shifts can affect communication, documentation, and decision-making. Recognizing these early signs allows adjusters to respond proactively and restore structure.

The responsibility for managing performance under strain rests with the adjuster.

Reorganizing claims takes time but restores clarity. Reviewing documentation, confirming next steps, and updating priorities reestablish direction. This brief reset reduces cognitive overload and supports consistent handling across multiple files.

Consistent routines further reduce strain. Structured approaches to documentation and communication reduce redundant decision-making and improve efficiency. When workflows are organized, adjusters can manage multiple claims without losing focus or continuity.

Recognizing strain is not a weakness; it is a signal to bring structure. Awareness, disciplined planning, and organized workflows help sustain performance during high-demand assignments.

Documentation as a Support Tool

Documentation not only protects the claim—it also supports the adjuster. Clear, organized notes help adjusters transition between claims without losing context. Recorded observations, timelines, and next steps reduce the need for repeated evaluation and help manage cognitive load.

The responsibility for maintaining that documentation rests with the adjuster.

Recording next steps preserves direction. Documenting follow-up actions ensures that pending tasks remain visible and organized. This clarity supports momentum across multiple files and reduces the risk of missed actions.

Documentation also strengthens continuity over time. When claims span days or weeks, clear records allow adjusters to revisit files and quickly understand a claim's status. This reduces confusion and supports consistent coordination with stakeholders.

Using documentation as a support tool reinforces resilience. Organized records, tracked follow-ups, and structured communication enable adjusters to sustain performance while maintaining clarity and control during high-stakes claims.

Maintaining Professional Consistency

Consistency supports resilience in high-stakes claims. When workflows remain structured, adjusters reduce cognitive strain and maintain clarity across multiple files. Predictable routines for documentation, communication, and prioritization help prevent confusion and support organized claim handling.

The responsibility for maintaining that consistency rests with the adjuster.

Consistent documentation and communication routines improve efficiency. When adjusters follow reliable processes for recording observations, identifying next steps, and providing updates, fewer decisions need to be revisited. This disciplined approach allows adjusters to focus on evaluation rather than reorganization.

Professional consistency also reinforces confidence. Clear, organized records serve as a dependable reference when revisiting claims. Adjusters can rely on documented information to guide decisions and communication, reducing uncertainty and supporting consistent performance.

Consistency sustains performance over time. Disciplined workflows, documented updates, and predictable communication help adjusters maintain clarity and control throughout extended assignments.

The Importance of Structured Breaks in Workflow

Resilience also depends on pacing. Continuous high-pressure work can reduce focus, increase cognitive fatigue, and impair decision quality. Incorporating structured breaks into the workflow helps adjusters reset, reorganize, and maintain clarity.

The responsibility for maintaining that pacing rests with the adjuster.

Using these intervals to review priorities, organize documentation, and confirm next steps helps restore direction. Even brief resets ensure that claims remain organized and pending tasks are clearly identified, reducing the risk of oversight.

Disciplined pacing does not slow progress; it protects it. Structured pauses promote consistency by helping adjusters maintain organization and clarity throughout the assignment. Regular workflow resets sharpen focus and reinforce sound decision-making.

Resilience includes maintaining structure over time. Planned pauses for organization and prioritization help sustain performance in demanding claims environments.

Sustaining Performance in Catastrophe Environments

Catastrophe assignments require sustained focus over extended periods. High claim volume, travel demands, and increased communication create constant pressure. In these environments, performance depends on the adjuster's ability to maintain organization and structure across multiple claims.

The responsibility for sustaining that performance rests with the adjuster.

Structured workflows help manage this demand. Grouping inspections by location, consistently documenting communications, and tracking next steps reduces cognitive load and improves efficiency. These practices enable adjusters to transition between claims without losing context, supporting continuity throughout the assignment.

Consistency in workflow also strengthens communication. When updates follow predictable patterns and documentation remains organized, stakeholders stay aligned. This reduces repeated inquiries and supports steady claim progression.

Sustaining performance in catastrophe environments requires disciplined handling. Structured documentation, organized scheduling, and consistent communication enable adjusters to manage high claim volume while maintaining clarity and control.

The Resilient Adjuster

Resilience in claims handling is built on organization, alignment, and discipline. Adjusters who maintain reliable workflows, document decisions clearly, and manage communication consistently can sustain performance over time. These practices reinforce professionalism in high-pressure environments.

The resilient adjuster recognizes the demands of high-stakes claims and responds with structure rather than reacting. Disciplined documentation, organized prioritization, and consistent communication maintain alignment even during extended assignments. This approach supports steady claim progression amid changing conditions.

Sustaining adjusters is essential to effective claims leadership. When adjusters maintain resilience, they coordinate stakeholders more effectively, manage workload demands more consistently, and guide claims forward with clarity. Organizational discipline strengthens both performance and professional credibility in demanding claims environments.

Practical Claim Leadership Actions

Sustaining the Adjuster: Resilience in High-Stakes Claims

High-stakes claims require sustained focus, clear communication, and disciplined decision-making over time. Extended deployments, emotionally charged conversations, and heavy workloads can undermine performance if not managed with structure. In these environments, resilience is operational. Organization, consistency, and disciplined habits protect both performance and alignment throughout extended assignments.

MAINTAIN STRUCTURED WORKFLOW

Organization reduces cognitive strain and supports consistent performance across multiple claims.

KEY ACTIONS:

Track claim status clearly
Document next steps consistently
Prioritize time-sensitive claims
Maintain organized file notes

GO-TO LINES:

"The claim status is being tracked to maintain clarity."
"Next steps have been documented for consistency."
"Priority actions have been identified and are being addressed."
"Documentation reflects the current stage of each claim."

MANAGE COMMUNICATION LOAD

High communication volume can disrupt focus and reduce efficiency. Structured communication maintains clarity and pacing.

KEY ACTIONS:

Schedule updates when possible
Confirm next steps during each interaction
Document key conversations
Avoid reactive communication

GO-TO LINES:

"Updates will be provided on a structured schedule."
"Here are the next steps based on our discussion."
"Key points from this conversation have been documented."
"Communication will remain structured as the claim progresses."

RECOGNIZE SIGNS OF DECISION FATIGUE

Sustained pressure can affect judgment. Awareness supports clarity and consistency.

KEY ACTIONS:

Review decisions before finalizing
Revisit complex conclusions
Document reasoning clearly
Confirm next steps deliberately

GO-TO LINES:

"This decision has been reviewed for accuracy."
"Additional review is being completed before finalizing."

"Reasoning has been documented to support this decision."
"Next steps have been confirmed following review."

SET REALISTIC WORKLOAD EXPECTATIONS

Managing expectations supports both sustainability and consistent performance.

KEY ACTIONS:

Communicate timelines realistically
Prioritize complex claims
Identify pending actions clearly
Maintain structured workflow

GO-TO LINES:

"Timelines are being set based on current workload and conditions."
"Priority claims are being addressed first."
"Pending actions have been identified and scheduled."
"The workflow is being managed to maintain consistency."

MAINTAIN PROFESSIONAL CONSISTENCY

Consistency stabilizes both the adjuster and the claims process over time.

KEY ACTIONS:

Provide predictable updates
Maintain documentation clarity
Communicate calmly under pressure
Close conversations with direction

GO-TO LINES:

"Updates will continue on a consistent basis."
"Documentation reflects the current claim status."
"Communication will remain clear and focused."
"Next steps have been outlined for continuity."

These practices help adjusters maintain clarity, professionalism, and performance in high-stakes claims environments. By maintaining structured workflows, consistent communication, and disciplined decision-making, adjusters protect both claim quality and personal effectiveness—even during prolonged periods of pressure and demand.

Resilience is not sustained by effort alone.

It is sustained by structure.

CLAIM LEADERSHIP SUMMARY

Key Takeaway

Sustained claim volume, travel demands, and emotionally charged conversations create ongoing pressure for adjusters. Over time, fatigue can impair communication, documentation, and decision-making. Maintaining resilience helps preserve alignment and reliability during extended deployments. When performance is sustained through structure and consistency, focus and clarity remain steady.

In Practice

Manage workload by pacing decisions, keeping documentation organized, and allowing time to confirm key details. Use brief resets to reorganize priorities and maintain focus between complex conversations. Disciplined routines support consistency and alignment throughout extended claim activity.

Questions for Reflection

1. Do I recognize when fatigue begins to affect my communication or decision-making?
2. What routines help me maintain consistency during extended deployments?
3. How do I reset to maintain clarity when dealing with demanding claims or conversations?

Claim Leadership Principle

Sustained resilience supports consistent leadership in claims. Clarity is maintained when structure, communication, and decision-making remain disciplined over time.

CHAPTER 20

The Future of Adjusting: Professional Leadership in Complex Claims

Event Spotlight — Increasing Claim Complexity Across Industries

Modern claims increasingly involve multiple parties, evolving information, and complex coverage considerations. Catastrophe events, liability exposure, and technical evaluations require cross-disciplinary coordination. Adjusters now operate in environments that demand both technical expertise and a consistent leadership presence.

Annual insured catastrophe losses now regularly exceed $100 billion, reflecting both increased event frequency and higher asset exposure. At the same time, material costs have increased, labor constraints have tightened, and supply chain disruptions have driven higher claim severity across property and commercial lines. These conditions require more detailed evaluation, longer timelines, and greater coordination among stakeholders.

Financial exposure across claims spans individual losses to large-scale catastrophic events. Engineers, attorneys, contractors, and other specialists often contribute to the evaluation process simultaneously. In addition, litigation involvement and third-party representation have become more common across a broader range of claims, requiring structured communication and disciplined documentation from the outset. Complexity is no longer the exception—it is the standard condition of modern claim handling.

Advancements in technology have also expanded the volume of available information. Tools such as remote inspections, aerial imagery, and estimating platforms provide additional data, but they do not reduce the need for structured evaluation. Adjusters remain responsible for organizing, interpreting, and applying that information to the claim. Information has increased, but clarity must still be created.

The adjuster's role continues to evolve in response to these conditions. What was once primarily a technical role now requires operational leadership. Adjusters must coordinate participants, maintain alignment among stakeholders, and guide claims through complex, often competing inputs. Communication, organization, and disciplined decision-making are now essential to professional adjusting.

The future of the role centers on alignment, reliability, and coordination. Adjusters who lead with structure and consistency help set the standard for modern claim handling. As complexity increases, the ability to maintain clarity among multiple participants becomes the distinguishing factor in effective claims leadership.

CHAPTER FOCUS

Professional adjusting requires leadership in complex environments. Adjusters who take ownership of the process influence outcomes and maintain organizational consistency across all stages of the claim. Leadership is demonstrated by the ability to sustain alignment, coordinate multiple inputs, and maintain reliability as conditions evolve. In modern claims environments, technical skill alone is insufficient—structured leadership defines effective claim handling.

The Future of Adjusting: Professional Leadership in Complex Claims

The adjuster's role continues to evolve beyond technical evaluation into professional leadership within the claim. What was once primarily a technical function centered on inspection and estimation has expanded to require coordination, communication, and disciplined decision-making. Modern claims involve multiple stakeholders, complex coverage considerations, and heightened expectations for documentation and responsiveness. As the claims environment grows more complex, the adjuster's role increasingly centers on guiding the claim from initial contact through resolution.

The future of adjusting is defined by complexity. Increased catastrophe activity, broader litigation awareness, and multi-party claim environments have reshaped how losses are handled. Policyholders expect clarity, responsiveness, and professionalism, while carriers require reliable documentation and consistent evaluation. These expectations place the adjuster in a position where leadership is no longer optional—it is required to maintain alignment.

The responsibility for that leadership rests with the adjuster.

Professional leadership in claims handling is demonstrated through structure. Adjusters maintain direction by organizing information, coordinating communication among stakeholders, and documenting decisions clearly. Alignment is not assumed—it is created through consistent communication, disciplined workflows, and reliable documentation.

The adjuster of the future is defined not by technical skill alone but by the ability to lead amid complexity. Guiding claims through multiple perspectives, evolving information, and competing expectations requires professionalism, organization, and consistency. These capabilities define modern adjusting.

Increasing Complexity in Modern Claims

Claims today often involve multiple components developing simultaneously. Property damage, business interruption, liability considerations, and mitigation activities may all be present in the same file. Each element requires documentation, evaluation, and coordinated communication. Managing these moving parts increases the level of organization required of the adjuster.

Multi-party involvement further complicates matters. Contractors, consultants, engineers, attorneys, and representatives may all participate in the claim, providing input and requesting updates. Each stakeholder may influence next steps or contribute documentation. Without structure, communication can become fragmented and misaligned.

The responsibility for maintaining that alignment rests with the adjuster.

Complex claims require consistent organization. Tracking communications, documenting decisions, and clarifying next steps ensure that information remains connected throughout the claim. Structured documentation provides continuity as conditions evolve, enabling the claim to progress with clarity and direction.

Increasing complexity underscores the need for structured claims leadership. Organization, communication, and disciplined documentation enable adjusters to manage claims effectively in modern environments.

Expanding Expectations of Policyholders

Policyholders increasingly expect clarity, responsiveness, and transparency throughout the claims process. They may request defined timelines, detailed explanations, and regular updates on claim status. These expectations shape how adjusters communicate and manage claims.

The responsibility for meeting these expectations rests with the adjuster.

Clear communication helps maintain alignment. Explaining inspection timing, outlining documentation requirements, and identifying next steps reduces uncertainty and supports productive interactions. When policyholders understand the process, conversations remain focused and organized.

Professional communication also builds confidence. Consistent updates and clear explanations show that the claim is progressing. When stakeholders understand how information is reviewed and what actions will follow, cooperation improves, and friction decreases.

Meeting expanding expectations requires leadership within the claim. Structured communication, documented updates, and clear direction help adjusters maintain alignment and guide the claim forward.

REAL WORLD
Technology and Human Judgment

An adjuster used automated tools to review claim data and identify initial patterns in a complex loss with multiple damage components. The system flagged potential areas of concern, but inconsistencies emerged between the automated output and the documented site conditions.

Rather than relying solely on automated results, the adjuster validated the data against inspection findings, reviewed supporting documentation, and compared the system's conclusions with observed conditions. Additional steps were taken to confirm accuracy, including revisiting key elements of the claim and clarifying how the data aligned with the physical loss.

As the evaluation progressed, the adjuster refined the claim scope using verified information, documenting both the system-generated insights and the rationale for any adjustments. Communication with stakeholders reflected both the efficiency of the tools used and the professional judgment applied in reaching final conclusions.

By combining technology with structured evaluation and disciplined decision-making, the adjuster ensured the claim remained accurate, consistent, and defensible. This example shows that although technology enhances efficiency, it does not replace professional judgment. Clarity, accuracy, and accountability remain the adjuster's responsibility.

Coordination Across Multiple Stakeholders

Complex claims often require coordination among multiple stakeholders. Engineers may evaluate structural components, contractors may provide estimates, and representatives may submit documentation at various stages of the claim. These inputs evolve over time and require consistent organization. The adjuster coordinates this information to maintain alignment.

The responsibility for that coordination rests with the adjuster.

Tracking stakeholder communication helps preserve clarity. Recording requests, responses, and follow-up actions ensures information remains consistent across all participants. These records help track claim development and reduce the risk of conflicting updates. Structured documentation supports continuity as the claim evolves.

Structured updates further support alignment. Communicating the current status, identifying pending items, and outlining next steps keep stakeholders focused on claim progression. Clear, consistent messaging strengthens coordination and reduces confusion.

Coordination is a leadership function in claims handling. Adjusters who organize communication, document developments, and guide next steps ensure that complex claims remain structured, aligned, and understandable.

Documentation as Professional Leadership

Documentation plays a central role in complex claims. Clear, structured notes capture observations, decisions, communications, and next steps. These records provide continuity as the claim progresses and help adjusters maintain clarity when multiple participants are involved. Structured documentation supports organized claim handling.

The responsibility for maintaining that documentation rests with the adjuster.

Professional documentation strengthens coordination. Stakeholders rely on consistent records that capture inspection findings, communication updates, and pending actions. When documentation is clear and organized, misunderstandings decrease, and communication remains aligned. This supports continuity throughout the claim.

Documentation also demonstrates disciplined handling. Clear timelines, recorded decisions, and documented follow-up actions show the claim's progress. These records provide direction as conditions evolve and reinforce professionalism throughout all stages of the claim.

The future of adjusting positions documentation as a form of leadership. Clear, consistent records allow adjusters to coordinate stakeholders, manage complexity, and maintain alignment from initial evaluation through resolution.

Technology and the Adjuster's Role

Technology continues to shape claims handling. Remote inspections, digital photo documentation, estimating platforms, and communication tools are now standard components of the claims process. These resources expand operational capabilities and enable adjusters to manage information more efficiently among multiple participants.

The responsibility for applying that technology effectively rests with the adjuster.

Technology does not replace adjuster leadership—it requires it. Adjusters must interpret digital inputs, validate information, coordinate communication, and determine next steps. The effectiveness of technology depends on organization, structure, and professional judgment.

Using technology effectively requires disciplined documentation. Recording digital communications, tracking uploaded materials, and documenting decisions based on available information ensure continuity. These practices allow digital inputs to be integrated into the claim in a structured, reliable way.

Technology expands capabilities, but leadership maintains clarity. Adjusters guide the claim by organizing information, documenting developments, and coordinating next steps across digital and human inputs.

Decision-Making in Complex Environments

Complex claims require disciplined decision-making. Multiple inputs, evolving conditions, and stakeholder communication can all influence evaluation. Adjusters must review information carefully while maintaining forward progress. A structured decision-making approach supports clarity and consistency.

The responsibility for maintaining that clarity rests with the adjuster.

Documenting decision rationale strengthens transparency. Recording the observations considered, the information reviewed, and the next steps identified ensures that decisions remain understandable as the claim evolves. These records support continuity and provide a clear reference for future evaluation.

Structured decision-making also promotes consistency. Systematically reviewing available information and identifying pending items helps maintain alignment among participants. This approach reduces uncertainty and strengthens professional judgment.

Decision-making in complex environments reflects the adjuster's leadership role. Clear documentation, structured evaluation, and consistent communication guide the claim through complexity and maintain direction.

Communication as a Leadership Tool

Communication remains central to modern adjusting. Clear explanations align stakeholders, especially when claims involve multiple participants and evolving information. Disciplined updates reduce uncertainty and ensure that all parties understand the claim's current status. Consistent communication provides direction.

The responsibility for maintaining that communication rests with the adjuster.

A professional tone supports cooperation. Adjusters who communicate clearly and respectfully help guide conversations, even when challenges arise. Calm, structured messaging keeps discussions focused on observations, timelines, and next steps, reducing escalation and supporting constructive dialogue.

Documenting communication ensures continuity. Recording updates, clarifications, and follow-up actions maintains consistency across interactions. These records serve as a reference for future discussions and help track claim progression.

When structured and documented, communication serves as a leadership tool. Adjusters guide the claim with clarity, consistency, and organized messaging.

The Shift from Processing to Guiding

Historically, adjusting often emphasized processing. The role focused on inspection, documentation, and resolution within more contained claim structures. Modern claims environments have introduced greater complexity, requiring a shift from task execution to disciplined claim leadership.

The responsibility for guiding that process rests with the adjuster.

This shift involves setting direction, documenting decisions, and coordinating stakeholders. Adjusters maintain structure by clarifying next steps, tracking communications, and managing timelines. These practices ensure the claim remains organized as conditions evolve.

The transition from processing to guiding defines the modern role of the adjuster. Rather than simply advancing a file, adjusters now coordinate multiple inputs and keep participants aligned. This requires structured communication, consistent documentation, and reliable organization.

Guiding the claim supports efficient handling. When adjusters lead with structure and clarity, complex claims move forward consistently, aligned, and with professional direction.

Professional Judgment in Complex Claims

Complex claims require disciplined professional judgment. Adjusters must evaluate information, prioritize tasks, and communicate next steps while coordinating with multiple stakeholders. Decisions often unfold in stages as additional information becomes available. A structured evaluation approach supports clarity and consistency throughout the claim.

The responsibility for that judgment rests with the adjuster.

Documentation strengthens professional judgment. Recording observations, information reviewed, and the reasoning behind decisions ensures transparency. These records track the claim's evolution and provide continuity across discussions. Clear documentation supports consistent decision-making.

Professional judgment also supports alignment. Systematically reviewing available information and identifying next steps helps maintain direction among participants. This structured approach reduces uncertainty and supports organized claim progression.

The future of adjusting positions professional judgment as a form of leadership. Adjusters guide claims through disciplined evaluation, clear documentation, and consistent communication.

Maintaining Structure in Evolving Claims

Claims evolve as new information emerges. Additional damage may be identified, documentation may be submitted, and new stakeholders may become involved. Adjusters must adapt to these changes while maintaining structure. Organization supports continuity as conditions shift.

The responsibility for maintaining that structure rests with the adjuster.

Recording changes helps track claim development. Documenting updated observations, revised timelines, and new follow-up actions ensures that progression remains clear. These records connect earlier decisions to new information, reducing confusion and preserving continuity.

Communicating updates supports alignment. Stakeholders benefit from understanding why changes were made and what next steps will follow. Clear, structured communication maintains professionalism and supports cooperation throughout the claim.

Maintaining structure amid evolving claims reflects leadership. Adjusters who document changes, communicate updates, and guide next steps ensure that claims progress clearly and consistently.

The Modern Adjuster as Claim Leader

The future of adjusting centers on leadership within the claim. Modern adjusters do more than inspect and document—they guide the claim by coordinating stakeholders, documenting decisions, and maintaining structured communication. This leadership ensures that complex claims remain organized and understandable from initial assignment through resolution.

The responsibility for that leadership rests with the adjuster.

Complex claims require disciplined handling. Multiple participants, evolving information, and time-sensitive decisions demand consistent coordination. Adjusters who track communication, document developments, and clarify next steps provide direction throughout the process. This organization supports efficient claim progression and reduces uncertainty.

Professional leadership within the claim environment defines modern adjusting. Adjusters who manage complexity effectively sustain alignment and reliability across stakeholders. Disciplined documentation, objective communication, and thoughtful decision-making ensure that the claim remains focused and controlled.

The future of adjusting belongs to professionals who lead through structure and consistency. Adjusters who provide direction, maintain organization, and document decisions clearly can manage complexity professionally.

The future of adjusting will not be defined by tools or volume.

It will be defined by the ability to sustain alignment, reliability, and leadership in increasingly complex environments.

Practical Claim Leadership Actions

The Future of Adjusting: Professional Leadership in Complex Claims

The future of adjusting requires a balance of technical expertise, communication, and professional leadership. Increasing complexity, litigation exposure, and stakeholder coordination require adjusters to guide claims with structure and alignment. As claims environments evolve, leadership is defined by the ability to sustain alignment, reliability, and coordination amid complexity.

LEAD WITH STRUCTURE

Modern claims require adjusters to establish direction early and maintain consistency throughout the claim.

KEY ACTIONS:

Establish claim structure at the outset
Clarify roles and responsibilities across stakeholders
Identify next steps consistently
Maintain a defined communication timeline

GO-TO LINES:

"Here is how the claim process will be structured."
"Roles and responsibilities have been clearly identified."
"These are the next steps moving forward."
"Updates will follow a consistent communication timeline."

INTEGRATE COMMUNICATION AND DECISION-MAKING

Professional leadership requires clear communication supported by documented decision-making.

KEY ACTIONS:

Explain decisions clearly
Document reasoning thoroughly
Confirm stakeholder understanding
Provide structured updates

GO-TO LINES:

"This decision is based on documented findings."
"Here is how the evaluation supports this outcome."
"Please let me know if clarification is needed."
"Updates will reflect the current status of the claim."

MANAGE INCREASING CLAIM COMPLEXITY

Complex claims require consistent organization and coordinated communication.

KEY ACTIONS:

Track claim progress clearly
Document developing information
Align communication across stakeholders
Maintain a consistent workflow

GO-TO LINES:

"The claim is being tracked to maintain clarity across all elements."
"Information is being documented as it develops."

"Communication is aligned across all stakeholders."
"The workflow is structured to support consistency."

MAINTAIN DEFENSIBLE PRACTICES

Modern claims environments require disciplined documentation and consistent handling.

KEY ACTIONS:

Record observations objectively
Document communication clearly
Identify pending evaluations
Reconfirm expectations

GO-TO LINES:

"Documentation reflects observed conditions and evaluation."
"All communication has been recorded for consistency."
"Pending evaluations have been identified and tracked."
"Expectations have been reconfirmed as the claim progresses."

OPERATE AS A CLAIM LEADER

Professional leadership defines modern adjusting. The adjuster's role is to guide the claim with clarity and consistency.

KEY ACTIONS:

Provide direction early
Maintain structured communication
Document decisions clearly
Guide claims through resolution

GO-TO LINES:

"I will continue to guide the claim through each stage."
"Communication will remain structured and consistent."
"Decisions are being documented to support clarity."
"The claim is progressing toward resolution as planned."

These practices enable adjusters to operate effectively in increasingly complex claims environments while maintaining professional leadership. By combining structured processes, clear communication, and disciplined decision-making, adjusters set the standard for modern claims handling. Claims remain clear, consistent, and aligned not because complexity is reduced, but because leadership is applied throughout the process.

CLAIM LEADERSHIP SUMMARY

Key Takeaway

The adjuster's role continues to evolve as claims grow more complex and collaborative. Multi-party coordination, technical evaluation, and evolving information require both technical expertise and leadership presence. Adjusters who provide structure and alignment help guide claims toward reliable outcomes. As complexity increases, alignment becomes the defining standard of professional adjusting.

In Practice

Focus on coordination, communication, and organized documentation. Clarify stakeholder roles, track emerging information, and provide consistent updates. Structured leadership helps manage complexity, ensuring the claim remains aligned, understandable, and able to progress as conditions evolve.

Questions for Reflection

1. How do I maintain clarity when claims involve multiple stakeholders?
2. Do I track evolving information consistently?
3. Am I guiding the claim through clear communication and structure?

Claim Leadership Principle

Professional leadership defines modern adjusting. Clarity is sustained when communication, documentation, and coordination remain structured, consistent, and aligned throughout the life of the claim.

PRELUDE

Sustaining the Adjuster in High-Stakes Claims

Claims work places sustained demands on adjusters. High-volume environments, complex losses, and continuous decision-making create pressure that builds over time. Maintaining professionalism in these conditions requires more than technical expertise. It also requires reliability, resilience, and disciplined work practices that support consistent performance in high-stakes situations.

The human side of claims work is often less visible yet equally critical. Adjusters manage conversations about loss, uncertainty, and frustration while navigating evolving information and competing expectations. Maintaining composure in these environments requires structured communication, organized workflows, and the ability to stay aligned under pressure.

The responsibility for sustaining performance rests with the adjuster.

Sustaining the adjuster supports long-term effectiveness. As workload and complexity increase, disciplined practices help reduce decision fatigue and preserve clarity. Organized workflows, predictable communication, and thoughtful pacing help maintain professionalism during extended deployments and demanding claims.

This section focuses on sustaining adjusters in high-stakes claims environments. The goal is to support long-term alignment, professionalism, and leadership as adjusters navigate complex losses. Sustained performance enables adjusters to guide claims effectively while maintaining reliability throughout the process.

PART V

Sustaining the Adjuster in High-Stakes Claims

Claims work is demanding not only because of its technical complexity but also because of the human realities behind each file. Adjusters regularly interact with policyholders facing disruption, financial uncertainty, and significant loss. These conversations take place while managing multiple claims, tight timelines, and evolving conditions. The role requires empathy, professionalism, and clarity, delivered consistently in every interaction. Over time, sustained exposure to these conditions can affect communication, focus, and decision-making. The emotional weight of claims handling may be less visible than the technical work, yet it plays a critical role in maintaining professional consistency.

The pace of modern claims handling has intensified these pressures. Increased catastrophe activity, complex losses, and staffing constraints often result in extended deployments and high-volume assignments. Adjusters may work long hours, coordinate with multiple stakeholders, and manage emotionally demanding conversations in rapid succession. These conditions demand sustained attention, disciplined documentation, and consistent communication. Maintaining professional standards in this environment requires more than technical knowledge. It also requires structured workflows, clear prioritization, and resilience to sustain steady performance over time.

Sustainability in adjusting has become a professional necessity. Fatigue, burnout, and turnover can undermine claim continuity, documentation quality, and communication clarity. Organizations depend on experienced adjusters to guide complex claims, yet sustained pressure can erode retention. When experienced professionals leave, remaining adjusters absorb additional workload and responsibility. This cycle increases strain and reduces capacity for thorough evaluation and consistent documentation. Sustainable practices help protect both performance and claim quality over extended periods of demand.

The human aspect of claims work also requires balancing empathy with professionalism. Policyholders may be experiencing stress, uncertainty, and frustration. Adjusters must acknowledge these conditions while maintaining structured communication and clear direction. Emotional awareness supports effective interaction, but boundaries preserve objectivity. Documenting discussions, clarifying next steps, and maintaining consistent communication help sustain alignment. Professional composure stabilizes the claim environment and supports productive dialogue.

Sustainability also encompasses professional responsibility and license integrity. High-pressure environments can affect pacing, documentation, and decision-making. Maintaining consistent standards protects both the claim and the adjuster. Clear documentation, disciplined communication, and structured evaluation support defensibility. License integrity reflects consistency, neutrality, and sound judgment. These practices ensure that professional standards remain intact even under pressure.

Continuing education and professional development further support long-term sustainability. Claims environments continue to evolve, requiring adjusters to stay current with regulatory expectations, documentation standards, and communication practices. Ongoing learning strengthens technical capabilities and reinforces disciplined handling. It also builds confidence in managing complex claims and adapting to changing conditions. Maintaining competence helps sustain professional consistency over time.

Sustainable claims handling also depends on structured workflow management. Prioritizing inspections, tracking communications, and documenting updates reduces cognitive strain. Defined workflows help adjusters stay aligned as workloads increase. Organized files preserve continuity when claims extend over time. These practices support focus, reduce oversight, and maintain clarity across multiple files.

This section examines the human demands of claims work and underscores the importance of sustainable professional practices. The chapters that follow address emotional strain, workload pressures, turnover trends, burnout risk, license integrity, and long-term sustainability. These topics reflect the realities of modern claims environments.

Effective claims handling depends not only on technical skill but also on the ability to sustain alignment, resilience, ethical judgment, and reliable leadership over time. By maintaining structured workflows, professional composure, and disciplined documentation, adjusters protect both the claim and their long-term effectiveness. Sustainable practices ensure that professional standards remain consistent—even in high-pressure environments.

CHAPTER 21

The Human Cost of Claims Work

Event Spotlight — Stress and Mental Health in Claims Roles

Insurance claims professionals work in high-pressure environments characterized by heavy workloads, emotionally charged conversations, and time-sensitive decisions. Adjusters routinely handle situations involving loss, disruption, and financial uncertainty while maintaining professionalism and accuracy. Over time, sustained exposure to these conditions creates emotional and mental strain that can affect performance and long-term career sustainability.

Workforce research consistently shows elevated stress across industries, with a majority of professionals reporting ongoing workplace stress and burnout, recognized by the World Health Organization as an occupational phenomenon. In the insurance industry, these pressures are intensified by heavy workloads and complex claims. Adjusters frequently manage dozens of active claims simultaneously, with volumes surging during catastrophe deployments. In addition, industry reports point to rising emotional fatigue and anxiety, along with a growing need for mental health support. In today's claims environment, stress is not an exception; it is a consistent operating condition.

The human cost of claims work is often less visible than financial exposure. Adjusters balance empathy with professionalism while managing deadlines, documentation, and communication. Continuous decision-making, combined with a high workload and emotionally demanding interactions, contributes to cognitive strain over time. Maintaining clarity under pressure requires not only technical skill but also sustained personal stability.

The impact extends beyond individual performance. Retention challenges in claims roles reflect the long-term effects of sustained pressure, as experienced adjusters leave the profession and remaining professionals absorb increased workloads. These conditions underscore that resilience is not optional; it is essential to maintaining professional standards.

The human cost of claims work must be recognized as part of the profession. Sustained performance depends on the ability to manage workload and personal capacity. Emotional awareness, structured workflows, and disciplined communication help adjusters maintain clarity, consistency, and professional leadership.

CHAPTER FOCUS

Claims work carries emotional and mental demands that extend beyond technical skill. Understanding the human cost of adjusting helps professionals maintain clarity, consistency, and professional leadership. Sustained performance depends on effectively managing both workload and personal capacity.

The Human Cost of Claims Work

Claims handling is often discussed in terms of inspections, estimates, documentation, and timelines. Yet behind every claim lies disruption, uncertainty, and change. Adjusters routinely work in environments where policyholders are navigating loss, displacement, and financial concerns. Over time, sustained exposure to these conditions builds cumulative pressure. Understanding the human cost of claims work is essential to sustaining professional performance.

The human cost of claims work extends beyond policyholders. Adjusters also work under demanding conditions. High claim volume, travel requirements, time-sensitive decisions, and complex communication create sustained pressure. These demands require emotional discipline, sustained focus, and consistent professionalism.

The responsibility for managing that pressure rests with the adjuster.

Modern claims handling requires both technical expertise and human awareness. Adjusters must manage documentation, coordinate communication, and maintain composure in dynamic environments. This balance enables claims to progress effectively while preserving clarity and alignment.

Recognizing the human cost of claims work supports resilience. Adjusters who understand these demands are better equipped to maintain consistency and professionalism under pressure. The human cost of claims work is not separate from performance—it directly shapes reliability, sound judgment, and professional leadership over time.

Exposure to Loss and Disruption

Adjusters routinely encounter property damage, business interruption, and, in catastrophe events, community-wide impact. These environments may involve widespread loss across neighborhoods, commercial districts, or infrastructure. Sustained exposure to these conditions can affect focus, clarity, and decision-making.

Policyholders navigating these situations often face uncertainty about displacement, repair timelines, and financial recovery. Adjusters must maintain professionalism while guiding communication during these conditions. This requires composure, clarity, and structured interaction.

Repeated exposure to disruption creates cumulative pressure over time. Without structure, this pressure can undermine communication and consistency. Organized documentation, clear communication, and defined next steps provide stability and help maintain alignment.

Understanding the impact of repeated exposure to loss helps adjusters manage these conditions more effectively. Structure supports clarity, and clarity supports professionalism in demanding claims environments.

Emotional Labor in Claims Handling

Emotional labor is an inherent part of claims handling. Adjusters are expected to maintain professionalism even when conversations involve frustration, urgency, or uncertainty. Policyholders may be dealing with disruption, financial concerns, or time-sensitive needs. Responding with calm, structured communication helps stabilize discussions and supports the progression of claims.

The responsibility for managing that emotional demand rests with the adjuster.

Policyholders may raise concerns about timelines, documentation requirements, or scope decisions. Adjusters must listen, clarify concerns, and respond with clear, structured explanations. This requires emotional discipline and sustained focus. When communication remains organized, conversations stay centered on the claim rather than on emotional reactions.

Maintaining a professional tone reduces escalation and supports alignment. Calm, respectful communication reinforces clarity and sustains constructive dialogue. When adjusters communicate consistently and reliably, stakeholders are more likely to remain aligned with the claim process.

Emotional labor is therefore a core component of professional claims handling. Disciplined communication supports alignment, preserves professionalism, and enables claims to progress in an organized and consistent manner.

REAL WORLD
Emotional Impact of Repeated Loss Exposure

An adjuster handled multiple severe loss claims over a short period, including total losses and emotionally demanding conversations with policyholders. Repeated exposure to high-stress situations led to emotional fatigue, which began to affect tone, focus, and decision-making.

Recognizing the impact early, the adjuster implemented structured practices to maintain stability. Boundaries were reinforced through disciplined workflows, and intentional resets—such as briefly stepping away between claims, maintaining regular routines, and using simple decompression strategies—helped restore focus.

Communication was approached with greater intention. Difficult conversations were prepared for in advance rather than handled reactively. Consistent documentation and repeatable processes reduced cognitive strain and supported more stable decision-making across files.

By combining structured work practices with deliberate attention to personal well-being, the adjuster maintained professionalism and clarity. This example shows that sustained exposure to loss requires more than technical skill. Maintaining performance over time depends on the ability to manage both the demands of the claim and those placed on the professional handling it.

High-Pressure Communication Environments

Claims handling often involves multiple conversations occurring simultaneously. Policyholders, contractors, consultants, and internal stakeholders may request updates at different times. Communication volume can increase significantly, particularly during catastrophe events or high-stakes claims. In these environments, organization is essential to maintaining clarity.

The responsibility for managing that communication rests with the adjuster.

High communication demands require focused, structured responses. Adjusters must balance responsiveness with the time needed for evaluation and documentation. Consistent updates and clear next steps help maintain alignment without disrupting workflow. Structured communication supports clarity and continuity.

Documenting communication reduces repetition and preserves consistency. Recording updates, pending items, and follow-up actions provides a reliable reference. These records help adjusters maintain consistent messaging and avoid reworking prior discussions. Documentation improves efficiency and supports organized claim handling.

High-pressure communication environments require disciplined structure. Consistent updates, documented communication, and clearly defined next steps enable adjusters to manage volume while maintaining performance and professionalism.

Decision Responsibility and Mental Load

Adjusters make continuous decisions throughout the claim lifecycle. Prioritization, documentation, inspection scheduling, and communication all require professional judgment. Sustained decision-making increases cognitive load, particularly during high-volume assignments. Recognizing this demand supports resilience and consistency.

The responsibility for managing that decision load rests with the adjuster.

Mental load often rises during catastrophe deployments. Travel demands, high claim volume, and continuous communication add complexity. Adjusters must switch between claims while maintaining clarity, accuracy, and consistency. Without structure, decision quality can decline under sustained pressure.

Disciplined workflows reduce cognitive strain. Consistent documentation, clear prioritization, and structured communication routines minimize the need for repeated evaluation. Recording next steps and tracking pending actions help adjusters maintain direction without reprocessing information. Organization supports both efficiency and decision quality.

Understanding decision responsibility helps adjusters manage cognitive load effectively. Structured handling, disciplined documentation, and organized communication sustain performance in demanding claims environments.

Maintaining Professional Detachment

Adjusters must remain objective in emotionally charged environments. Policyholders may be experiencing displacement, disruption, or financial concerns, and conversations may reflect urgency or frustration. Professional detachment enables adjusters to focus on evaluation, documentation, and next steps while maintaining calm, structured communication. This clarity supports the claim.

The responsibility for maintaining that detachment rests with the adjuster.

Detachment does not eliminate empathy. Adjusters can acknowledge concerns while maintaining structured communication and objective evaluation. This balance keeps discussions constructive and focused on claim progression. Organized communication supports professionalism and alignment.

Objectivity strengthens decision-making. Documented observations, recorded timelines, and clearly defined next steps provide a stable foundation for evaluation. When decisions are grounded in documentation, adjusters can navigate complex conversations consistently and clearly, reducing uncertainty.

Maintaining professional detachment helps manage the human demands of claims work. Calm communication, structured handling, and objective evaluation support resilience and sustained performance in demanding environments.

The Impact of Sustained Workload

High claim volume often persists for weeks or months, especially during catastrophe assignments. A sustained workload can undermine focus, prioritization, and organization if not managed systematically. Adjusters must manage their workload deliberately to maintain clarity and performance.

The responsibility for managing that workload rests with the adjuster.

Tracking next steps preserves continuity. Recording pending inspections, documentation requests, and follow-ups on communications ensures tasks remain visible and organized. Clear documentation reduces the need for repeated evaluation and supports efficient workflow management.

Prioritization strengthens workload control. Identifying urgent tasks, time-sensitive mitigations, and scheduled inspections provides direction for daily decision-making. Structured prioritization helps adjusters maintain efficiency even when volume remains high.

Understanding the impact of sustained workloads supports resilience. Documentation, prioritization, and organized workflows enable adjusters to maintain consistency, clarity, and professional performance throughout extended assignments.

Community-Wide Loss Events

Catastrophe events can affect entire communities. Adjusters may inspect multiple losses in the same area while coordinating travel, scheduling, and communication. In large-scale events tracked by organizations such as the National Oceanic and Atmospheric Administration, losses regularly reach billions of dollars and affect wide geographic regions. Adjusters may manage dozens of claims concurrently during these deployments, increasing operational pressure and the need for disciplined organization.

Community-wide loss events also raise expectations. Policyholders experiencing similar damage often seek prompt resolution and regular updates. Communication is critical to maintaining alignment in a high-volume environment. Structured messaging helps manage expectations and reduce confusion.

Consistent updates and documented communication promote clarity. Recording inspection timing, next steps, and pending items helps track claim progression across multiple files. These practices ensure that claims remain organized even during sustained high-volume activity.

Community-wide loss events underscore the human cost of claims work. Structure, documentation, and consistent communication uphold professionalism in demanding environments.

Managing Personal and Professional Boundaries

Adjusters often work with policyholders experiencing significant disruption. Maintaining professional boundaries sustains performance and keeps communication focused on the claim. Structured communication promotes clarity and consistency, especially in high-pressure environments where expectations may shift.

Avoiding informal assurances helps prevent misunderstandings. Statements about outcomes, timelines, or scope should remain grounded in documented evaluation. Service research consistently shows that unclear expectations lead to escalation and repeated inquiries. Maintaining factual, process-focused communication supports transparency and reduces misalignment.

Professional boundaries also reinforce objectivity. When adjusters stay focused on observations, documentation, and next steps, discussions remain structured and productive. This helps guide the claim while preserving professionalism.

Managing boundaries helps mitigate the human cost of claims work. Clear communication, objective evaluation, and consistent documentation support resilience and disciplined claim handling.

Recognizing Cumulative Pressure

The impact of claims work often builds gradually. A sustained workload, repeated exposure to disruption, and continuous communication demands create cumulative pressure over time. Workforce research indicates that a majority of professionals report ongoing stress, and the World Health Organization recognizes burnout as an occupational phenomenon. In claims roles, these conditions are intensified by high volume and decision-making responsibility.

Adjusters may not recognize these effects immediately, but they can affect focus, prioritization, and decision-making. Continuous decision-making contributes to cognitive fatigue, especially when managing multiple files simultaneously. Recognizing cumulative pressure enables adjusters to respond with structure rather than reacting.

Reviewing documentation and confirming priorities restores clarity. Revisiting next steps, updating timelines, and organizing pending items help reestablish direction. These brief resets reduce cognitive strain and support consistent performance.

Structured workflows also reduce redundant decisions. Consistent documentation routines, prioritized follow-ups, and organized communication allow adjusters to rely on the process rather than on repeated evaluation. This supports resilience in demanding environments.

Recognizing cumulative pressure supports sustained performance. Awareness, organization, and disciplined workflows help maintain clarity throughout extended assignments.

Documentation as Stability

Documentation provides consistency in demanding environments. Clear notes help adjusters transition between claims without losing context. Documented observations, timelines, and follow-up actions reduce the need to reconstruct information, helping manage cognitive load.

Recording next steps maintains direction. Documenting pending items ensures tasks remain visible and that claim progression continues. Structured documentation supports continuity across multiple claims and reduces inefficiency from repeated review.

Documentation also strengthens professional confidence. When decisions, communication, and observations are clearly recorded, adjusters can rely on documented information rather than memory. This reduces uncertainty and supports consistent judgment.

In high-pressure environments, documentation serves as a stabilizing force. Clear records, structured timelines, and documented next steps sustain performance and support organized claim handling.

Sustaining Professional Performance

Managing the human cost of claims work requires organization, alignment, and discipline. Adjusters who maintain structured workflows reduce cognitive strain and improve continuity across claims. Disciplined handling reinforces professionalism in demanding environments.

Effective communication helps manage expectations and reduce uncertainty. Regular updates, a calm tone, and documented conversations help maintain alignment. Clear communication reduces repeated inquiries and supports steady claim progression.

Claims handling involves both technical and human demands. Adjusters must evaluate documentation, coordinate with stakeholders, and manage emotionally charged conversations. Recognizing these combined demands supports composure and sustained performance.

The human cost of claims work is real and measurable. Sustained performance depends on the ability to manage both workload and personal capacity. Structured documentation, organized workflows, and reliable communication protect long-term effectiveness and reinforce professional leadership.

Practical Claim Leadership Actions

The Human Cost of Claims Work

Claims work often involves sustained exposure to disruption, loss, and emotionally demanding conversations. Over time, these conditions can affect communication, clarity, and decision-making. Structured professional habits allow adjusters to maintain stability and consistency while managing the human dimension of claims work. In high-pressure environments, structure preserves clarity even when emotional demands remain constant.

MAINTAIN PROFESSIONAL COMPOSURE

Emotionally charged conversations require calm, structured communication. Maintaining composure stabilizes the claim process and supports productive dialogue.

KEY ACTIONS:

Use calm, professional language
Focus on facts and process
Avoid reactive responses
Confirm next steps clearly

GO-TO LINES:

"I want to ensure we keep communication clear and professional."
"Let's focus on the process and next steps."
"This is based on the information available at this time."
"Here are the next steps moving forward."

SET COMMUNICATION BOUNDARIES

High communication volume can disrupt clarity and pacing. Structured boundaries maintain consistency and protect workflow.

KEY ACTIONS:

Establish communication expectations early
Provide defined update timing
Document key conversations
Maintain consistent messaging

GO-TO LINES:

"Updates will be provided on a consistent schedule."
"Here is when you can expect the next update."

"This communication reflects the current claim status."
"We will continue to follow a structured communication process."

USE STRUCTURE TO MAINTAIN CLARITY

Organization prevents emotional strain from affecting claim direction. Structured workflows maintain alignment across all stages of the claim.

KEY ACTIONS:

Track claim status clearly
Document next steps consistently
Maintain organized file notes
Reconfirm timelines as needed

GO-TO LINES:

"The claim status is being tracked to maintain clarity."
"Next steps have been documented for consistency."
"Documentation reflects the current stage of the claim."
"Timelines are being reconfirmed as needed."

RECOGNIZE EMOTIONAL IMPACT ON DECISION-MAKING

Emotional fatigue can influence pacing and judgment. Awareness supports consistency and protects decision quality.

KEY ACTIONS:

Review complex decisions carefully
Document reasoning clearly
Avoid rushed conclusions
Confirm next-step direction

GO-TO LINES:

"This decision has been reviewed for accuracy."
"Additional review is being completed before finalizing."
"Reasoning has been documented to support this decision."
"Next steps have been confirmed following review."

MAINTAIN CONSISTENCY ACROSS CLAIMS

Consistency reinforces both professionalism and long-term sustainability. Reliable processes reduce cognitive strain and support performance across multiple files.

KEY ACTIONS:

Provide predictable updates
Maintain documentation clarity
Communicate expectations clearly
Close conversations with direction

GO-TO LINES:

"Updates will continue on a consistent basis."
"Documentation reflects the current claim status."
"Expectations have been clearly communicated."
"Next steps have been outlined for continuity."

These practices help adjusters maintain clarity, professionalism, and stability while navigating the human side of claims work. By combining structured communication, consistent documentation, and disciplined decision-making, adjusters sustain performance and claim quality—even when emotional demands persist, and pressure builds over time.

CLAIM LEADERSHIP SUMMARY

Key Takeaway

Claims work entails sustained exposure to stress, emotionally charged conversations, and time-sensitive decision-making. Adjusters regularly support policyholders navigating disruption while managing workloads and documentation requirements. Recognizing the human cost of claims work helps professionals maintain alignment, resilience, and long-term effectiveness. When these demands are managed deliberately, performance and focus remain consistent over time.

In Practice

Manage workload intentionally, pace decisions appropriately, and maintain clear professional boundaries. Reset between emotionally demanding conversations and prioritize organization to reduce unnecessary strain. Ongoing self-awareness supports sustained performance and alignment throughout extended claim activity.

Questions for Reflection

1. Do I recognize the emotional demands of my claims workload?
2. How do I reset after difficult conversations?
3. Am I managing my workload in a way that supports long-term consistency?

Claim Leadership Principle

Sustainable claim leadership requires awareness of the human cost. Clarity is maintained when energy, communication, and decision-making are consistently managed and disciplined over time.

CHAPTER 22

Turnover, Burnout, and Sustainability in Adjusting

Event Spotlight — Claims Turnover and Burnout Trends

Burnout has become a measurable operational risk across claims organizations. Workforce research, including findings from the World Health Organization, recognizes burnout as an occupational phenomenon linked to sustained workplace stress. In high-volume claims environments, professionals under continuous workload pressure are more likely to consider leaving their roles. Increasing claim complexity, rising catastrophe frequency, and staffing constraints continue to intensify these demands. In modern claims environments, workforce sustainability is directly tied to the ability to manage sustained operational pressure.

Turnover trends further illustrate this strain. Insurance workforce data reflect ongoing retention challenges, particularly in claims roles that require high-volume decision-making and emotionally demanding communication. Industry analyses also indicate that a significant share of the insurance workforce is approaching retirement, suggesting a loss of experienced adjusters in the coming years. As experienced professionals exit, the workload is redistributed across remaining teams, increasing pressure on those still handling active claims.

In high-volume environments, turnover cycles can accelerate. Staffing gaps increase the workload, contributing to fatigue and burnout, which in turn increases the likelihood of further turnover. This cycle affects claim continuity, training costs, and operational reliability. What begins as workload pressure becomes a systemic risk to performance and consistency.

Sustainability is therefore no longer optional—it is required to maintain professional standards. When sustainability is not upheld, reliability, alignment, and claim quality are directly affected. Organizations and professionals must recognize that sustained performance depends on structured workflows, disciplined communication, and the ability to manage workload over time.

CHAPTER FOCUS

Long-term success in adjusting requires sustainability. Managing workload, maintaining resilience, and protecting professional capacity support reliable leadership in claims environments. Sustained performance depends on maintaining alignment, clarity, and consistency over time, even as workload demands increase.

Turnover, Burnout, and Sustainability in Adjusting

The claims industry has seen rising turnover in recent years. High claim volume, catastrophe deployments, litigation exposure, and communication demands have reshaped the role. What was once primarily technical now requires leadership, coordination, disciplined documentation, and continuous decision-making. These expanding responsibilities create sustained pressure.

Burnout among adjusters often develops gradually. Extended deployments, heavy caseloads, and continuous communication demands contribute to fatigue. Adjusters may work long hours, transition rapidly between files, and manage complex conversations. In the field, additional risks may include travel fatigue, hazardous inspection conditions, and the potential for physical injury. Over time, this sustained pace can affect focus, decision-making, and long-term reliability.

Sustainability in adjusting requires organization and discipline. Adjusters who manage workload, document decisions, and communicate reliably are better positioned to sustain performance. These practices reduce cognitive strain and support long-term effectiveness.

Understanding turnover and burnout is critical to the future of adjusting. Sustaining adjusters helps preserve professional claims handling and reliable leadership within the claims environment. Sustainability does not reduce workload—it ensures that workload does not erode alignment, reliability, and professional performance over time.

The Causes of Adjuster Turnover

Adjuster turnover is influenced by multiple factors, beginning with workload demands. Catastrophic events often require extended deployments, high claim volumes, and rapid transitions between assignments. Adjusters may move from one loss environment to another with limited recovery time. Over time, this sustained pace can undermine long-term sustainability and contribute to turnover.

Communication demands also play a role. Policyholders, contractors, consultants, and internal stakeholders may request updates at the same time. Managing these interactions requires focus, organization, and consistent messaging. Without structure, communication volume can become difficult to manage, increasing stress and reducing efficiency.

Decision responsibility is another contributing factor. Adjusters must evaluate documentation, prioritize claims, coordinate inspections, and communicate next steps. Sustained decision-making increases cognitive load, and over time, this cumulative mental demand contributes to fatigue and reduced performance.

Field conditions introduce additional complexity. Adjusters may encounter damaged structures, unstable environments, and travel-related fatigue during catastrophe deployments. Physical risk, combined with workload pressure, further increases the demands of the role.

Social dynamics may also influence the work environment. In some situations, adjusters may encounter challenging interactions, such as bias, hostility, or lack of cooperation from stakeholders. These interactions can complicate communication and heighten emotional strain. Maintaining professionalism in these situations requires composure, structured communication, and adherence to process.

Organizational factors further contribute to turnover. Inconsistent workflows, unclear expectations, and reactive communication environments can heighten frustration and reduce efficiency. When structure is absent, workload pressure becomes harder to manage.

Understanding these combined factors helps explain turnover in adjusting. Structured workflows, consistent documentation, organized communication, and professional boundaries support sustainability and reduce strain in complex claim environments.

REAL WORLD
High Turnover in a Desk Environment

A claims team experienced high turnover driven by sustained workload pressure and reactive communication patterns. Constant interruptions, unclear expectations, and inconsistent updates created an environment in which adjusters struggled to maintain focus and manage their workload effectively.

As volume increased, communication became fragmented. Team members addressed issues as they arose rather than following a structured process, resulting in repeated work, unclear priorities, and growing frustration. Over time, this reactive pattern contributed to burnout and ongoing staff turnover.

To address this, structured workflows were introduced to standardize daily operations. Clear task prioritization, defined processes, and organized documentation reduced confusion and limited rework. Communication expectations were also reset, with consistent update cycles, clearer timelines, and fewer reactive escalations.

As the structure increased, the team gained greater control over workload and communication flow. Adjusters could focus on completing tasks rather than responding to interruptions, improving alignment and reducing operational strain.

By shifting from reactive patterns to disciplined operations, the team improved stability and reduced burnout. This demonstrates that sustainability in high-volume environments is not achieved by reducing workload alone, but by improving the organization, alignment, and reliability of work management.

Burnout in High-Volume Claims Environments

Burnout often develops in high-volume claims environments. Adjusters may manage dozens of active files simultaneously while coordinating inspections, documentation, and communication. Travel demands, extended hours, and evolving claim conditions further intensify the workload. In these environments, sustained pressure requires disciplined handling and structured workflows.

The responsibility for managing that pressure rests with the adjuster.

Signs of burnout may include difficulty prioritizing tasks, delayed documentation, and reduced communication effectiveness. Adjusters may revisit decisions or struggle to maintain organization across multiple files. These responses reflect sustained cognitive demand and align with broader workforce research identifying burnout as a response to prolonged workplace stress, as recognized by the World Health Organization. Recognizing these indicators supports proactive adjustment.

Defined workflows reduce strain and improve consistency. Reliable documentation routines, tracked next steps, and scheduled communication intervals reduce redundant decision-making. Structured handling helps adjusters maintain alignment and clarity even during sustained high-volume periods.

Burnout is closely tied to workload and organizational factors. Structure, prioritization, and consistent communication support resilience and sustain professional performance.

The Impact of Catastrophe Deployments

Catastrophe deployments significantly increase workload intensity. Adjusters may inspect multiple losses per day while coordinating communication, documentation, and scheduling. Travel between locations, exposure to damaged environments, and evolving claim conditions add complexity. Maintaining organization is essential to sustaining performance.

The responsibility for maintaining that organization rests with the adjuster.

Extended deployments may shorten recovery time. Adjusters often move continuously among inspections, documentation, and stakeholder communication, with little opportunity to reset. Sustaining performance over extended assignments requires structured workflows, disciplined pacing, and consistent prioritization.

Tracking inspections, documenting communication, and identifying next steps provide stability in these environments. Clear records enable adjusters to transition between claims without losing context, reducing cognitive strain and improving continuity.

Catastrophe deployments highlight the need for sustainability in adjusting. Organization, structured communication, and consistent documentation enable adjusters to maintain clarity, resilience, and professional performance during high-demand assignments.

REAL WORLD
Managing Volume and Emotional Load in a Desk Adjuster Role

An adjuster managed a high-volume desk assignment with continuous inbound calls, status requests, and claim updates across multiple files. Conversations often involved frustrated or stressed policyholders seeking immediate answers.

As volume increased, communication became more reactive, and the adjuster experienced mental fatigue from repeated conversations and constant task switching—conditions consistent with research indicating that frequent interruptions and multitasking heighten cognitive strain and reduce efficiency.

To stabilize the workload, the adjuster established regular communication intervals, consistently documented key updates, and organized claims by status. Clear messaging reduced duplicate inquiries, and structured documentation improved continuity across files.

By introducing structure and maintaining a professional tone, the adjuster reduced cognitive strain and improved consistency. This approach supported sustained performance in a high-volume, emotionally demanding environment.

Communication Overload and Cognitive Strain

Communication volume can spike during complex claims. Policyholders, contractors, consultants, and internal stakeholders may request updates simultaneously. Adjusters must respond to these inquiries while continuing their evaluation, documentation, and scheduling. This overlapping demand increases cognitive strain and requires structured handling.

The responsibility for managing that communication load rests with the adjuster.

Without organization, communication demands disrupt workflow. Frequent interruptions reduce focus and limit the ability to complete documentation or review information effectively. Repeated context switching increases mental workload and can reduce decision quality, a pattern supported by cognitive research on multitasking and sustained attention. Disciplined handling is essential to maintaining clarity.

Establishing communication routines reduces overload. Providing updates at defined intervals, clarifying next steps, and documenting conversations limit repeated inquiries. Stakeholders remain informed, and adjusters retain dedicated time for focused evaluation. Documentation preserves continuity across interactions and supports consistent messaging.

Managing communication overload supports sustainability. Defined updates, documented interactions, and organized follow-up actions maintain alignment in high-demand environments.

Workload Management and Longevity

Sustainability in adjusting requires managing workload over time. High claim volume, evolving conditions, and communication demands often extend over weeks or months. Structured organization allows adjusters to maintain clarity and consistency throughout extended assignments.

The responsibility for managing that workload rests with the adjuster.

Prioritizing claims sharpens focus. Identifying urgent inspections, time-sensitive mitigation, and pending documentation enables adjusters to allocate attention effectively. Structured prioritization improves efficiency and reduces the risk of overlooked tasks.

Tracking next steps preserves continuity. Recording pending items, scheduled inspections, and follow-up communications keeps claims organized. Documentation reduces the need for repeated evaluations and supports consistent workflow management.

Workload management supports longevity in adjustment. Organized documentation, structured prioritization, and consistent communication enable adjusters to sustain performance over time while upholding professional standards.

Professional Boundaries and Sustainability

Maintaining professional boundaries supports sustainable claims handling. Adjusters communicate clearly and avoid informal commitments outside the claims process. Clear, structured communication ensures that expectations remain aligned with documented evaluations and claim progression.

The responsibility for maintaining those boundaries rests with the adjuster.

Boundaries also support workload management. Defined timelines, documented updates, and consistent communication reduce redundant conversations. When stakeholders understand the next steps, fewer clarifications are needed. This improves efficiency and reduces cognitive strain.

Professional boundaries preserve focus. Communication remains centered on observations, documentation, and next steps rather than on informal discussion. This structured approach supports clarity, consistency, and long-term performance.

Sustainability requires disciplined communication and clear boundaries. These practices enable adjusters to manage their workload effectively while maintaining professional standards.

Organizational Support and Claims Structure

Sustainability is also influenced by claims structure. Clear workflows, documentation expectations, and communication guidelines reduce cognitive strain and support consistent performance. When processes are defined, adjusters rely on structure rather than making repeated decisions.

The responsibility for applying that structure remains shared between the organization and the adjuster.

Organized claims environments improve continuity. Documentation provides context, identifies next steps, and tracks communication, enabling adjusters to transition between files without reassembling information. This reduces inefficiency and supports workflow stability.

Structured claims handling also helps reduce burnout. Clear expectations, consistent documentation, and defined communication processes create stability during high-volume assignments. Adjusters can focus on evaluation while relying on established systems.

Organizational support and structured claims handling promote sustainability. Clear workflows, documented communication, and organized evaluation reduce strain and enhance long-term effectiveness.

Recognizing Early Signs of Burnout

Recognizing early signs of burnout helps adjusters maintain alignment during demanding assignments. Difficulty organizing claims, delayed documentation, reduced communication effectiveness, and increased decision fatigue may signal emerging strain. These responses reflect sustained workload and cognitive pressure rather than a lack of capability.

Awareness supports proactive adjustment.

Reestablishing structure helps restore clarity. Reviewing documentation, confirming priorities, and organizing pending actions reduce cognitive strain and support a consistent workflow. These deliberate resets help maintain performance during extended assignments.

Documenting decisions further reduces mental load. Clear records enable adjusters to transition between claims without reconstructing information, improving efficiency and supporting consistent decision-making.

Recognizing early signs of burnout supports sustainability. Awareness, organization, and structured planning help adjusters maintain clarity, consistency, and professional performance in high-demand environments.

Documentation as a Sustainability Tool

Documentation supports both the claim and the adjuster. Clear, consistent notes enable adjusters to transition between files without re-evaluating prior information. When observations, communications, and next steps are reliably recorded, continuity is maintained across multiple claims, reducing cognitive strain.

The responsibility for maintaining that documentation rests with the adjuster.

Recording next steps preserves direction. Pending inspections, follow-up communications, and documentation requests remain visible and organized. This structured tracking reduces the need for repeated decisions and supports efficient workflow management.

Documentation also strengthens communication. Clear records reduce redundant discussions and support consistent messaging across stakeholders. When updates are documented, adjusters can respond efficiently while maintaining alignment throughout the claim.

Using documentation as a sustainability tool supports long-term performance. Structured notes, tracked next steps, and consistent communication records help adjusters manage their workload effectively and maintain clarity over time.

Building a Sustainable Adjusting Career

Sustainability in adjusting is built through organization, alignment, and discipline. Adjusters who maintain reliable workflows reduce cognitive strain and improve efficiency. Consistent documentation and communication routines sustain alignment, even in high-volume environments.

Clear communication and structured documentation also support workload management. Providing regular updates, tracking next steps, and prioritizing tasks help adjusters remain responsive without sacrificing organization or consistency.

A sustainable career in adjusting requires balancing responsiveness with structure. Adjusters who guide claims through disciplined documentation, organized communication, and clear prioritization maintain consistency throughout extended assignments. This approach supports both performance and professional longevity.

The responsibility for sustaining that performance rests with the adjuster.

The future of adjusting depends on sustainability. Adjusters who maintain resilience, organization, and structured workflows are better positioned to lead complex claims and remain effective throughout their careers.

Practical Claim Leadership Actions

Turnover, Burnout, and Sustainability in Adjusting

Turnover and burnout affect claim continuity, communication, and documentation. Sustainable practices enable adjusters to maintain performance and support long-term professional effectiveness. Structure and consistency are essential in high-demand claims environments. In sustained, high-volume conditions, structure stabilizes both performance and workload over time.

MAINTAIN STRUCTURED WORKFLOW

Organization reduces workload strain and supports consistent performance across multiple claims.

KEY ACTIONS:

Track claim status clearly
Document next steps consistently
Prioritize time-sensitive claims
Maintain organized file notes

GO-TO LINES:

"The claim status is being tracked to maintain clarity."
"Next steps have been documented for consistency."
"Priority actions have been identified and are being addressed."
"Documentation reflects the current stage of each claim."

MANAGE COMMUNICATION VOLUME

High communication demands contribute to burnout. Structured communication preserves clarity and supports sustainability.

KEY ACTIONS:

Provide scheduled updates
Confirm next steps clearly
Document conversations promptly
Avoid reactive messaging

GO-TO LINES:

"Updates will be provided on a structured schedule."
"Here are the next steps based on our discussion."
"Key points from this conversation have been documented."
"Communication will remain structured to maintain clarity."

SET REALISTIC EXPECTATIONS

Unrealistic timelines increase pressure and create misalignment. Clear expectations support stability and reduce unnecessary escalation.

KEY ACTIONS:

Communicate timelines realistically
Identify pending evaluations
Reconfirm expectations
Update stakeholders as conditions change

GO-TO LINES:

"Timelines are based on current workload and conditions."
"Pending evaluations have been identified and are in progress."

"Expectations will be reconfirmed as the claim develops."
"Updates will be provided as timelines are adjusted."

MAINTAIN DOCUMENTATION CONSISTENCY

Clear documentation reduces rework and supports continuity across the life of the claim.

KEY ACTIONS:

Record observations clearly
Document decision reasoning
Track follow-up actions
Maintain chronological notes

GO-TO LINES:

"Documentation reflects observed conditions and evaluation."
"Decision reasoning has been recorded for clarity."
"Follow-up actions have been documented for continuity."
"All updates are recorded in chronological order."

SUPPORT LONG-TERM PROFESSIONAL STABILITY

Consistency sustains performance in demanding environments. Disciplined habits protect both the adjuster and the claim.

KEY ACTIONS:

Maintain structured workflow
Communicate calmly under pressure
Document decisions clearly
Close conversations with direction

GO-TO LINES:

"Workflow is being managed to maintain consistency."
"Communication will remain calm and structured."
"Decisions are documented to support clarity."
"Next steps have been outlined for continuity."

These practices help adjusters sustain performance, reliability, and professional standards in high-demand claims environments. By combining structured workflows, disciplined communication, and consistent documentation, adjusters protect both claim quality and long-term effectiveness—ensuring that increasing workload does not compromise alignment or professional standards.

CLAIM LEADERSHIP SUMMARY

Key Takeaway

Turnover and burnout continue to affect claims environments where workload, complexity, and emotional demands remain high. Sustained pressure can influence consistency, communication, and long-term professional effectiveness. Sustainable adjusting requires balancing performance expectations with resilience and structured workload management. As demands increase, sustainability becomes essential to maintaining clarity, consistency, and professional standards over time.

In Practice

Maintain organization, make decisions deliberately, and communicate clearly, even during high-volume periods. Prioritize consistency over speed and recognize when the workload requires a structured adjustment. Disciplined habits support long-term performance, ensuring clarity and effectiveness are sustained as demands increase.

Questions for Reflection

1. How do I maintain consistency during high-volume claim periods?
2. Do I recognize when workload begins to affect my performance?
3. What habits support long-term sustainability in my claims work?

Claim Leadership Principle

Sustainable leadership in claims requires disciplined practices. Clarity is maintained when workload, communication, and decision-making are consistently managed and structured over time.

CHAPTER 23

License Integrity and Professional Responsibility

Event Spotlight — License Responsibility in High-Pressure Claims

License integrity has become increasingly critical in modern claims environments. As claims grow more complex and timelines tighten, adjusters must make decisions based on evolving information while managing high volumes. These conditions require that documentation, communication, and professional judgment withstand later review. Claim files may be revisited months or years after closure, particularly in the context of litigation, reinspection, regulatory inquiry, or internal audit. In today's claims environment, accountability extends beyond the life of the claim.

The responsibility for that accountability rests with the adjuster.

Regulatory expectations reinforce this obligation. Adjusters hold licenses that impose individual accountability for professional conduct, documentation, and decision-making. Even within team structures or under operational directives, the adjuster remains responsible for the work performed under their license. This establishes a professional standard that requires clarity, consistency, and defensibility in every claim. The license represents personal accountability for how the claim is evaluated, documented, and communicated.

High-pressure environments can challenge this standard. Catastrophe deployments, staffing constraints, and elevated claim volume may pressure decision-making or documentation. However, when claims are later reviewed, those conditions are not always apparent. The claim file becomes the definitive record of professional judgment, communication, and reasoning.

Industry conditions further heighten scrutiny. Litigation exposure, regulatory oversight, and internal quality audits continue to raise expectations for claims handling. Adjusters are expected to demonstrate how decisions were reached, what information was considered, and how communication was managed throughout the life of the claim. These expectations underscore the importance of maintaining license integrity, regardless of workload or environment.

License integrity is not separate from sustainability—it is a core component. Maintaining professional standards protects both the adjuster and the claim. Clear documentation, structured communication, and disciplined decision-making support defensibility and consistency over time. As claims environments continue to evolve, protecting license integrity becomes central to professional adjusting. Consistent standards ensure that the claim remains clear, defensible, and aligned, regardless of when it is reviewed.

CHAPTER FOCUS

Professional adjusting entails individual responsibility. Maintaining license integrity requires disciplined documentation, consistent communication, and sound decision-making under pressure. Protecting the license supports long-term credibility, defensibility, and sustained professional performance. Accountability is demonstrated by the consistency with which claims are handled, documented, and communicated over time.

License Integrity and Professional Responsibility

License integrity is one of the most important yet often overlooked aspects of professional adjusting. While claims environments focus on timelines, documentation, communication, and resolution, every decision within a claim ultimately ties back to the adjuster's professional responsibility. The license represents more than a qualification. It reflects accountability, judgment, and adherence to professional standards.

Modern claims environments require decisions made under pressure. Information evolves, timelines compress, and expectations remain high. These conditions require adjusters to balance operational demands with professional responsibility. License integrity becomes the anchor that supports consistency. It guides decision-making, shapes documentation, and defines how communication is delivered.

The responsibility for maintaining that standard rests with the adjuster.

Adjusters often work in teams, follow operational direction, and collaborate with multiple stakeholders. Despite this shared environment, responsibility for claim handling remains individual. The adjuster's license reflects personal accountability for professional conduct and decision-making. This responsibility extends to documentation, communication, and the reasoning behind conclusions. Maintaining license integrity requires consistency, even under demanding conditions.

The license does not simply authorize the work—it holds every decision, communication, and outcome to a professional standard that must withstand scrutiny over time.

The License Represents Professional Accountability

The adjuster's license reflects a professional commitment. It signifies that the adjuster is qualified to evaluate claims, interpret policy language, communicate decisions, and document findings clearly and consistently. This responsibility does not change with workload, deployment conditions, or operational pressure.

In practice, decisions must be supported by clear reasoning. Documentation must reflect observed conditions rather than assumptions. Communication must remain professional, structured, and consistent. These practices ensure that the claim reflects sound judgment and defensible handling.

Adjusters may manage multiple claims simultaneously, work in catastrophe environments, and navigate evolving conditions. Even in these situations, the responsibilities associated with the license remain constant. Maintaining consistency under pressure is not an exception—it is a professional expectation.

Pressure and Professional Responsibility

Modern claims environments involve competing demands. Timelines may be compressed, claim volume may increase, and stakeholders may request faster decisions. Adjusters are often expected to move claims forward even as information continues to develop.

The responsibility for managing that pressure rests with the adjuster.

These conditions create tension between speed and precision. Moving too slowly may delay resolution, while moving too quickly can lead to incomplete documentation or unsupported reasoning. License integrity guides this balance, ensuring that progress does not compromise alignment, clarity, or defensibility.

Pressure may also stem from differing perspectives within the claim. Contractors may advocate for scope expansion, policyholders may request clarification or reconsideration, and internal stakeholders may seek updates or decisions. Adjusters must carefully evaluate these inputs while maintaining professionalism and objectivity.

Maintaining license integrity in these situations requires documenting observations, explaining the reasoning, and communicating clearly. These practices ensure that decisions remain consistent, defensible, and aligned with the claim.

Documentation and Defensibility

Documentation is central to protecting license integrity. The claim file serves as the record of professional judgment. It documents what was observed, how conclusions were reached, and how communication was managed. Clear documentation supports both understanding and accountability.

In modern claims environments, files may be reviewed by supervisors, stakeholders, or legal professionals. When this happens, documentation must stand on its own. The rationale for decisions should be clear, communication should be traceable, and observations should be clearly recorded.

The claim file becomes the evidence.

Brief or unclear documentation creates gaps in understanding. Structured documentation provides clarity. This does not require excessive detail—it requires disciplined decision-making and clear communication. Recording what was known at the time and why conclusions were reached strengthens both the claim and its defensibility.

Adjusters who treat documentation as a leadership tool promote accuracy, consistency, and accountability. This approach protects the claim and reinforces professional responsibility.

Communication and Professional Integrity

Communication is directly tied to license integrity. Adjusters interact with policyholders, contractors, experts, and internal teams. Each conversation shapes understanding, and each explanation shapes expectations.

Professional communication requires clarity and consistency. Adjusters must explain what is known, what remains under review, and the steps that will follow. This approach reduces uncertainty and promotes transparency for all stakeholders.

Inconsistent communication leads to misalignment. When expectations are unclear, stakeholders may interpret information differently, increasing the risk of escalation and delays. Clear, structured communication maintains direction and supports claim progression.

Documenting communication strengthens professional integrity. Recording key conversations ensures expectations, decisions, and next steps remain traceable. This consistency supports alignment throughout the life of the claim and reinforces defensibility.

Decision-Making Under Professional Responsibility

Adjusters often make decisions based on incomplete information. Inspections may be pending, expert reports may not yet be available, and conditions may continue to evolve. Despite these limitations, decisions must be made to move the claim forward.

The responsibility for those decisions rests with the adjuster.

License integrity guides this process. Adjusters evaluate available information, exercise professional judgment, and document the rationale for each decision. As new information emerges, decisions may be revisited. This structured flexibility supports clarity, consistency, and defensibility.

Sound decision-making requires balancing speed and accuracy. Delayed decisions can slow claim progression, while rushed decisions can lead to inconsistency or unsupported conclusions. Adjusters must evaluate what is known, identify what remains pending, and communicate next steps precisely.

Professional responsibility includes explaining the basis for decisions. A clear explanation promotes understanding, maintains alignment, and ensures that decisions remain defensible over time.

Leadership Without Authority and License Responsibility

Adjusters often work in collaborative environments where authority is shared. Contractors, engineers, attorneys, and policyholders contribute to the claims process. Decisions may involve multiple perspectives, evolving input, and competing priorities.

The responsibility for maintaining professional standards does not shift in these environments.

License integrity remains central. Adjusters guide the claim by organizing information, documenting observations, and clearly explaining their reasoning. This structured approach maintains alignment among stakeholders and supports consistent claim progression.

Leadership in this context is demonstrated through influence rather than control. Adjusters set direction through communication, documentation, and consistency. This practical leadership reinforces professional integrity and ensures the claim remains organized, defensible, and aligned.

Sustainability and Long-Term Professional Standards

Maintaining license integrity also supports sustainability. High-volume claims, catastrophe deployments, and emotionally demanding conversations can erode clarity over time. Fatigue may affect communication tone, and workload pressure may reduce documentation accuracy. Recognizing these risks reinforces the need for disciplined, structured handling.

The responsibility for maintaining that consistency rests with the adjuster.

Structured workflows and consistent practices preserve professional standards. Adjusters who document observations clearly, track next steps, and maintain organized communication reduce the risk of error. Discipline in workflow supports both claim quality and long-term professional performance.

License integrity extends beyond individual claims and reinforces long-term credibility. Consistent documentation, clear communication, and structured decision-making demonstrate reliability across diverse claim environments. Over time, these practices strengthen trust and professional reputation.

Sustainability and professional standards are closely linked. Adjusters who maintain organization and clarity protect both immediate claim outcomes and long-term career stability.

The Role of Ethical Judgment

Ethical judgment is central to license integrity. Adjusters must evaluate information objectively, communicate honestly, and document decisions clearly. These practices promote fairness, consistency, and accountability throughout the claims process.

Ethical judgment does not require certainty—it requires clarity. Adjusters must distinguish among what is known, what is still developing, and what remains under review. Transparent communication of evolving information preserves credibility and reduces the risk of misunderstanding.

Maintaining ethical standards reinforces trust. Policyholders, carriers, and stakeholders rely on consistent, accurate communication. Clear documentation promotes understanding, and objective evaluation ensures fairness. These practices guide claims handling in a responsible and professional manner.

Ethical judgment reinforces professional responsibility. Structured communication, transparent documentation, and objective evaluation help maintain integrity in complex, high-pressure claims environments.

REAL WORLD
Maintaining Professional Standards Under Pressure

An adjuster faced pressure to expedite a claim decision before all documentation and evaluations were complete. The urgency created risk, as moving too quickly could compromise accuracy, consistency, and the claim's defensibility.

The responsibility for maintaining professional standards did not change.

Rather than advancing the claim prematurely, the adjuster maintained disciplined handling by continuing to thoroughly document findings and ensuring that all required evaluations were completed. Communication remained clear and consistent, with the adjuster explaining what information was still pending, how it would affect the decision, and when the next update would be provided.

The adjuster emphasized that the decision would be based on a complete evaluation, not on timeline pressure. Each step in the process was documented, including the rationale for delaying the decision until sufficient information was available. This approach preserved clarity, transparency, and alignment with professional expectations.

By adhering to a structured process and disciplined communication, the adjuster protected both the claim and their professional responsibility as licensed. This demonstrates that maintaining standards under pressure is not optional—it ensures decisions remain accurate, consistent, and defensible regardless of external demands.

Protecting the Claim and the Professional

License integrity protects both the claim and the adjuster. Clear documentation supports defensibility. Structured communication maintains alignment, and thoughtful decision-making ensures consistency.

The responsibility for maintaining these standards rests with the adjuster.

Adjusters who apply these practices create stability in complex claims environments. They guide the process with clarity, discipline, and professionalism. This approach strengthens individual performance and reinforces overall claim quality.

Modern claims environments will continue to evolve. Complexity will persist, and expectations will continue to rise. License integrity provides a consistent foundation. It supports professional judgment, ethical decision-making, and long-term credibility amid changing conditions.

Maintaining license integrity is not separate from claim leadership—it defines it.

Continuing Education and Professional Responsibility

License integrity extends beyond individual claims. Maintaining professional competence is a core responsibility. Continuing education requirements reinforce the expectation that adjusters stay current with policy interpretation, regulatory standards, and evolving claims practices.

The responsibility for maintaining that competence rests with the adjuster.

Claims environments change over time. Coverage interpretations evolve, documentation standards develop, and communication expectations rise. Continuing education supports awareness of these changes and helps ensure consistency in professional practice.

Renewal cycles reinforce accountability. The license is not permanent—it requires ongoing attention, adherence to standards, and active participation in continuing education. Adjusters who view continuing education as more than a requirement strengthen their judgment, communication, and decision-making.

Professional development promotes clarity, consistency, and credibility. It reinforces the responsibilities of holding a license and ensures that claims handling remains aligned with current expectations.

Practical Claim Leadership Actions

Practical Guardrails for License Integrity

Maintaining license integrity requires consistent professional habits. Adjusters operate under individual professional responsibility, and decisions made during the claim may be reviewed later. Clear documentation, structured communication, and thoughtful decision-making help protect both the claim and the adjuster. These guardrails support clarity, defensibility, and long-term professional credibility. In high-pressure environments, consistency in documentation and communication is what protects professional accountability over time.

DOCUMENT DECISION REASONING CLEARLY

When information is evolving, documenting the reasoning behind key decisions helps ensure the claim file reflects professional judgment. Clear explanations support defensibility and continuity.

KEY ACTIONS:

Document basis for key decisions
Identify information relied upon
Note pending or unknown factors
Clarify next steps in documentation

GO-TO LINES:

"This decision is based on the following documented findings."
"The evaluation reflects the information available at this time."
"There are factors still under review and pending evaluation."
"Next steps have been documented to maintain clarity."

COMMUNICATE EXPECTATIONS CONSISTENTLY

Clear expectations reduce misunderstanding and help maintain alignment across stakeholders. Consistent communication reinforces professionalism.

KEY ACTIONS:

Clarify timelines and next steps
Communicate limitations clearly
Reconfirm expectations when conditions change
Document expectations discussed

GO-TO LINES:

"Here is what to expect as the claim progresses."

"These limitations are based on current information available."
"Expectations will be updated as conditions change."
"This has been documented to ensure alignment."

AVOID ASSUMPTIONS IN DOCUMENTATION

Documentation should reflect observations and supported conclusions. When uncertainty exists, it should be acknowledged.

KEY ACTIONS:

Record observations objectively
Avoid speculative language
Identify pending evaluations
Document developing information

GO-TO LINES:

"Documentation reflects observed conditions only."
"This remains under evaluation at this time."
"Pending reviews have been identified and are in progress."
"Information is being documented as it develops."

MAINTAIN PROFESSIONAL WRITTEN COMMUNICATION

Emails, notes, and reports may be reviewed later. Professional language supports credibility and consistency.

KEY ACTIONS:

Use clear, neutral language
Avoid emotional or reactive wording
Confirm facts before documenting
Maintain consistent tone

GO-TO LINES:

"Communication reflects the current claim status."
"This is based on verified information available."
"All details have been confirmed prior to documentation."
"The tone and content remain consistent with professional standards."

REVISIT DECISIONS WHEN INFORMATION EVOLVES

New findings may require adjustment. Revisiting conclusions reflects sound professional judgment.

KEY ACTIONS:

Review decisions as information develops
Document updated conclusions
Communicate changes clearly
Reconfirm next steps

GO-TO LINES:

"This decision has been updated based on new information."
"The evaluation is being revisited as findings develop."
"Changes have been documented for clarity."
"Next steps have been reconfirmed following review."

RECOGNIZE WORKLOAD IMPACT ON CLARITY

High volume can affect pacing and documentation quality. Structured habits help maintain integrity.

KEY ACTIONS:

Slow down for key documentation
Review complex decisions carefully

Confirm reasoning before closing notes
Maintain organized documentation

GO-TO LINES:

"This documentation has been reviewed for accuracy."
"Additional review has been completed before finalizing."
"Reasoning has been confirmed prior to closure."
"The file has been organized to maintain clarity."

USE DOCUMENTATION AS CLAIM STRUCTURE

Documentation helps maintain direction and supports professional responsibility.

KEY ACTIONS:

Track claim status clearly
Document next steps consistently
Maintain chronological notes
Record communication timelines

GO-TO LINES:

"The claim status is being tracked to maintain consistency."
"Next steps have been documented for continuity."
"All updates are recorded in chronological order."
"Communication timelines have been documented for clarity."

These practices help maintain license integrity even in fast-moving claims environments. By combining structured documentation, disciplined communication, and consistent decision-making, adjusters protect both the claim and their professional responsibility—ensuring that every decision remains clear, supported, and defensible regardless of when it is reviewed.

CLAIM LEADERSHIP SUMMARY

Key Takeaway

License integrity is central to professional adjusting. Decisions made under pressure, documentation produced during high-volume periods, and stakeholder communications may all be subject to later review. Maintaining alignment, reliability, and sound professional judgment protects both the claim and the adjuster. Clear documentation and deliberate decision-making support defensibility and long-term credibility. When license integrity is upheld, the claim file stands as a complete and reliable record of professional judgment.

In Practice

Document the reasoning clearly, especially when decisions are made with evolving information. Communicate expectations consistently and record key conversations. Avoid assumptions or implied conclusions. In fast-moving conditions, prioritize precision and professionalism so the claim file clearly reflects the basis for each decision and supports reliable interpretation over time.

Questions for Reflection

1. Am I clearly documenting the reasoning behind key claim decisions?
2. Would my claim file stand on its own if reviewed months later?
3. Do my communication notes accurately reflect what stakeholders were told and when?

Claim Leadership Principle

License integrity defines professional claim leadership. Alignment is sustained when documentation, communication, and decision-making consistently reflect sound professional judgment in all circumstances.

Extending Claim Leadership Beyond Property

While many examples in this book focus on property and catastrophe claims, the leadership principles apply across all lines of adjusting.

In commercial claims, adjusters manage higher financial exposure, business interruption considerations, and coordination among multiple stakeholders, including business owners, contractors, accountants, and legal teams. These claims require disciplined communication, structured documentation, and alignment as conditions evolve.

In auto claims, adjusters work in fast-paced environments where liability, coverage, and communication must be addressed promptly. The pace and volume demand immediate clarity in decision-making and communication. Conversations often occur in real time, and documentation must accurately reflect those decisions. Clear communication and disciplined documentation promote consistency and reduce disputes.

In workers' compensation claims, adjusters navigate medical documentation, ongoing treatment, and extended timelines. These claims require consistent communication and coordination among multiple parties, including employers, medical providers, and legal representatives. Maintaining continuity over time is essential.

In liability and litigation-aware claims, documentation, communication, and decision-making are subject to detailed review. These environments require disciplined handling, a professional tone, and clearly documented reasoning to support defensibility.

Across all claim types, the core responsibilities remain the same. Adjusters must document clearly, communicate consistently, and guide the claim professionally. While the details of each claim may differ, the standard does not.

The responsibility remains with the adjuster.

The modern adjuster leads with consistency. The claim environment may change, but the leadership standard remains the same.

CONCLUSION

The Standard You Set

Throughout this book, one theme has remained consistent: the role of the adjuster has evolved. Modern claims require more than inspection and estimation. They require coordination, communication, documentation, and professional judgment. Adjusters are no longer simply processing claims. They are guiding them.

The standard you set as an adjuster shapes the claim environment. Your communication, documentation, and decision-making influence how the claim progresses. Stakeholders look to the adjuster for direction. When structure is maintained, the claim remains organized. When communication is clear, expectations align. When documentation is consistent, decisions are supported.

Professional adjusting is defined by the standard of practice. Adjusters who establish clarity early reduce confusion. Those who document thoroughly support continuity. Those who communicate consistently reduce escalation. These practices create stability within the claim. When the standard is consistent, the claim environment becomes predictable, structured, and professionally aligned.

Leadership Within the Claim

Leadership in adjusting does not require authority over every participant. It is demonstrated by how the claim is managed. Adjusters lead by setting expectations, coordinating communication, and maintaining documentation. This leadership aligns stakeholders and supports structured claim progression.

When multiple parties are involved, structure is essential. Contractors, consultants, engineers, and policyholders may all contribute to the claim. The adjuster provides direction. Clear communication and documented decisions support coordination and reduce uncertainty.

Leadership within the claim prevents reactive handling. Structured guidance keeps discussions focused on evaluation, documentation, and next steps, supporting claim progression and reducing confusion. The standard you set determines how effectively the claim advances. Leadership is demonstrated through consistency, not control.

Consistency Builds Professional Confidence

Consistency is one of the most valuable tools in claims handling. When adjusters use structured workflows, they reduce uncertainty throughout the claim lifecycle. Documentation provides continuity, and communication supports alignment among stakeholders.

Consistency builds confidence. Policyholders know what to expect. Contractors and consultants rely on documented decisions. Internal stakeholders benefit from organized communication. This clarity strengthens the claims environment.

Professional confidence is not based on speed alone. It is built through organized handling and a disciplined workflow. Consistent adjusters guide claims effectively and uphold professionalism in complex environments. The standard you set is reflected in consistent professional behavior. Consistency transforms individual actions into a reliable professional system.

Documentation Defines the Claim

Documentation plays a central role in professional adjusting. Clear notes capture observations, decisions, and next steps. These records support continuity as claims evolve and reduce the need to revisit information.

As claims develop over time, documentation provides context. Adjusters can track new information, updated timelines, and stakeholder communications. This supports alignment and reduces confusion.

Documentation also supports communication. Clear records reduce misunderstandings and allow decisions to be referenced with clarity and consistency. The standard you set includes documentation discipline. Documentation is not just recordkeeping—it provides the structure that supports every decision in the claim.

Communication Shapes the Claim Experience

Communication shapes how claims unfold. Structured updates manage expectations, and clear explanations reduce uncertainty. A professional tone fosters cooperation and guides discussions.

Adjusters who communicate consistently build alignment. Policyholders understand next steps, contractors stay informed, and internal stakeholders can track progress. This supports claim progression and reduces duplicate inquiries.

Communication also helps manage conflict. Calm, structured messaging stabilizes conversations and reduces escalation. The standard you set includes clear communication. Effective communication strengthens claims handling and supports leadership in the claim.

Professional Judgment and Decision-Making

Adjusters make decisions throughout the claim lifecycle. Prioritization, evaluation, and communication require professional judgment. Structured decision-making promotes clarity and consistency.

Documenting reasoning maintains transparency. Recording observations and next steps supports continuity and reduces confusion as claims evolve. Professional judgment is strengthened by organization. Adjusters who document decisions, communicate clearly, and maintain structured workflows effectively guide claims. The standard you set reflects disciplined decision-making. Well-structured decisions preserve clarity, even when conditions are uncertain.

Sustaining Performance Over Time

Claims handling often involves sustained workload. Catastrophe events, complex losses, and multi-party coordination create ongoing demands. Maintaining performance requires organization and discipline.

Documentation, communication routines, and prioritization reduce cognitive strain. These practices build resilience and help adjusters manage high-volume environments effectively.

Sustaining performance is part of professional adjusting. The standard you set is measured over time, not just within individual claims. Sustained performance comes from disciplined, repeatable professional habits—not effort alone.

The Modern Adjuster

The modern adjuster is a claims leader. This role extends beyond inspection and estimation to include guiding communication, documenting decisions, and coordinating stakeholders. Professional adjusting is defined by organization and discipline. When adjusters maintain structure, document observations, and communicate reliably, claims move forward with clarity and alignment.

The adjuster's influence is evident in how claims unfold. Documentation preserves continuity, communication stabilizes discussions, and disciplined decisions yield reliable outcomes. The standard you set shapes the claim environment. The modern adjuster leads through alignment, not control.

Raising the Standard

Raising the standard in adjusting does not require overhauling the entire process. It requires applying structure consistently across communication, documentation, and decision-making. Adjusters who apply these practices reduce escalations, improve alignment, and maintain clarity throughout the claim process.

The standard you set becomes the model for handling. Reliability builds trust. Structured workflows ensure consistency. Over time, disciplined handling strengthens both individual claims and professional credibility.

The future of claims adjusting depends on leadership within the claim. Adjusters who guide claims through alignment, organization, and consistent communication do more than manage claims—they define the profession's standard.

REFERENCES

Industry data, regulatory guidance, and widely reported catastrophe events informed the development of this book. The following sources provide additional context on claims handling, catastrophe losses, aviation incidents, and litigation trends.

Catastrophe Events and Loss Data

National Oceanic and Atmospheric Administration. *Billion-Dollar Weather and Climate Disasters Database.*

Insurance Information Institute. *Catastrophe Losses and Insurance Industry Data.*

Swiss Re Institute. *Sigma Reports: Natural Catastrophes and Man-Made Disasters.*

Munich Re. *NatCatSERVICE Loss Database.*

Claims Handling and Regulatory Guidance

National Association of Insurance Commissioners. *Unfair Claims Settlement Practices Model Regulation.*

Federal Emergency Management Agency. *Disaster Assistance and Claims Coordination Resources.*

Aviation Incidents and Investigation

National Transportation Safety Board. *Aviation Accident Reports and Investigation Summaries.*

Federal Aviation Administration. *Aviation Safety Data and Regulatory Guidance.*

International Civil Aviation Organization. *Standards and Recommended Practices for Aviation Safety.*

Legal and Liability Frameworks

Montreal Convention. *Convention for the Unification of Certain Rules for International Carriage by Air (1999).*

Florida Office of Insurance Regulation. *Property Insurance Market and Litigation Reports.*

Industry Practice and Professional Context

Information presented in this book also reflects general industry practices, catastrophe response environments, and multi-party claims coordination commonly observed across property and aviation claims handling. The content draws on industry data, publicly available reports, and professional claims handling practices across multiple sectors.

CONTINUING YOUR PROFESSIONAL DEVELOPMENT

Professional adjusting continues to evolve. Claims environments shift, stakeholder expectations expand, and complexity across loss types increases. As the role grows, professional development becomes essential to maintaining alignment and reliability. Adjusters who continue to develop communication, documentation, and decision-making capabilities are better prepared to manage complex claims.

Professional development in adjusting extends beyond technical knowledge. While policy interpretation, estimating, and inspection remain essential, modern adjusting also requires leadership within the claim. This includes coordinating stakeholders, managing communication, and maintaining disciplined documentation. Strengthening these capabilities supports long-term effectiveness.

Ongoing development enables adjusters to adapt to emerging challenges. Catastrophe events, multi-party claims, and litigation-aware environments require thoughtful execution. Adjusters who refine their approach sustain alignment in these conditions.

Continuing professional development reinforces reliability. It enables adjusters to maintain organization, professionalism, and confidence over time.

Strengthening Communication Skills

Communication remains central to modern claims handling. Clear explanations help align stakeholders and reduce misunderstandings. A professional tone supports cooperation and guides conversations during complex or time-sensitive claims. Adjusters benefit from continually refining their communication skills throughout their careers.

This includes explaining timelines, outlining next steps, and documenting discussions. Structured communication helps prevent escalation and keeps stakeholders aligned. Consistency in messaging supports clarity and reduces repeated inquiries.

Practicing communication also helps manage complex conversations. Policyholders may request clarification, contractors may seek direction, and stakeholders may express concerns. Adjusters who communicate clearly help guide discussions toward resolution while maintaining professionalism.

Strengthening communication skills supports professional development and improves overall claims leadership.

Enhancing Documentation Discipline

Documentation plays a key role in claims handling. Clear notes reflect observations, decisions, and next steps. Continuing to refine documentation practices supports consistency across files and over time. Structured documentation helps maintain continuity.

Professional documentation helps track claim progression. When claims evolve, recorded information provides context for new developments. Stakeholders benefit from consistent records that reflect communication, evaluation, and decisions.

Improving documentation discipline also supports decision-making. Recorded reasoning helps maintain transparency and reduces uncertainty. Clear documentation allows adjusters to reference prior evaluations and maintain consistency.

Enhancing documentation discipline is an important part of professional development. Organized records strengthen clarity, efficiency, and professionalism.

Developing Decision-Making Consistency

Adjusters make decisions throughout the claim lifecycle. Prioritization, evaluation, and communication require professional judgment. Developing consistent decision-making supports clarity and improves claims handling.

Structured evaluation guides decisions. Reviewing documentation, confirming observations, and identifying next steps support disciplined judgment. Documenting reasoning ensures continuity as claims evolve.

Refining decision-making skills also helps manage pressure. Adjusters who use structured workflows reduce redundant evaluations and maintain consistency across claims. This structured approach supports efficiency and professionalism.

Developing decision-making consistency supports professional growth. Adjusters who maintain structured judgment guide claims effectively and strengthen long-term performance.

Expanding Knowledge of Complex Claims

Complex claims require coordination, organization, and structured decision-making. Multi-party losses, catastrophe events, and litigation-aware claims often involve engineers, contractors, consultants, and representatives. Adjusters benefit from continuing to build knowledge in these areas to maintain clarity and professionalism.

Understanding how to coordinate communication, document decisions, and track evolving information supports structured handling. As complexity increases, organized workflows help guide the claim and reduce uncertainty. Expanding technical and procedural knowledge strengthens claim leadership.

Expanding knowledge also supports confidence. Adjusters who understand complex claim environments can communicate clearly, maintain organization, and guide stakeholders effectively. This strengthens claims handling and professional performance.

Continuing to build knowledge supports long-term professional development.

Learning From Claim Experience

Each claim presents an opportunity for growth. Reviewing communication, documentation, and decision-making after claim activity helps refine the approach. Adjusters can identify where the organization improved understanding and where additional discipline may strengthen handling.

Reflecting on claim handling reinforces reliability. Reviewing workflows, communication timing, and documentation practices strengthens organization and reduces recurring challenges, improving efficiency in future assignments.

Learning from experience also builds confidence. Disciplined reflection helps adjusters sustain alignment and develop reliable practices. Over time, experience strengthens professional judgment and reliability.

Experience is a critical development tool. Continuous reflection supports professional growth.

Maintaining Professional Consistency

Reliability supports professional growth. Adjusters who apply defined workflows reduce uncertainty across claims. Documentation and communication routines sustain alignment even in complex environments.

Maintaining reliability across claims refines handling. Adjusters develop disciplined practices for prioritization, documentation, and communication. These practices improve efficiency and reduce redundant decision-making.

Professional reliability strengthens performance. Defined workflows support organization, alignment, and disciplined decision-making. Over time, consistent execution improves both claim outcomes and professional development.

Reliability supports ongoing growth and long-term effectiveness.

Collaboration and Professional Learning

Collaboration also supports development. Discussing claim-handling approaches with peers can provide perspective on communication strategies, documentation practices, and workflow organization. Shared experience helps refine claim handling.

Learning through collaboration helps adjusters evaluate different approaches. Exposure to alternative communication methods or documentation structures may strengthen clarity. This supports professional growth.

Collaboration also supports consistency. Shared practices across teams can improve communication, reduce confusion, and strengthen structured handling. Adjusters benefit from collective knowledge.

Professional learning contributes to development. Collaboration, reflection, and continued knowledge-building help adjusters refine skills and maintain professional clarity over time.

Adapting to Industry Changes

The claims industry continues to evolve. Technological advancements, shifting communication expectations, and increasing complexity influence how adjusting work is performed. Ongoing professional development enables adjusters to adapt while maintaining alignment and reliability.

Learning new tools and workflows supports efficiency. Remote inspections, digital documentation platforms, and coordinated communication systems improve organization when applied with discipline. Adjusters who adapt to these changes sustain effective handling and reduce uncertainty.

Adapting to industry changes also strengthens professional confidence. Adjusters who stay current with evolving practices manage claims more effectively and coordinate stakeholders more precisely. This reinforces professionalism in complex environments.

Adapting to industry changes is part of professional development. Continuous learning helps adjusters maintain relevance, organization, and structured decision-making.

Building Long-Term Professional Capability

Professional development is an ongoing process. Adjusters who refine communication, documentation, and decision-making capabilities build long-term effectiveness. These foundational practices sustain alignment across both simple and complex claims.

Defined workflows reinforce reliability over time. Adjusters who continue to develop their approach strengthen organization, improve communication, and sustain disciplined decision-making. These practices support professionalism across diverse claim environments.

Long-term capability also supports resilience. Adjusters who maintain alignment, disciplined documentation, and reliable communication are better positioned to manage sustained workload and evolving claim conditions. This strengthens performance and professional longevity.

Continuing professional development helps sustain a strong career in adjusting. Adjusters who invest in communication, documentation, and structured workflows build the capability to guide complex claims effectively over time.

OTHER BOOKS BY DR. KARISSA THOMAS

Dr. Karissa Thomas is the author of multiple titles in leadership, communication, and professional development across claims, education, and global leadership. Her work focuses on emotionally intelligent leadership, communication under pressure, and guiding professionals through complex environments.

Leadership and Professional Development

The Mosaic Way™ — Emotional Intelligence for Inclusive Leadership in a Changing World
The Mosaic Way™ Field Glossary — Language for Leading with Identity, Inclusion, and Cultural Intelligence
Composed: A Mosaic Advantage to Lead Without Losing Yourself
Leading After the Storm — How to Communicate, Calm, and Coordinate in the Wake of Disaster

Insurance and Adjuster Leadership

Claim the Lead™ — Transformational Leadership for Insurance Adjusting Managers
Communicate, Connect, and Lead™ — A New Standard for Insurance Adjusters

Personal Development and Foundational Work

The Look of Success — Redefining Achievement, Identity, and Fulfillment on Your Own Terms

These titles extend the ideas presented in this book by exploring leadership under pressure, communication in complex environments, emotionally intelligent decision-making, and professional resilience across industries.

The Look of Success focuses on the internal dimension of achievement, challenging traditional definitions of success and encouraging readers to align identity, purpose, and fulfillment. It explores how individuals move beyond external validation to develop clarity, confidence, and a more sustainable sense of personal and professional success.

ABOUT THE AUTHOR

Dr. Karissa Thomas is an award-winning author, leadership strategist, and creator of the Mosaic Intelligence Method™, an operating architecture designed to help professionals navigate complexity, pressure, and change. Her work examines how communication, emotional awareness, and disciplined leadership support sound decision-making in high-stakes environments. Her books are used by leaders across industries, including insurance, education, corporate leadership, and crisis response.

Her work focuses on the evolving demands of modern leadership. Through practical guidance and real-world insight, she equips professionals to operate effectively in complex environments while maintaining composure and direction. She is known for translating emotionally intelligent leadership into structured, actionable practices that can be applied in demanding professional settings.

Dr. Thomas is the author of multiple titles spanning leadership, communication, and claims handling, including *The Mosaic Way*, *Leading After the Storm*, *Lead Anyway*, and *Claim the Lead*. Her writing emphasizes communication under pressure, disciplined decision-making, and leadership without formal authority—capabilities increasingly essential in complex, fast-moving environments.

Drawing on cross-sector experience, Dr. Thomas writes for professionals who work in settings where coordination, communication, and judgment are critical. Her work supports readers in strengthening communication, maintaining professionalism, and guiding complex situations with confidence.

Through her books and professional resources, Dr. Thomas advances a consistent message: leadership today is defined not by title, but by alignment, communication, and the ability to guide others through uncertainty.

www.ingramcontent.com/pod-product-compliance
Lightning Source LLC
Chambersburg PA
CBHW031334230926
51848CB00002B/235
* 9 7 8 1 9 6 8 2 7 7 6 1 1 *